Health and the Rhetoric of Medicine

HEALTH
and the Rhetoric of Medicine

JUDY Z. SEGAL

Southern Illinois University Press
Carbondale

Library of Congress Cataloging-in-Publication Data
Segal, Judy.
Health and the rhetoric of medicine / Judy Z. Segal.
   p. cm.
Includes bibliographical references and index.
   1. Medicine—Language. 2. Rhetoric. I. Title.
[DNLM: 1. Persuasive Communication. 2. Authorship.
3. Semantics WZ345 S454h 2005]
   R123.S38 2005
   610'.1'4—dc22
   ISBN 0-8093-2677-9 (cloth : alk. paper)   2005011674

Printed on recycled paper. ♻

The paper used in this publication meets the minimum
requirements of American National Standard for Information Sciences—Permanence of Paper for Printed Library
Materials, ANSI Z39.48-1992. ∞

For my mother,
who thought I could do anything,
. . . something I did.

Contents

Acknowledgments

Over the years of work that have gone into this book, I have had the support of the Social Sciences and Humanities Research Council of Canada and the Hampton Fund of the University of British Columbia. I have received funding from other sources as well: Riverview Hospital (Port Coquitlam, British Columbia), the Canadian Institutes of Health Research, and the Peter Wall Institute for Advanced Studies. I thank them for their support. For their research assistance, I also thank the Wellcome Institute for the History and Understanding of Medicine. I am grateful, too, for the resources of the libraries of the University of British Columbia.

Over these years, I have presented some of my work in the form of conference papers and other talks. I appreciate the comments of audience members I encountered at meetings of the American Association for the Rhetoric of Science and Technology; Conference on College Composition and Communication; Society for the Social Studies of Science; Centre for Health Economics and Policy Analysis; Canadian Society for the Study of Rhetoric; International Society for the Study of Narrative; Conference on Narratives of Disease, Disability, and Trauma; UBC Faculty of Nursing; UBC Faculty of Pharmaceutical Sciences; Green College Science and Society Lecture Series; and the Vancouver General Hospital Interdisciplinary Lecture Series.

Chapter 5 contains versions of two published essays: "Contesting Death, Speaking of Dying," *Journal of Medical Humanities* 21 (Winter

2000): 29–44; and "What Is a Rhetoric of Death?: End-of-Life Decision-Making at a Psychiatric Hospital," *Technostyle* 16 (Winter 2000): 67–86. Portions of chapter 6 were published as "Public Discourse and Public Policy: Some Ways that Metaphor Constrains Health (Care)," *Journal of Medical Humanities* 18 (1997): 217–31. Thanks to both journals for permission to reprint portions of these essays.

I have enjoyed life in a community of rhetorical scholars, whose members have contributed to and improved my work. First among them are Nan Johnson and Andrea Lunsford, who made it possible for me to do the work at all—and Karen Burke Lefevre, Anthony Paré, Richard Coe, Carolyn Miller, Randy Harris, Carol Berkenkotter, Joan Leach, Bill Keith, and Philippa Spoel. I am grateful for comments on work in progress and for conversations more generally on health and medicine to Leah Ceccarelli, Tom Couser, Susanna Egan, John Gilbert, Ian Gummeson, Maurice Bloch, Sholom Glouberman, Alan Bernstein, and Eric Cassell. For conversation and encouragement, I also thank Barry Luger, David Lotto, Barbara Dresner, Michael Barden, Sybil Faigin, Jessica Emed, and Marcia Segal. Further thanks go to my students, especially in graduate and majors seminars, for all the thinking we have done together. Colleen Derkatch deserves special thanks.

I have, for the duration of the project, been a faculty member in the English department at the University of British Columbia. I thank, especially, the PhDivas—Patsy Badir, Miranda Burgess, Siân Echard, and Sandy Tomc—for making life there quite a lot of fun.

I am fortunate to have had the most wonderful research assistants. Nora Lusterio saw me through the first part of the project, and Katja Thieme took over after a while. They both were creative, reliable, and indefatigable collaborators on the book.

I am grateful for the expert suggestions of Celeste Condit and Mary Lay Schuster, the manuscript's anonymous reviewers, who are now revealed. Thanks also to Karl Kageff and Carol Burns at Southern Illinois University Press and to Mary Lou Kowaleski, my amazing copyeditor.

Stephen Straker was my colleague, advisor, neighbor, and friend, and, more than he knew, he made this book possible.

Alan Richardson read and talked to me about every chapter. He gave me ideas and time and care. No one could be smarter or more generous.

My final thanks are to Moberley and Gabriel Luger, clearly the world's best children, for love and patience, constancy and company. They make me want to work and, thank goodness, also make me want not to.

Health and the Rhetoric of Medicine

Introduction: The What, Why, and How of a Rhetoric of Medicine

This book is for a range of readers: rhetorical theorists, rhetoricians of science, medical anthropologists, historians of medicine, and other scholars; health practitioners and health researchers with a special interest in the book's topics (for example, migraine, health anxiety, end-of-life decision making, values in health policy, patient "compliance"); health practitioners and health researchers with a critical interest in their own discourse and practice; and other persons interested in health and medicine more generally. The premise of the book is that rhetorical study—essentially, the study of persuasion[1]—is a good means of illuminating and recasting problems in health and medicine. *Health* is the more encompassing term for our study; typically in Western culture, *medicine* provides the set of terms through which health is primarily understood.

The rest of this introduction is in three parts. The first considers the what and the why of studying health and medicine rhetorically; the second considers the how of it; the third part is a chapter outline of the rest of the book.

What and Why

Persuasion is a central element in many medical situations. Patients may have to persuade physicians that they are ill and in need of care; physicians seek to persuade patients to adhere to courses of treatment; experts persuade the public to count some states and behaviors as pathological and others not; pharmaceutical companies persuade consumers to request their products, and physicians to prescribe them. Moreover, the very terms in which persuasion takes place in health and medicine themselves condition outcomes. The phrase *social anxiety disorder* persuades the very shy person that he or she may be a candidate for drug treatment; the word *breakthrough* persuades the public to imagine medical research as a dramatic sort of enterprise; the phrase *fighting disease* persuades persons that they have failed at something when they cannot stop being ill; the term *survivor* leaves the dead person looking somehow culpable. *Caregiver* creates a class of care receivers and tips the economy of families; *antibacterial* enters public discourse as a term of general praise. Rhetorical criticism identifies the persuasive element in the discourse of health and medicine and asks, "Who is persuading whom of what?" and "What are the means of persuasion?" The goal of rhetorical criticism is a greater understanding of human action. Rhetorical theory, as a whole, has considerable explanatory power in a world in which we act upon each other by influence.[2]

The relations of rhetoric and medicine are various and webbed. As my mentor in rhetoric, Nan Johnson, taught me, you can start rhetorical investigation anywhere, and you can get everywhere from there. The first questions of my own studies in rhetoric and medicine were about strategies of influence in medical authorship, about the means by which medical authors persuade medical readers on matters of disease etiology, diagnosis, and treatment. In order to write my doctoral dissertation, I read hundreds of medical journal articles in a rhetorical-analytic mode. S. Michael Halloran has said, in a landmark essay in the rhetoric of science, that while many theorists claimed that scientific writing was rhetorical, few scholars had actually examined the writing to describe how, exactly, it was so. The purpose of my dissertation was to isolate and describe persuasive strategies in medical journal articles and then to suggest a procedure for reading medical prose as rhetoric, as a motivated discourse with persuasive force. My project was theory-based, but it was not itself theoretical; rather, it was analytic and descriptive (see Segal, "Reading Medical Prose as Rhetoric").

Analysis and description are never very far from criticism, though, or theory. I discovered that the rhetorical features of medical journal articles are particularly well suited to biomedicine and, in a sense, enact its values. The textual markers of certainty, for example, are tied to conventions of medical authority; statistical argumentation plays out the scientific bent of biomedicine; the inquiring mind is a trope aimed at securing professional cooperation, and so on. Furthermore, medical texts perform much of their rhetorical work on a large scale, generically, with or without the intentions of particular authors.

Medicine is not only rhetorical as it is reproduced in published texts; it is also rhetorical as a system of norms and values operating discursively in doctor-patient interviews, in conversations in hospital corridors, in public debate on health policy, and in the apparatus of disease classification. So, for example, rhetorical theory is a means of understanding hypochondrias of a time and a place. The question of why about half of physician office visits each year are made for complaints for which there is no known organic cause may be reformulated as a question about how people become persuaded that they are ill when by some accounts they are not.

Rhetoric and medicine sometimes converge fairly obviously. Consider, for example, the thinly veiled agendas of fee-for-service guidelines sent to health-maintenance-organization care providers or consider the campaigns of direct-to-consumer advertising for prescription pharmaceuticals. The obvious candidates for the rhetorical study of medicine are, however, not the primary concern of this book—simply because they *are* obvious. For example, two newspapers recently reporting on the same medical study offer completely different accounts of it because they are aimed at persuading readers in different directions. One headline says, "Unnecessary Operations May Be Rife, Study Finds" (Picard); in another newspaper, the headline says *about the same study*, "Elective Surgery Benefits Most Patients: Study" (Fayerman). The conflicting stories cite the same statistics: "Up to one-quarter of patients who undergo common operations . . . feel worse or no better after the procedure," reports the first article. "The vast majority of elective surgery patients . . . said they experienced huge benefits to their health and lives after surgery," reports the second. The stories even cite the same expert spokesperson. Dr. Charles Wright is reported in the first article as saying, "If some surgery is being done based on flimsy medical indications, it could mean a move to de-insurance" (Picard). Apparently, Wright also said, "[T]here is a tremendous advantage to a great majority of people who need and get elective surgery" (Fayerman).[3] Such obvious examples of a rhetorical medicine can be displayed, but others, less obvious, need to be teased out.

Rhetorical theory does not provide an exact procedure for teasing out the rhetoric of medicine, but it does suggest principles that can be used as instruments for the process. These principles both enable and structure observations about human encounters, once we have acknowledged there is a persuasive element in them. Each principle, as the following chapters demonstrate, is a strategy for interpretation in a world that, in the view of Kenneth Burke, is saturated with rhetoric. "You meet a new person, and the *first* sentence he utters on some controversial subject is spoken in such tonalities as though he were speaking *in conclusion*" (original emphasis). The point is made as a "barely detectable inflection, which you must strain to catch, but which unmistakably implies, 'This is the slant you have too, if you have the proper slant'" (*Rhetoric of Motives* 98). Such a subtle rhetoric is a means of influence in everyday life, and rhetorical principles are keys that turn it on and keys that unlock it, too.

This book as a whole, in making a case for the heuristic value of the principles of rhetorical theory in the critical study of health and medicine, argues for the relevance of rhetorical findings for clinical practice and health policy. It is thus part of a larger argument for the importance of humanities research in a health research agenda. The idea of a broadly interdisciplinary approach to health research is compelling. If we know, for example, and we do, that economic status is a prime determinant of health, then health research goes beyond the scope of basic biomedical and clinical research into research on the distribution of employment and education opportunities in populations. Since the last decades of the twentieth century, at least, the case for the inclusion of the social sciences in the project of health research has been relatively easy to make; currently, the notion of "social determinants of health" is a *sine qua non* of health research (see, for example, Evans, Barer, and Marmor). The case for the inclusion of the humanities has been harder to make.

The problem for the humanities may be answered by research that takes up a plan of being *useful* even if it is not necessarily *applied*. *Useful* and *applied* are importantly not synonymous terms. It is a *useful* project in rhetorical research, for example, to inquire about medicine's myriad persuasive strategies and to discover from those strategies what unarticulated goals they might serve. *Applied* rhetorical research, on the other hand, is instrumental; its purpose might be to render a specific persuasive program more effective. For example, it would be useful to scrutinize the notion of "safe sex" and examine its discursive force in a culture (see Scott) while an applied project in rhetoric might be aimed at making existing safe-sex messages more persuasive to the public (see Perloff). Applied research is at the same time useful; but useful research is not necessarily applied.

In suggesting a rhetorical account of certain problems in health and medicine, this book is a humanities contribution to health research and meant to be useful. While rhetoric is sometimes understood to suggest a procedure for analyzing a particular text (a political speech or an advertisement, for example), its theory requires no single procedure, and the object of analysis may be not a particular text but rather a discourse as a whole.

How Is Rhetorical Analysis of Health and Medicine Done?

This section explains how rhetorical analysis can both be a method and not be methodical and how rhetorical analysis can illuminate health and medicine.[4] Readers new to rhetoric will find in this section explanations of the nature, terms, and operations of rhetorical analysis; readers familiar with rhetoric will find here, I hope, a contribution to studies of methods of rhetorical criticism. Readers not interested in methodology may wish to skip this section.

The term *rhetoric* itself has well-known negative connotations in popular discourse. Where *rhetoric* is taken to be the opposite of *reality*, as it often is,[5] rhetorical analysis is taken to be a procedure for unmasking. So, for example, students may learn to perform rhetorical analysis so that they may develop some immunity to the persuasive strategies in advertising or politics that are deployed in the world to deceive and control them. When Burke wrote about the rhetoric of *Mein Kampf*, he did so, he said, in order that "we may know, with greater accuracy, exactly what to guard against" as a population in America (*Philosophy* 191).

Rhetorical analysis, however, is not only a procedure for unmasking, although, as my earlier account of the two newspaper articles on elective surgery suggests, there is sometimes unmasking to be done. Language in use simply *is* rhetorical: the symbolic means, according to Burke, "*of inducing cooperation in beings that by nature respond to symbols*" (*Rhetoric of Motives* 43; emphasis in original). To analyze something rhetorically is not to suggest that it was wrong or deceitful or not real to begin with. Rhetorical analysis first needs to escape the taint of rhetoric.

Rhetoric's bad reputation is long held (it dates back at least to Plato's diatribes against the Sophists) and not entirely unearned (the means of persuasion are, indeed, generally taught without consideration of the ends of it). But *rhetoric* is, in the first instance, the persuasive element in discourse, and *rhetorical analysis* is an account of that element. Four groups of questions get at some of the difficulty of framing rhetorical method.

1. How inclusive is "rhetorical analysis" as a category of critical practice? Rhetorical critic Mark Klyn wrote in 1968, that "rhetorical criticism

is only intelligent writing about works of rhetoric" (147). Around the same time, Otis Walter wrote that rhetorical theory cannot "furnish a formula" for criticism; rather, "criticism that is brilliant is always criticism that could *not be easily prescribed*" (170; emphasis in original). Moreover, if rhetorical criticism is understood to be *criticism of rhetorical texts*, and if, by the terms of rhetorical theory itself, all texts are in some way rhetorical, then, can rhetorical criticism be construed broadly as a term for critical reading in general?

2. How is rhetorical criticism different from other schools of literary criticism? For example, when a rhetorical critic reads a text closely, how is he or she behaving differently from, say, a New Critical reader? The question is easy to answer *in theory*. The rhetorical critic, for example, asserts interest in authorial intention and audience affect while the New Critic eschews it; as M. H. Abrams says, the rhetorical critic is "pragmatic," looking at the work of art "chiefly as a means to an end" (15), while the New Critic is "objective," regarding the work of art as a "self-sufficient entity, constituted by its parts in their internal relations" (26). But the question is less easy to answer in terms of procedure: How does a rhetorical critic read differently from a New Critical one? Or, when a rhetorical critic attends to the persuasive force of generic textual elements hardly within the control of individual authors at all (as Martha Solomon does, for example, in her essay, discussed later in this chapter, on the rhetoric of the reports of the Tuskegee syphilis project), how does he or she differ in method from a deconstructionist critic interested in those elements? What, in other words, makes rhetorical criticism a special methodology within the realm of literary criticism?

3. How is the rhetorical critic different from discourse critics in other disciplines? If it is, in part, the socially situated nature of rhetorical analysis that distinguishes it from most other literary analysis[6]—the fact, as Burke says, that rhetoric is always "addressed"—then how is the rhetorical critic different from other critics of social texts? How is the rhetorical critic distinguishable from critics who *without* explicit knowledge of rhetorical theory are alert, for example, to the action of metaphor on public discourse? Several such critics appear in the coming chapters. George J. Annas, a physician, writes in the *New England Journal of Medicine* about the force of certain metaphors in debates on health policy; Paul Atkinson, a sociologist, writes about the reproduction of normal medicine through the discourse of medical education; Richard Melito, a psychologist, writes about the dominance of business metaphors in human-services delivery; Barbara Duden, a historian, writes about the discursive transformation

of pregnancy in the twentieth century (*Disembodying*). Are all of these actually rhetorical analysts writing under cover of some other discipline?

4. What are the features of a specifically branded rhetorical study? Once *rhetorical analysis* is understood to be a usefully limiting phrase, once a rhetorical approach is distinguished from other literary critical approaches, and once a rhetorical approach is distinguished from other social-critical approaches to discourse, then, what are the limits of a rhetorical brand of criticism? Steve Fuller writes of rhetorical study of science that the more it "looks like classical rhetoric, the less exciting its interpretations seem," but "the more [it] strays from classical sources, and the more provocative its readings become, the more interchangeable its methods seem with those used by sociologists and critical theorists" ("Rhetoric" 279). Broadly speaking, what counts as rhetorical theory, and what is the relation of rhetorical theory to rhetorical method?

These four groups of questions are important to the current study for the way they detail the larger question: What is rhetorical criticism? They point to a definition of rhetorical criticism that suggests both its variety and its cohesiveness: Rhetorical criticism is criticism performed by a rhetorical critic. The statement is more than tautological. A rhetorical critic is a person trained within a scholarly tradition on public discourse into a rhetorical subjectivity suggesting lines of inquiry and a procedure for thinking.[7] The rest of this section describes the history and the project of rhetorical analysis, outlines the conditions for rhetorical study of health and medicine, and gives an account of the sort of analysis that the remaining chapters of the book have to offer. In the course of discussion, many of the questions just raised about rhetoric as a discipline and a critical program are, at least provisionally, answered.

Recently, commentary on rhetorical criticism has added theoretical texture to a methodology that was declared a half-century ago to be at least pluralistic. Burke himself wrote that rhetorical criticism is a "naming of manoeuvres" in which the critic is obliged to "use all that is there to use" (*Philosophy* 23). In 1992, the *Quarterly Journal of Speech* published a "forum" on rhetorical criticism, in which noted critics exhibited a self-consciously variegated rhetoric for rhetoric. In 1994, a collection of essays edited by William L. Nothstine, Carole Blair, and Gary A. Copeland offered the personal reflections of rhetorical critics on the very different types of work that they do. Published around the same time, *Landmark Essays on Rhetorical Criticism* defined rhetorical criticism by displaying the range of its canonic examples. Its editor, Thomas W. Benson, wrote, "We might as well admit at the outset that what is defined as 'rhetoric' and what passes as meeting the requirements of 'criticism' are themselves contested issues" (xi); "rhetorical action, and rhetorical theory and criticism, can never be codified and completed" (xiii).[8] Sonja K. Foss's *Rhetorical Criticism: Exploration and Practice* includes sections on (by name) neo-Aristotelian criticism, cluster criticism, fantasy-theme criticism, feminist criticism, generic criticism, ideological criticism, metaphoric criticism, narrative criticism, Burkean pentadic criticism, and generative criticism: rhetorical criticisms, all.[9]

Default rhetorical criticism in the twenty-first century is, however, still neo-Aristotelian. When students learn to do rhetorical analysis, in general they are learning to convert an Aristotelian framework for producing speeches into an analytic method for receiving them (see Gross and Keith, for example, on the production/reception distinction). Aristotle describes three occasions for speeches (deliberative, forensic, and epideictic—roughly, political, legal, and ceremonial), two kinds of arguments (artistic and nonartistic), two types of reasoning (deductive and inductive), two primary argumentative structures (the *enthymeme*, which is a rhetorical syllogism, and the example), three types of appeal (*ethos*, the character of the speaker; *pathos*, the emotions of the audience; and *logos*, the appeal of "the arguments themselves"), thirty-two lines of argument (called *topoi*, on the metaphor of location: We search for arguments in places), four parts of the speech (introduction, narration, proof, and conclusion), two principal virtues of style (clarity and correctness), and two main constituents of delivery (voice and gesture). With these elements, Aristotle supplies an apparatus for commentary.

Even within an Aristotelian framework, part of the theoretical project has been to leave rhetorical criticism openended, underdescribed, to allow to arise what will arise out of each critical situation. Rhetoric responds to exigence, and so does rhetorical criticism.

In 1925, Herbert A. Wichelns first described a neo-Aristotelian model for rhetorical criticism. According to another rhetorical critic, Donald Cross Bryant, Wichelns's "Literary Criticism of Oratory" set the pattern for rhetorical criticism and "had a greater and more continuous influence upon the development of the scholarship of rhetoric and public address than any other single work published in this century" (*Rhetorical Idiom* 5).[10] However, what Wichelns offered, in detail, was not an algorithm for Aristotelian criticism so much as a critical approach trained on Aristotelian theory with an interest in speaker, audience, arguments, expression, and delivery. Wichelns was reluctant to constrain the imaginations of critics in their pursuit of insights. As Charles J. Stewart notes in his history of rhetorical criticism in the twentieth century, Wichelns catalogued appropriate foci of interest on a classical model, but he did not explain *"how the critic should [proceed]"* (6; emphasis in original).

Writing some years after Wichelns, rhetorician Edwin Black proposed an alternative to neo-Aristotelian criticism, suggesting an approach based on rhetoric as *transaction* rather than *argumentation*. Rhetorical transactions, Black says, are the relations of rhetorical situation, rhetorical strategies, and audience effects—and critics should attend to ratios among these elements, according to a "scale" for the rhetorical process as a whole. But, like Wichelns, Black does not say how to do the analysis.

Black is a key figure in a history of enabling a rhetorical study of health and medicine, because he brings a theoretical and methodological unorthodoxy to the task of rhetorical criticism and because he opens up the question of what constitutes an appropriate text for rhetorical study: "[T]he subject matter of rhetorical criticism is persuasive discourse" (14), but "persuasive . . . refers to intent, not necessarily to accomplishment. Rhetorical discourses are those discourses, written or spoken, which aim to influence men" (15). With this, Black shifts his attention from *analysis of rhetorical texts* to *analysis of the rhetorical element in any text*. This is an important move for rhetorical criticism. Black had already with Lloyd Bitzer said that rhetoric extends beyond the realm of public address: "Rhetorical studies are properly concerned with the process by which symbols and systems of symbols [exert] influence upon values, attitudes, and actions, and they embrace all forms of human communication, not exclusively public address" (208). By the 1970s, then, even within traditional speech communication circles, the purview of the rhetorical critic expanded to include "texts" of all sorts and the persuasive element in them.

In this expansionist critical context, Bryant writes about the distinction for the rhetorical critic between "the treatment of artifacts as significant primarily for what they *are* and the treatment of them as primarily significant for what they *do*" (*Rhetorical Dimensions* 27). Here, Bryant follows the lead of Edward P. J. Corbett, who had described the rhetorical project for literature as "more interested in a literary work for what it *does* than for what it *is*" (*Rhetorical* xxii; emphasis in original). Moreover, by being interested in rhetoric as "the rationale of the informative and suasory *in* discourse," Bryant opened up texts literary and nonliterary, public and private, explanatory and suasory, written and spoken as possible objects of rhetorical critical study. Like Wichelns and Black, Bryant is more focused on the nature and quality of rhetorical criticism than on a procedure for it.

It is this very idea—that the *what* and the *why* of rhetorical criticism are actually more important than precisely the *how* of it—that Klyn and Walter articulate in passages I cited earlier in which they decry method. Arguing for critical pluralism against the monism of neo-Aristotelianism, Klyn, for example, writes that rhetorical criticism "does not imply a prescriptive mode of writing, any categorical structure of judgment, or even any judgmental necessity" (147). The best rhetorical critics have "functioned as *free* men . . . unfettered by any coercive critical doctrine, unconfined by any pedagogical imperative, able to reason inductively from their material and to explore their insights as independent, disinterested thinkers" (156). This, on the same point, is Walter:

> To assume that rhetorical theory can furnish a formula complete with a step-by-step procedure to be followed by the otherwise thoughtless critic, is likely in error. Formulas may work well in elementary physics, but in the humanities, formulas somehow result in mindless mechanicalness, giving evidence sometimes of hard work but less often of brilliance. Scholarship and hard work are not the same thing; but criticism that is brilliant is always criticism that could *not be easily prescribed*, that is somewhat unexpected, that fits the unique speech for which it is designed and perhaps no other speech, that is the most appropriate thing to say at *this* time about *that* speech. (170; emphasis in original)[11]

Rhetorical criticism, then, is an intentionally underspecified procedure, with certain characteristic interests, for the study of persuasive elements, in a wide range of texts, especially in the realm of social action or public discourse.
Two shifts had to take place in rhetorical criticism for health and medicine to become a realm of study for rhetoric and for rhetoric to become a means for the study of health and medicine. The first was that rhetorical criticism had to come to include not only observations along Aristotelian lines but also observations along the lines of other theories of persuasive action. The second was that rhetorical attention had to be directed not only to political, legal, or ceremonial speeches as objects of study but also to rhetorical "texts" more broadly defined. Rhetorical texts in this broader definition might be works of art or conversations with oneself or the reports of scientists writing for professional journals.

Two further theoretical shifts had to take place as well and did. Burke and Thomas S. Kuhn are key figures here—metonymically, because they stand in for other theorists as well, but not only metonymically. Burke opened up rhetoric to science, and Kuhn opened up science to rhetoric.

Burke is the twentieth-century rhetorical theorist who develops a critical approach coherent enough to stand with Aristotelianism. After Burke, rhetorical critics, who were not even asked to abandon their Aristotle (Burke did not abandon his), have a new set of terms—including "terministic screens," "dramatism," "identification," "division," "consubstantiation," "symbolic action," "courtship," "magic," "motive"—to describe a revised rhetorical attention.[12]

While Burkean theory suggests a possible procedure for rhetorical analysis and while, indeed, students are often taught a Burkean lexicon as a guide to textual analysis, Burke's criticism is itself not systematic. Burke sees all relations as discursive, all discourse as action, all action as motivated. With this view, nothing but the most fluid and wide-ranging criticism would serve. Marie Hochmuth Nichols indicates the range of resources for Burke's analysis of Adolf Hitler's *Mein Kampf*:

> [Burke's] knowledge of psychoanalysis is useful in the analysis of the "sexual symbolism" that runs through the book. . . . His knowledge of history and religion is employed to show that the "*materialization*" of a religious pattern is one "terrifically effective weapon . . . in a period where religion has been progressively weakened by many centuries of capital materialism." . . . Conventional rhetorical knowledge leads him to call attention to the "power of endless repetition." ("Kenneth Burke" 143; emphasis in original)[13]

Burke's own criticism, that is, is not, reductively, "Burkean." It is at once neo-Aristotelian, Freudian, metaphoric, ideological, pentadic, and more. Much of the variety that is codified in accounts of rhetorical criticism is performed in this single analysis by Burke.

In particular, two features of Burkean practice enable a rhetorical criticism for health and medicine. First, Burke's attentions are seamlessly both traditional and "new rhetorical." According to Burke, "The key term for the old rhetoric was 'persuasion' and its stress was upon deliberate design. The key term for the 'new' rhetoric would be identification, which can include a partially unconscious factor in appeal" ("Rhetoric—Old and New" 203).

> Persuasion ranges from the bluntest quest of advantage . . . to a "pure" form that delights in the process of appeal for itself alone, without ulterior purpose. And identification ranges from the politician who, addressing an audience of farmers, says, "I was a farmboy myself," through the mysteries of social status, to the mystic's devout identification with the source of all being. (*Rhetoric of Motives* xiv)

The rhetorical quality of Burkean criticism is explicitly not in his procedure but in his world view. He has sought, he says, to write a philosophy of rhetoric, theoretically expansive and methodologically unrestrained.

The second enabling feature of Burkean criticism is its inclusiveness. No discursive action lies outside its purview, and it deliberately includes science. Burke opens a rhetorical view of science not only because he entreats us to "realize how ubiquitous [deliberative] 'oratory' is today, particularly in written forms that often pass for sheer 'information,' 'knowledge,' 'science'" (*Rhetoric of Motives* 73) and not only because he makes it difficult to refute him on "the necessarily *suasive* nature of even the most unemotional scientific nomenclatures" (*Language* 45; emphasis in original). Burke opens a rhetorical view of science also because his rhetorical theory as a whole is a plausible account of scientific knowledge-making.

Burke defines rhetoric as an art of influence, "the use of words by human agents to form attitudes or to induce actions in other human agents" (*Rhetoric of Motives* 41). In Burke's view, rhetoric is the act of identification itself, in which the rhetor and the audience, having overcome their "division," *act together*, having "common sensations, concepts, images, ideas, attitudes" (*Rhetoric of Motives* 21). This rhetoric of identification as the starting place, the means, and the goal of discourse is among other things a theory of scientific discourse if the model of science is the model suggested by Kuhn, and widely accepted, of science proceeding within knowledge communities, sharing a language, an explanatory theory, rules of practice, puzzles, instruments, and standards of instrumentation.[14]

Kuhn's theory of scientific knowledge-making is so well known as not really to need rehearsal here, but his understanding of the role of *persuasion* in science is especially important to any account of intellectual history toward a rhetoric of health and medicine.

It is not as if there would be no rhetoric of science without Kuhn. But, as Randy Allen Harris and others have said, Kuhn provides a kind of touchstone for rhetorical inquiry because he actually uses the word *persuasion* to talk about how scientists are won over from one "disciplinary matrix" to another. When philosophers of science such as Michael Polanyi wrote about the value-ladenness of theory and the theory-ladenness of observation, they created the conditions also for a rhetoric of science. Rhetoric is another word for *tendency* in language. Some of the rhetorical view of science in the 1970s took the form of chastisement of scientists, on the idea that science should not be rhetorical but is (Cox and Roland; Weigert). However, some criticism took up the necessarily rhetorical element in social science and science itself (Weaver, "Concealed";

Simons, "Are Scientists?") and gave accounts consistent with those of science studies in other disciplines.

Kuhn makes rhetoric a featured element of the conduct of science. *The Structure of Scientific Revolutions* describes scientific progress occurring not simply by evolution or an accretion of scientific knowledge but by revolution—the overthrowing of one paradigm by another.[15] Certainly, a question pertinent to rhetorical inquiry is "What is the process by which scientists are brought from support of one paradigm over to support of another?" Kuhn's answer is "persuasion." Even without the invocation of persuasion by its name, however, Kuhnian science bears the stamp of rhetoric. Burke has said: "We must use terministic screens since we can't say anything without the use of terms; whatever terms we use, they necessarily constitute a corresponding kind of screen; and any such screen necessarily directs the attention to one field rather than another" (*Language* 50). He resonates with Kuhn:

> No part of the aim of normal science is to call forth new sorts of phenomena; indeed those that will not fit the box are often not seen at all. Nor do scientists normally aim to invent new theories, and they are often intolerant of those invented by others. Instead, normal-scientific research is directed to the articulation of those phenomena and theories that the paradigm already supplies. (*Structure* 24)

Paradigms gain their status, according to Kuhn, because they are "more successful [at puzzle solving] than their competitors" (23). Science as usual, "normal science," proceeds; an "anomaly" presents itself, a problem that normal science cannot solve; the discipline enters a state of "crisis"; and a new paradigm presents itself, forcing a choice among the discipline's initiated. "Paradigm shift" follows "the comparison of both paradigms with nature *and* with each other" (77; emphasis in original) and is the result of a rhetorical contest. The new paradigm must win adherents, and its establishment as the new normal science is evidence of rhetorical success:

> [I]f a paradigm is ever to triumph it must gain some first supporters, men who will develop it to the point where hardheaded arguments can be produced and multiplied. . . . Because scientists are reasonable men, one or another argument will ultimately persuade many of them. . . . [I]f the paradigm is one destined to win its fight, the number and strength of the persuasive arguments in its favor will increase. More scientists will then be converted, and the exploration of the new paradigm will go on. (158, 159)

Kuhn's theory of scientific revolutions is rhetorical, then, both implicitly, in its account of scientific training and trained observation, and explicitly, in its account of persuasion as a force in paradigm shift. In Kuhn's account, the figure of the impersonal, disinterested, value-free scientist is replaced by the rhetorically interesting figure of the persuading scientist in the social life of a scientific community. Burke explains a great deal of Kuhn. Scientific inquiry is legitimated by the inquirer's membership in a scientific community. Actions performed to acquire and maintain that membership are symbolic actions aimed at persuasion by identification and identification by persuasion. Membership is both a condition for and a consequence of participation. Now science is within the realm of rhetoric; and scientific conduct, knowledge production, and inquiry are material for rhetorical analysis.

That is, the 1960s and 1970s saw rhetorical theory converge with theory in the history, philosophy, and sociology of science, producing a rationale for the rhetorical study of health and medicine—a rationale and a call for such study. The convergence produced sociological studies that resembled rhetorical analysis (e.g., Latour and Woolgar; Gilbert and Mulkay; Knorr-Cetina) and produced rhetorical analysis that resembled sociology (e.g., Bazerman; Myers; Prelli). Rhetoric of science was not simply interdisciplinary. It was trans- and multi- and post-disciplinary, and it both enabled and suggested an approach for research on this question: *What can be learned about health and medicine by looking at them through the terministic screen of a theory of persuasion?*

Rhetorical study of health and medicine is, like rhetoric of science in general, Janus faced. It looks back to the sort of classical theory that produced its first terms of art and looks forward to newer theories offering an account of language in use.

Not many years ago, it might have been safe to say that most rhetorical critics held a certain set of beliefs about texts—in general, that texts reflect the intentions of authors, that authors communicate to readers through texts, that rhetorical acts are addressed, strategically, to audiences and have effects on the situations into which they are introduced.[16] By the late twentieth century, the rhetorical critic sees things a little differently. Most contemporary critics do not understand the rhetor to be simply a strategist with a purpose who speaks through crafted texts to an audience in order to change or make up their minds. In Burkean terms for contemporary theory, the rhetor is not only an *agent*, although he or she is one, but also an *agency*—for a language that is already in circulation. Contemporary rhetorical criticism is friendly to a poststructuralist account of language and to the idea of speech genres as themselves motivated forces in human interchange.[17] Rhetorical criticism is distinguishable from, but not incommensurable with, other contemporary critical programs. What is especially true of rhetoric is that it provides a theory for considering language in use, in Burke's "human barnyard"—broadly speaking (to invoke James Berlin's definition of rhetoric), "language in its service of power."

While a contemporary rhetorical criticism is in some ways poststructuralist, it is also, more than vestigially, humanist, and it may be that what distinguishes rhetorical criticism is also what has traditionally distinguished rhetoric, and that is that it has, as Weaver would say, "a sense of the *ought*" ("Language" 211; emphasis in original). Fuller bristles at so-called rhetoric critics who neglect their social obligation, *which is to say they have one*:

> Nowadays . . . rhetorical criticism is more literary analysis than sociology of reception. That is, rhetoricians often spend more time unearthing the "implied reader" of a text than tracking down the text's real readers and seeing what, if any, relation they have to the implied reader projected in the text. Unfortunately, this literary approach to rhetoric fails to capture the distinctiveness of rhetoric as a practice that has periodically interrupted, as well as represented, the normal flow of discourse. (*Philosophy* xii)

In the *QJS* forum on rhetorical criticism, Michael Leff distinguishes textual and ideological criticisms. Textual criticism, Leff says, centers on the interpretation "of the intentional dynamics of a text"; ideological criticism "studies the extensional, social and political force of discursive practice" (223). Leff proposes a dialectical relation between the two types of criticism, and he uses his own critical approach as an example of the dialectic: for Leff, "the text becomes stabilized as a field of rhetorical action through a calculus that subsumes its extensional thrust within its intentional dynamics" (226). That is, the critic looks outside a text by looking inside it; close reading repays theory, both rhetorical and ideological. Leff's invocation of ideology speaks to his own motive for rhetorical criticism, which is, clearly, to encourage the conditions for a better world, even (sometimes) with an idea of what would count as one. This is critic Roderick Hart on the same topic:

> Criticism is not something I do; it is something I am. I am a critic because I often do not like the language my contemporaries speak nor the policy opinions they endorse. I am a critic because I feel that rhetoric should move a society forward rather than backward, that it

should open and not close the public sphere, that it should make people generous and not craven. I am a critic, ultimately, because I am a citizen. (72)

Thomas B. Farrell says that the point of criticism is "to attend systematically to the qualitative differences among human artifacts" and that the end of criticism is "better artifacts, [r]icher human experiences, [e]nlightened civic participation" (4).[18]

While criticism is a form of advocacy for some rhetorical critics, others believe that description rather than approval and disapproval is the job of the critic but, yet, that the critic may ameliorate matters by describing them. One critic of the latter sort is Martha Solomon, whose account of the rhetoric of the medical reports of the Tuskegee syphilis project[19] draws attention to a "dehumanizing rhetoric" while Solomon herself says she refuses to be outraged by her own material:

> My goal has always been to explain rhetorical processes, not make social judgments. I recognize that all criticism is inevitably political and ideological to some extent, but I make an earnest effort to show how texts work rather than judge whether it is just that they should have worked at all. ("Commentary" 306)

What is true, however, of rhetorical criticism is that a will to amelioration pervades it. This will may be expressed through critical engagement, as in the case of Leff, or critical distance, as in the case of Solomon.

In the analysis itself, the rhetorical critic works uniquely from a *rhetorical subjectivity* that is constructed in the terms and history of a tradition that has always been concerned with moral action. It may be that every work of criticism is reflexively epideictic, singing its own praises as a work of analysis, but the special role of rhetorical criticism is self-consciously to serve a deliberative function as well.

My own analysis begins with a will to amelioration, though it claims no special purchase on what ought to be. Its purpose is to assist the understanding of human action in the realm of health and medicine by describing its rhetorical element. The analysis does this by inquiring about our persuasive lives in health and medicine, using some of the most basic principles of rhetorical theory, heuristically, as probes:

- Persuasion is contingent, fit to situation.
- Speakers construct and invoke their audiences.
- Speech genres, like speeches, are good places to look for values.
- Ambiguity is not a problem to be solved but a resource to be mined.

- Rhetoric per se only occurs where there is a contact of minds.
- The terms of a debate constrain what it is possible to argue at all.
- The character of a speaker is a means of persuasion.

The following chapters take their lead from these principles in turn and work in a rhetorical frame of mind.

Chapter Outline

Chapter 1 unpacks a first principle of rhetoric: *kairos*, the principle of contingency or fitness-to-situation. It considers the history of medicine as in part a study of shifts understood as rhetorical responses to changes in situation: a kairology. The period of interest is from the "birth of clinic" in the eighteenth century, as Michel Foucault describes it, through the institutionalization of contemporary biomedicine in the early twentieth century. The chapter is not a contribution to medical history itself, but it re-presents certain moments in medical history to suggest medicine's rhetorical element. The chapter is interested, for example, in the fall and rise of patients as knowledgeable interlocutors. The chapter serves as an introduction to medical history and offers *kairos* as a term to bear in mind in all of the chapters that follow.

Chapter 2 is an essay on the well-established rhetorical principle that the nature of discursive encounters is conditioned by speakers' constructions of their audiences. The chapter focuses especially on the physician's construction of one kind of patient: the headache patient. It argues that a patient who appears in a physician's office with a chronic and largely invisible complaint such as headache is a different sort of interlocutor than one who appears with a gaping wound or visible tumor. The chapter takes a historical view of physicians' characterizations of migraine patients especially and considers how these characterizations influence physician-patient encounters as well as treatments and treatment outcomes.

Chapter 3 is a study of pathography—the "autobiographical or biographical narrative about an experience of illness" (Hawkins, *Reconstructing* 229n1)—and it unfolds on the principle that in rhetorical productions reside community values. Aristotle used the term *epideictic* to designate speeches that most prominently display and perpetuate values: speeches such as funeral orations, whose primary work is to honor people for having embodied general virtues. (Aristotle's deliberative rhetoric is trained on the future, and its business is exhortation and dissuasion; his forensic rhetoric is trained on the past, and its business is accusation and defense.

Epideictic rhetoric is trained on the present, and its business is praise and blame.) Illness narratives are epideictic, surely. They may inscribe the virtue of a sense of optimism or a sense of irony or a sense of family. But, this chapter argues, the *genre* of pathography itself is epideictic, and so is much of pathography *scholarship*, which inscribes the virtue of a particular sort of response to illness—overall, an individual and apolitical one.

Questions of illness and meaning are further taken up in chapter 4 through the idea of hypochondria, a rhetorical disorder if ever there was one. Hypochondria is rhetorical in many dimensions simultaneously. Hypochondriacal complaints are meant to persuade, and so is public discourse structuring illness anxiety. Moreover, hypochondriacs are engaged in acts of self-persuasion, and they are the unpersuaded audiences of physicians intent on convincing them that they are well. The chapter explores where hypochondriacal complaints come from and how on various stages they perform. Burke's phrase "the *resources* of ambiguity" impels the interpretive work of the chapter (*Grammar* xix), and Burkean theory supplies some of the terms of investigation of this illness (if hypochondria is an illness) in which sufferers are at the same time agents, agencies, and scenes of distress.

The rhetorical principle at the center of chapter 5 is that the making up and changing of minds legitimately can only occur where there is a "contact of minds" (in the words of Chaim Perelman and Lucie Olbrechts-Tyteca). That is, two people are not engaged in a properly rhetorical enterprise but rather, perhaps, in a coercive one, when only one of them really knows what they are talking about, and the other only knows what the first one reveals. The sites of research in this chapter are the nursing home and the hospital, and the object of research is conversation about death and dying. The chapter focuses on encounters at patients' end of life between health care professionals on the one hand and patients and families on the other. It analyzes the persuasive action in such encounters but also makes the point that a developing public rhetoric of death-as-a-part-of-life is increasingly at odds with a biomedical rhetoric of death as medical failure. If biomedical and public discourses are, to some extent, incommensurable, then rhetorical study is itself a means of enabling fair persuasion to exist where it did not exist, really, before.

Chapter 6 is an essay on the language of health policy, specifically the metaphors that are "asleep" (see E. Martin, "Egg") in health-policy debate. Its rhetorical principle is Burke's principle of terministic screens (the salient quotation is a mantra to students of rhetoric—in effect, that a terminology is not simply a *reflection* of reality but necessarily also a *selec-*

tion and *deflection* of reality [*Language* 45]) and the corollary that the terms of a debate constrain what it is possible to argue at all. The chapter discusses, for example, these metaphors of health and medicine: *diagnosis is health, medicine is war, the body is a machine, medicine is a business, a person is genes.* The chapter argues that the outcomes of health-policy debate are constrained in part by the biomedical terms and metaphors in which the debate takes place. The purpose of the chapter is not to suggest an exchange of old metaphors for new ones but rather to take up Emily Martin's call to wake up sleeping metaphors, especially in science.

Chapter 7 considers similarities and differences among the concepts, *compliance* with physicians' orders, *adherence* to physicians' advice, and *concordance* between physicians and patients on matters of care. It argues that instead of primarily gathering compliance statistics for various conditions in various environments or announcing a "paradigm shift" to physician-patient equality to obviate the idea of "compliance" itself (see, for example, Burton and Hudson), health researchers might turn their attention to improving the conditions for getting best persuasion to occur. Here, as in chapter 5, questions are raised about trust, expertise, and decision making. While it is not certain that medical expertise is the primary necessary expertise in decision making on end-of-life care (a matter of quality of death), medical expertise may indeed be the most important expertise to have for decision making on matters of medical treatment: on the appropriateness of antibiotics, for example, or the advisability of childhood vaccinations. This chapter pivots on the rhetorical principle that *ethos*, the character of the speaker, is a central element in persuasion. The chapter notes that patients *will* have a role to play in decision making on matters of their own care and so considers the conditions for their persuasion.

The chapters of the book work together. The doctor-patient interview that is a topic for historical study in chapter 1 is the site of the problem of the headache patient as interlocutor in chapter 2 and of the compliance problem in chapter 7. The information in play in informed decision making problematized for end-of-life care in chapter 5 and for treatment adherence in chapter 7 is subject to the metaphoric leanings described for policy in chapter 6. The ambiguously trusted physician described in chapter 1 is the expert on whom questions of patient concordance turn in chapter 7. The notion that terms contain their obverses—the way, for example, *biopsychosocial* is both the refusal and the next iteration of *biomedical*—is a feature of both the account of the doctor-patient interview and the account of health-policy debate. If the patient is reimagined as consumer, there are implications for policy and for compliance most obviously but also for the reception of the migraine patient and the entitlements of the hypochondriac. The injection of terms into a living discourse is a questionable process in chapter 6 that demands especially to be taken seriously in chapter 7 in the case of compliance, adherence, and concordance. Pathography is an epideictic genre, and so is the medical journal's review article.

The book's conclusion confirms that rhetoric is a resource for critical common sense in everyday life. It has heuristic value for the analysis of lives lived increasingly in the idiom of health and illness. More and more, our identities are health identities. We think of ourselves as healthy or not, able-bodied or not—but also as fit or not, vegetarian or not, sexually "safe" or not, menopausal/andropausal or not. Some of us think of ourselves as cosmetically repaired and surgically altered or not. As we age, our hair (which is thinning), our teeth (which are yellowing), our bones (which are brittling), our eyes (which are failing) and our skin (which is wrinkling) are all sites of medical intervention, product promotion, and public information. What are possible lines of rhetorical thinking about this *medical us*, and what are possible rhetorically based interventions in customary discursive practice? Hart has said, "I am a critic because I often do not like the language my contemporaries speak nor the policy opinions they endorse" (72). Barbara Warnick writes that the "advocate critic," engages texts polemically and seeks "to persuade, to change readers' perspectives through the process of criticism" (233). The book's final chapter takes Hart and Warnick as the most optimistic of scholars and offers rhetorical theory as a means of criticism-for-use in the everyday lives of health researchers, health professionals, and patients—and the partial or incipient patient in all of us.

1   A Kairology of Biomedicine

Some sure evidence that biomedicine, notwithstanding its scientific basis, is subject to the vagaries—and the rhetoric—of situation is the instability of the nosology, the catalogue of illnesses. Both Edward Shorter and Elaine Showalter, for example, say that certain diseases, such as chronic fatigue syndrome and Gulf War syndrome, represent points of convergence of symptoms that articulate distress at a place and a time; Showalter, controversially, calls these diseases "hysterical epidemics." Andrew Malleson, writing especially about whiplash and associated disorders, says that diagnoses of particular conditions may multiply for reasons that have little to do with science. Diagnoses of whiplash, he says, are more frequent where soft-tissue injury is compensable by insurers than where it is not. What counts as illness, in Malleson's view, has a lot to do with money. According to Joseph Dumit,

> The very meaning of "definable illness" and especially the entailments of that definition—whether a person with symptoms receives help or blame or dismissal—depend upon who is doing the assessing, where they are doing it from, and within what regime of social good and compassion they are operating. . . . We may not like the implication that a person is sick in one place but not in another, but socially this may be a fact. ("When" 209)[1]

The most salient narrative of medical history is the narrative of progress, the narrative that says, "We used to have things wrong, and now we have

21

them right, or are on the road to having them right."[2] But a rhetorically informed medical narrative is a narrative of fitness. The history of medicine is a history of shifts that can be understood as responses to changes in situation where situation includes the record of scientific discovery.

The rhetorical principle undergirding this chapter is the principle of *kairos*, the principle of contingency and fitness-to-situation. Arguments are persuasive, said the Sophists, early rhetoricians, when they aptly meet conditions of time, place, and audience; arguments have a quality of truth *in those situations*. In a well-known example of Sophistic thinking, death is said to be bad for those who die but not bad absolutely, because it is good for undertakers and gravediggers. While Plato tells us that tyranny is bad for everyone (both the tyrannized, obviously, and tyrants, whose actions are bad for their immortal souls), the Sophist is willing to say that tyranny may be good for someone. Indeed, it might be true, for example, that tyranny is good when it spurs the tyrannized to seek a better state. Furthermore, for the Sophist, the *dialogue* on the possible benefits of tyranny is good in itself, a means of deriving knowledge about values.

In its dyslogistic, or negative, form, *kairos* is the principle of moral relativism, and, in fact, moral relativism is a criticism of Sophism mined by Plato. *Kairos* is rehabilitated in contemporary rereadings of classical rhetoric where Sophists are credited with having a pleasingly dialogic sense of truth (see Jarratt). As a part of a contemporary epistemology, *kairos* gives a good account of local and present knowledge in contrast to a Platonic and perhaps obsolete notion of absolute knowledge.

Kairos has heuristic value for understanding health and medicine both historically and currently. A compelling account of the coming and going of disorders in both medical fashion and patient experience is provided by Ian Hacking, who writes about "transient mental illness," an example of which is fugue, a dissociative disorder prompting travel, occurring primarily although not exclusively among European men of the late nineteenth century (*Mad Travelers*). Not only disorders but also medical institutional structures take hold at a time and a place, according to Michel Foucault, who writes about the "birth of the clinic" in eighteenth-century Europe and about attendant changes in ideas of the hospital, the home, medicine, and the body. The shifts Hacking and Foucault describe are among other things, by the account of the authors themselves, discursive shifts. Changes in practice are importantly reciprocal with changes in the terms of practice. They are for the same reason *rhetorical* shifts.

Rhetorical theory is below the surface in the accounts of Hacking and Foucault. Neither uses the lexicon of rhetorical theory predominately.

Kairos delivers some explanatory advantage, however, revealing medicine as a scene for persuasion and persuasion as a scene for medicine. Kenneth Burke describes a world seething with rhetoric. Naming shifts in diagnostic habits or medical institutional structures as kairotic opens up medicine as a Burkean world of motives and symbolic action. What captures the rhetorically minded historian's attention is not only a *chronology* of events but also a *kairology* of them: a study of historical moments as rhetorical opportunities.

A kairotic account of medical history is more Hacking-esque than Foucauldian. Foucault's account of things answers to a kind of teleology: It is an account of a world moving in a certain direction, away from some things and toward others, as from a more human medicine to a more mechanistic one. Hacking's account, on the other hand, features vectors. Hacking writes about mental illnesses as thriving in "ecological niches" identified by four vectors. An illness *is* an illness by fitting into a taxonomy of illness (the medical vector), by being situated in a certain way between cultural elements (the cultural polarity vector), by being visible as a disorder (the observability vector), and by providing some otherwise unavailable release (*Mad Travelers* 1–2). Similarly, a kairology is not a fatalistic account of things.

Kairology will be our term for a rhetorically tilted medical history. This chapter will focus on a key period in Western medicine—from the birth of the clinic in the eighteenth century through the institutionalization of contemporary biomedicine in the early twentieth. The chapter will be interested, for example, in the narrative thread of the fall and rise of patients as knowledgeable interlocutors. The chapter seeks not to contribute to medical history—it relies very much on existing accounts—but, rather, to consider medical history from a rhetorical point of view. When in later chapters we look at shifts over time in the characterization of the migraine patient (chapter 2), changes in the medical representation of the hypochondriac (chapter 4), and the discursive transformation of patient compliance into doctor-patient concordance (chapter 7), it will help to think of medicine as having this kairotic element. So, while other chapters are relatively specific in their applications of rhetorical principles to medical situations, this chapter uses a rhetorical principle, the principle that things are persuasive when they are fit to situations, to illuminate medicine more generally.

The history of medicine in the West is the history of *bio*medicine. According to Howard F. Stein, biomedicine is the "official" medicine of the Western world. It is referred to variously as "Western," "scientific," and "modern" medicine and is described by many authors. Sociologist Elliot Mishler describes biomedicine by referring to four assumptions that underlie it: (1) that diseases consist in deviations from measurable biological norms; (2) that diseases have specific and discoverable causes or origins; (3) that diseases have characteristic features that are universal; and (4) that physicians are bioscientists, ideally objective and neutral ("Viewpoint"). It may seem paradoxical to take as rhetorical what must be to be itself arhetorical; by its definition, biomedicine is not subject to the vicissitudes of persuasion. However, a considerable body of literature in rhetoric of science makes the case that the rhetoricity of arhetoricity is not really a paradox but rather only a bit of an irony.[3] Medicine cannot help but be rhetorical; it just doesn't know it.[4]

At mid-eighteenth century, Western medical practice consisted largely in the action of "heroic" medicine, based primarily on the traditional doctrine of humors, passed from Hippocrates through Galen. The humoral theory was a general theory of medicine, holding that all disease, regardless of symptoms, resulted from an underlying condition involving the body as a whole. Therapeutics encouraged balance within the body among blood, phlegm, yellow bile, and black bile. Bleeding, sweating, and purging and dosing with a variety of concoctions were the common prescriptions for restoring or inducing a healthy balance. The damage done by physicians practising in the humoral tradition is not well documented although it must have been considerable. Anemics were among those bled to relieve their symptoms; without antisepsis, physicians created running wounds to drain patients' bodies of impure fluids. Yet, "regular" physicians—that is, physicians practising allopathic medicine[5]—garnered by the eighteenth century considerable professional authority and prestige. They competed successfully for the loyalty of clients with other medical workers, such as, surgeons, barbers, midwives, and apothecaries, and with other physicians, such as homeopaths. Regular physicians of the time were not especially well respected or well paid, but their authority was established long before they could make the most convincing claims to be improving the health of their charges.

In their brief history of modern medicine, Barbara Ehrenreich and Deirdre English write that "heroic" medicine was a powerful weapon if not in the fight against disease then in the fight against other practitioners. One purpose of interventions as dramatic as bleeding, they say, was to produce the strongest possible effect on the patient, to leave "no question but that the doctor was doing something: something visible, tangible, and roughly measurable" (45). In the tradition of heroic medicine, the physician's authority is derived in part at least rhetorically: One might consult a physician and improve and be persuaded by rhetorical fallacy— the *post hoc ergo propter hoc* fallacy—that one improved *because of* the physician. Many who were subjected to emerging Western medicine would get better as long as their doctors did not make them worse. As Herbert Benson and others have documented, even in contemporary medical practice, most illnesses (about three-quarters of them) do not respond to physicians' specific agents and procedures. The illnesses "either get better by themselves or are related to nonspecific mind-body interactions" (13).

Paul Starr has noted that physicians' authority comes not only from their abilities of cure and prognosis but also from their ability to read the body, to say what symptoms mean. According to Starr, physicians shape patients' understandings of health or illness such that they "create the conditions under which their own advice seems appropriate" (14). Historian Barbara Duden reports that the authority of physicians in the first half of the eighteenth century depended not primarily on the knowledge that separated them from their patients, their special knowledge as physicians, but on the knowledge that bound them to their patients, a shared knowledge of the body. Physicians, that is, specialized in what everyone knew.

Duden gives an account of the records of physician Johann Storch practising in Eisenach, Germany, in the first half of the eighteenth century. Her history allows us to read shifts in health experience and medical practice as kairotic shifts. We might say, relying on Duden's history, that the medical rhetoric of the early eighteenth century was *epideictic*, its main action being to affirm the values of the community in which it is offered— specifically, to perpetuate those values by the motions of praise and blame. Medical encounter in Storch's practice affirmed what informed persons already knew. Medical authority, then, was a function of the epideictic nature of the discourse of care; it was, furthermore, a shared authority.

For example, it was common knowledge in Eisenach that "cold wind on bare skin closed the pores and drove the blood inward, thus explaining violent cramps and epileptic seizures" (Duden, *Woman* 140). The experienced body is an element in and an effect of the rhetorical conditions of medicine. Duden's history makes clear that physicians collaborate with the people they treat to construct the body they both construe. Storch's records reveal what women's bodies were before they were constructed in the rhetoric of modern medicine. Storch's patients describe the body as a "porous place, a place of metamorphosis" (109). "Their freckles transformed themselves into bad breath; sweat smelled of urine; stopped-up menstrual blood left the body through bloody sputum" (109).

In many cases, Storch was called upon to explain the anatomically and physiologically impossible, but he had little trouble doing this, so compelling were patients' eyewitness accounts of the phenomena of their living bodies and so willing was he to take his patients at their word.

Duden demonstrates that the body in Eisenach was known as fully in its own terms as our body is known now; it was not waiting to be discovered by scientific medicine. Just as patients are said currently to get sick in accordance with advertised disease processes—and "symptom pools" (see Shorter; Showalter; and Malleson)—so, too, did the women of Eisenach. Their diseases and their body experiences were, as ours are, saturated with context. Although Duden does not offer an explicitly rhetorical account of medical history, she does suggest an element of rhetorical inevitability in the particularities of ways of being sick. Some descriptions will be more effective than others in persuading physicians of a place and a time that one is ill. Duden explains even that it is a possessiveness of a time and a place that invites us to talk about the bodies the women of Eisenach *had*. To "have" a body, she says, is a consequence rather than a given of medical perception after 1750. A rhetoric of medicine is bound, that is, reciprocally, to a rhetoric of the body.[6]

The traditional body of Duden's accounts, fluid and wanting to be opened and drawn out, was replaced in the nineteenth century by a medical body, invented, as Foucault says, by the "clinical gaze." This body was the object and the creature of clinical observation and pathological anatomy and only became possible when the patient was relocated from the home and the hospital and came to inhabit the clinic. It is this new body—hardbound, anatomized, and deferent to the institution—that, having been made, has come to be understood as the one we were looking for all along.

Foucault's translator, A. M. Sheridan Smith, uses the term *clinic* to denote both clinical medicine and the teaching hospital. The clinic was different from the traditional hospital, which housed more indigent cases than interesting ones. The primary function of the hospital was patient care, but the primary function of the clinic was physician education. Diseases were represented there, residing in exemplary human specimens:

> [I]n the hospital one is dealing with individuals who happen to be suffering from one disease or another. . . . In the clinic, on the other hand, one is dealing with diseases that happen to be afflicting this or that patient. . . . In the hospital, the patient is the *subject* of his disease, that is, he is a *case*; in the clinic, where one is dealing only with

examples, the patient is the accident of his disease, the transitory object that it happens to have seized upon. (Foucault 59)

In the clinic, Foucault says, "[T]he individual in question was not so much a sick person as the endlessly reproducible pathological fact to be found in all patients suffering in a similar way" (97).

The birth of the clinic removed the person from his or her lifeworld and reset him or her in the institution. Thus, in a transformation from personhood to patienthood, the individual exchanged one kind of isolation for another. He or she gave up the isolation of the diseased person in the larger community to become an exemplary member of what was a disease community. At the same time, he or she was isolated by dislocation. The transformation, in any case, constituted "progress" in medicine: It allowed the scientific and epidemiological study of disease.

Foucault underscores the discursive nature of the shift in the focus of practice from treatment of the person to study of the exemplar. Now the "text" to be read is not the person but the disease. The ideal of medicine was that "all pathological manifestations would speak a clear, ordered language" (94–95), a language that is not referential but is reality itself. The rhetorical ideal was a visual and embodied version of seventeenth-century scientific language, described by Thomas Sprat in his 1667 *History of the Royal Society*, as a language of "primitive purity and shortness . . . where men deliver'd so many things almost in an equal number of words" (314). Medical language was thus essentially anatomical. The reliability of medical description depended on the effacement of the patient. "Medical certainty is based not on the *completely observed individuality but on the completely scanned multiplicity of individual facts*" (Foucault 101; emphasis in original).[7]

As the discourse of medicine changed, it also became differently persuasive. It became persuasive from a new authority the more it was associated with the rhetoric of science. Modern medicine was born in the clinic itself and at the meeting of the clinic and the morgue. While Storch only decades before did not customarily examine, or sometimes even meet, his patients (but rather relied on the reports of patients brought by messengers and on patients' various transported bodily productions), physicians by the end of the eighteenth century looked at, listened to, and palpated the bodies of their charges in the interest of diagnosis. A theory of particular diseases, different and localized in particular organs and tissues, had appeared in the sixteenth century and again in the seventeenth century, but when, in the eighteenth century, bedside observations were correlated with death-house observations, diagnoses of particular diseases really became possible. In the eighteenth century, anatomists suggested that lesions found at autopsy could be correlated with antemortem symptoms and the findings of physical examinations.

The Galenic notion of general disease then collapsed, at least in theory, against a new nosology that arose from pathological anatomy. Again, as rhetoric is plastic, there is a medical rhetoric of the moment that both responds to and helps to materialize a new sort of patient and a new relation between patient and physician. As disease was localized in specific organs and tissues, the whole patient was replaced by the fractured or exploded patient, medically not more than the sum of his or her parts (see Young, "Narrative Embodiments," on the "disarticulated" body). The living body of the patient was read with a hermeneutics of death. Both objectification of the patient and separation from him or her were inevitable, then, if the physician did not want to identify with a corpse.

Rhetorician Charles M. Anderson notes that medical students encounter patients first as cadavers, "shorn of the possibilities of pain and pleasure and language" (9). Identification of the diseased person and the dead one is one reason, perhaps, for *division* (in the Burkean sense, the opposite of *identification*) in the encounter of patient and physician although it is not the only reason. The physician may separate himself or herself from patients, as Kathryn Montgomery Hunter suggests, to ensure provision of medical services fairly and indiscriminately; or separation may be a device of self-protection, a defence against sadness or loss. Indeed, division is a standard feature of medical rhetoric, not only in patient-physician communication but also in physician-physician communication and in physician self-talk. (Medical sociologist Sue Fisher reports that when she queried a medical resident on his choice of reproductive oncology as a specialty, he replied that he wanted to work on diseases from which he was necessarily immune [7].)

Pathological anatomy not only mapped the body, it also inscribed the metaphor of mechanism onto it. The mechanized-industrialized body is something to notice in a kairological account of medicine, because it can be seen to arrive and, recently, to begin to depart. The body of the late twentieth and early twenty-first centuries is described increasingly with gene metaphors—the body is code on display, genes are the incipient body—and with computer metaphors. Once, my doctor found me "run down"; now, he says my "hard drive is full."

With studies in pathological physiology in the nineteenth century, the body was not only a machine but also a laboratory where chemicals were synthesized from increasingly known elements, and entry into both machine and laboratory was made possible by nineteenth-century instrumentation. The nineteenth century saw a proliferation of scopes (stethoscopes, ophthalmoscopes, laryngoscopes) that could be used in examining patients and of other new technologies of the gaze (x-rays, microscopes) that could be used in the diagnosis of illness even in the absence of the patient. The microscope brought the physician's gaze to the level of the cell. These technologies further scientized the practice of medicine; they also scientized the rhetoric of medicine. They created more distance between patient and physician, and they made the physician a more powerful interlocutor.[8]

Duden and Foucault provide well-textured histories of the movement away from reliable patient accounts, but the shift away from full-bodied patients at the center of medical practice is a commonplace of medical history. Historian Mary Fissell writes:

> [In the] context of increasing medical autonomy . . . the patient's narrative of illness was made utterly redundant. Hospital medicine came to focus on signs and symptoms, which provided doctors with a disease-orientated diagnosis conducive to the demands of hospital practice and reflective of its social structure. (93)

Fissell reports that the erosion of the patient's narrative was underway by 1800. Over the course of nineteenth century, "[d]octors begin to sound like doctors, and patients' voices disappear" (99).

Medical historians, such as Richard H. Shryock, note that the stethoscope, originally just a wooden tube for amplifying sound, might have been invented centuries earlier but was not in part because examination of the chest was of no interest to doctors before a theory of specifically localized disease. The stethoscope went through a variety of design changes and improvements before it became an instrument the physician could *wear*, an element of biomedicine's visual rhetoric, a metonym for the doctor and a sign of his or her special capabilities.

Although it is still associated with the figure of the physician, the stethoscope has already had its rhetorical moment. The stethoscope stood for the physician's diagnostic power especially when pronouncements of tuberculosis and other bronchial disease were the prophecy of death. Now, much of the most terrifying diagnostic work of medicine is done far away from patients, in radiography rooms and laboratories, and doctors are, more often than before, seen without the defining accessory.[9]

Stethoscopes were, inter alia, a means of the nineteenth-century doctor overcoming the intimacy of physical proximity in the doctor-patient relationship. Roy Porter cites this personal account from Laennec, the inventor of the stethoscope:

> In 1816 I was consulted by a young woman presenting general symptoms of disease of the heart. Owing to her stoutness little information could be gathered by application of the hand and percussion. The patient's age and sex did not permit me to resort to [direct application of ear to chest]. I recalled a well-known acoustic phenomenon: namely, if you place your ear against one end of a wooden beam the scratch of a pin at the other extremity is distinctly audible. It occurred to me that this physical property might serve a useful purpose in the case with which I was then dealing. (*Greatest Benefit* 309–10)

According to Laennec, intimacy was overcome by this invention. Also overcome was the subjective report of the patient; it was trumped by the objective report of the new technology. Diagnosis was rendered objective by instrumentation that allowed the doctor to "bypass the patient's unreliable account" (R. Porter, *Greatest* 309). To illustrate, Porter contrasts an eighteenth-century account of consumption by physician William Heberden "based upon a lifetime of taking histories and close observation" (309) and a nineteenth-century account by Leannec "homing in on physical change beneath the skin and manifesting the disease-centredness of the new medicine" (310).

Thus, a diagnostic protocol develops in the nineteenth century that more and more excludes patient narrative. Stanley Reiser observes that with the stethoscope, the physician "isolated himself in a world of sounds, inaudible to the patient" (43). The physician's attention turned literally away from the patient to the sounds of the body, sounds that the patient himself or herself could not interpret or even hear. Commenting on more recent diagnostic technology, Duden in *Disembodying Women* describes prenatal uterine ultrasound as a means of directing the physician's attention, again away from the patient, now to the videographic image of her womb, rendering the woman both a medium for and an obstacle to the viewing of the foetus; she is an object whose opacity must be overcome.

By the end of the nineteenth century, the patient's account, so valuable to Storch not much more than a century before, was not the key to diagnosis; it was, in fact, something of an impediment to it. The patient as a reliable person was disappearing. His or her story was suspect in principle, as subjective rather than objective; as well, the patient might be the scene of asymptomatic disease (such as venereal disease) or be an unwitting carrier of disease (such as smallpox) or be duped by pain referred from one location to another. Whereas Storch and his patients knew the same body, by the nineteenth century, scientific—"real"—knowledge of the body was available to the physician alone, and the patient had become a little stupid. Fissell mentions that the move from English to Latin as the primary language of diagnosis was swift and occurred at the end of the eighteenth century. "Cough" became "*tussis*"; "wound" became "*vulnus*," and so on. In the late 1770s, 70 percent of all diagnoses were in English, and 19 percent were in Latin (the rest were diagnoses without precise linguistic equivalents); by the turn of the century, 79 percent of diagnoses were in Latin, and only one percent were in English.

The patient's narrative itself came to need translation—from patient's story to doctor's story. It came to need retelling in a way consistent with established medical knowledge. The meaning and the means of the shift are discussed by historians, like Fissell, and by scholars from other disciplines—by literary specialist Hunter, sociologist Aaron V. Cicourel, and anthropologist Young. All of these scholars have documented the thinning and restyling of patients' stories as they are translated into the generic terms of disease classification.

Duden has lamented the loss of the primacy of experience as patients themselves wait for affirmation from technology to know what they are experiencing. It is true that many of us ourselves have waited for the reading on the thermometer to find out if we are sick (or the reading on the electrocardiogram to find out if we are dead). A kairology suggests that the symbolic moment of the credulous patient may also be passing, much like the symbolic moment of the stethoscope has, for the most part, passed. Direct-to-consumer advertising for prescription pharmaceuticals (more on this later in the chapter), disease support groups, childbirth and menopause movements, health information Web sites, popular pathographies, and patients' rights legislation are all part of a somewhat different rhetoric of patienthood. Democracy and publicity in matters of health may not actually solve the problems of alienation that attend medical technologies—Duden has suggested that the very means of patient empowerment can actually foster feelings of alienation[10]—but the shift itself in patient roles is further evidence that medical history is a history of movements and moments that by their nature come and go.

The practice of medicine became both safer and more effective in the nineteenth century with the dual discoveries of anaesthesia and antisepsis. The discovery of ether in 1846 made surgery a common medical intervention. Around 1865, Joseph Lister began spraying incisions with carbolic acid, lowering the rate of postsurgical infection and increasing

31

the desirability of surgery. By the end of the nineteenth century, surgical instruments and surgeons' hands were also sterilized, making surgery more lifesaving than life-threatening. So, surgeons and physicians gradually traded places in the medical hierarchy. Earlier, surgeons were associated with barbers, and their practice was restricted to operations on broken bones, visible tumors, and the like. By the end of the nineteenth century, their purview included the once-invisible interior of the body. Internal medicine was now in the hands of surgeons.[11]

Discoveries continued apace. Between 1875 and 1900, specific bacteria were identified as causal factors in typhoid, cholera, tuberculosis, pneumonia, and diphtheria, and soon, the spread of these diseases was controlled. Public health measures were largely responsible for slowing the spread of contagious disease during this period, with water purification and improved food handling being the most significant improvements. Still, the medical profession was due much of the credit for disease control, for it was the discovery of prevention by immunization that checked the spread of diseases such as smallpox, diphtheria, and yellow fever. Life expectancy in the United States went from forty-one in 1850 to fifty in 1900, then to sixty-five by 1955 (Shryock 260). This last jump was due in part to the development of curative drugs, such as antibiotics and insulin, in the first half of the twentieth century.[12]

The emerging authority of physicians came only in part from the measurable benefits of their treatments. Their authority came also from the work of professional inclusion and exclusion performed by guilds and organizations of allopathic physicians. Much of this work was done in the twentieth century and institutionalized biomedicine as we know it. Professional "boundary work" is itself a sort of rhetorical work and has been written about as such by Lawrence J. Prelli, for one, who is interested in strategies deployed to establish who counts as a scientist and who does not (see also Gieryn, whom Prelli cites). Boundary work is in part the process by which arguments are marshalled to move some people to the center of legitimate professional life and some to the margins of it and some right outside. The American Medical Association had been formed in 1847, but the ranks were not fully closed until the AMA's Council on Medical Education joined forces with the philanthropic Carnegie Foundation to order a study of medical education. The resulting report—the Flexner report of 1910—is widely believed to be a turning point in medical history. It made Johns Hopkins the prototype medical school and closed the doors of scores of schools that did not meet its standards. By 1915, the number of schools had fallen from 131 to 95, and the number of graduates from 5,440 to 3,536. By 1922, the number of medical schools had fallen to 81 and graduates to 2,529 (numbers are from Starr 120–21).

Eighteenth-century medicine had been characterized by the populist notion of "every man his own physician"—the short title, in fact, of a widely circulating book by John Theobald, *Every Man His Own Physician. Being a Complete Collection of Efficacious and Approved Remedies. For Every Disease Incident to the Human Body. With Plain Instructions for Their Common Use. Necessary to Be Had in All Families, Particularly Those Residing in the Country*, published in 1764. Historian Charles Rosenberg says that until the mid-eighteenth century, books on health for laypeople fell into two broad categories: books on regimen and long life, written to be read more than used, and more pragmatic books, "consisting essentially of recipes or lists of medicaments and their applications in the home treatment of perceived illness," written to be used more than read (34–35). William Buchan's *Domestic Medicine*, published in 1769, broke away from those conventions, being a book to be both read and used, recruiting readers to the project of health maintenance and illness care, assuming a "broad diffusion of medical knowledge among . . . Britons" (Rosenberg 38). The book was, nonetheless, intent on "setting the plausible boundaries between medicine and its lay competitors" (39).

John C. Gunn's *Domestic Medicine, or a Poor Man's Friend, in the Hours of Affliction, Pain, and Sickness*, published in 1830, continued in the tradition of a "world in which knowledge and competence were not segregated in credentialed heads and hands" (Rosenberg 57). Edward B. Foote's *Plain Home Talk*, published about forty years later, embraced, as its subtitle announces, "medical common sense," applied to "causes, prevention, and cure of chronic diseases," and more. By the end of the nineteenth century, however, medical competence was in the hands of licensed practitioners in a proprietary frame of mind, and self-help books notwithstanding, physicians sought more explicitly to deprive their patients of, rather than equip them with, the sense that they could look after themselves. In his *Book on the Physician Himself: And Things That Concern His Reputation and Success* (published c. 1890), D. W. Cathell advised physicians:

> Especially avoid giving self-sufficient people therapeutic points that they can thereafter resort to. . . . It is not your duty to cheat yourself or other physicians out of legitimate practice by supplying this person and that one with a word-of-mouth pharmacopoeia for general use. If compelled to give a person remedies under a simple form, study to do so in such a way as not to increase his self-conceit and make

him feel that he knows enough to practice self-medication and dispense with your services. (qtd. in Starr 87)

Status asymmetry between physicians and their patients as a concomitant or a feature of their knowledge asymmetry was perfected in the twentieth century. Anderson writes in the 1980s about the vertical rather than horizontal rhetoric of physician-patient dialogue in broadly contemporary medicine, and Moira Stewart and Debra Roter write about "high physician control and low patient control"; Candace West provides a review of social science literature on asymmetry in the doctor-patient relationship. More recently, both Barron H. Lerner ("From Careless") and James A. Trostle give historically informed accounts of paternalism and the ideology of physician control. While a paternalism consequent to peculiar asymmetries seems to be a well-established feature of biomedicine, it is also a kairotic one. That is, relational elements of medical practice are themselves not fixed. As chapter 7 (on the shift from patient compliance to doctor-patient concordance) notes, medical paternalism itself may be replaceable by some other value.

Certain (nonpaternalist) values of health care are implied and actualized by direct-to-consumer advertising for prescription pharmaceuticals, advertising aimed at patients and patients-to-be who are addressed as consumers. In the *British Medical Journal*, Silvia N. Bonaccorso and Jeffrey L. Sturchio argue, in support of direct-to-consumer advertising, that multiple persuasions are at work all the time in health and medicine and that pharmaceutical company persuasion is best considered first as information-giving, a force against both paternalism of physicians and the paternalism of any organization that would seek to protect patient-consumers from advertising itself:

> [Opponents of direct-to-consumer advertising] would argue that the information offered by a pharmaceutical company must be biased in ways in which information from doctors and public agencies will not be. Certainly, all stakeholders have different agendas. Companies will want to increase the market for their medicines; doctors will want to guard professional territory; and the government will want to minimise the cost to the exchequer. But it seems condescending to assume that consumers have no consciousness of these mixed motives and that their scepticism will be dissolved in their anxieties about health and illness. (910)[13]

The informed-consumer model of health care to which Bonaccorso and Sturchio subscribe seems to run counter to a vertical medicine and to suggest a different *ethos* for the physician—notably, as partner rather than as father or god.[14] It does not *necessarily* do so, however. "Shared responsibility" is, in part, a refreshing new direction for health care and, in part, a rhetorical manoeuver to watch. What seems to be a challenge to paternalism may be a cagey new version of it. That is, in shared-responsibility medicine, patients have a voice because they are *granted* a voice; patients are decision makers because they are recruited to decision making by experts who tell them what decisions are to be made and what the terms are in which to make them (see chapters 5 and 7 on medical decision making)[15]; medicine empowers patients while what counts as patienthood is established in advance. Some of the differences between the new physician and the old one are, that is, rhetorical. There are ways in which the new physician is still the god-like practitioner but one whose job description includes caring what the patient thinks.

As kairology is an account of contingency, there are further plots and subplots to be registered in a fitness narrative of medical history. Geoffrey C. Bowker and Susan Leigh Star, for example, provide a history of the *International Classification of Diseases* (ICD) that may be read as a rhetorical history. Starvation, they report, takes on new meaning as a cause of death in the first part of the twentieth century when the World Health Organization distinguishes between the starvation of an adult ("misfortune" is the cause of death) and the starvation of a child ("homicide" is the cause of death) (19). These are changes in classification that both reflect and effect changes in how medicine is practised; a persuasive force of classification responds to and produces values governing notions of illness and death. David Healy's history of the pharmaceutical industry in antidepressants may also be read as a rhetorical history, partly because Healy describes the reciprocity of psychiatric conditions and the pharmaceutical treatments for them (Does depression persuade us in the direction of Prozac, or does Prozac persuade us in the direction of depression?) and partly because the discourse of drugs, those that cure us and those that "enhance" us, is itself a rhetorical discourse. Peter Kramer (*Listening*), Carl Elliot (*Better Than Well*), and Brendan I. Koerner all write as well about enhancement therapies in ways compatible with rhetorical thinking.

On the rhetoric of drugs themselves, this is Jacques Derrida:

[T]here are no drugs "in nature." There may be natural poisons and indeed naturally lethal poisons, but they are not as such "drugs." As with addiction, the concept of drugs supposes an instituted and an institutional definition: a history is required, and a culture, conventions, evaluations, norms, an entire network of intertwined discourses, a rhetoric, whether explicit or elliptical. (2)

Nikolas Rose's discussion of the "pharmacotherapeutics of desire" is part of a larger account of the molecularization of disease and the return in psychiatry of the *gaze*, now the prosthetic gaze of visualizing technologies. Rose's analysis, too, can be read with persuasion as a keyword; his analysis also returns us to Foucault. The histories of particular ailments from cancer (see Sontag, *Illness*) to migraine (see my chapter 2) are also rhetorical histories, as are histories of explanation from humors to genes.

Kairos is a way of making sense of both the medical past and the medical present. It helps illuminate the current medico-cultural moment when popular and medical interests converge on certain themes as they seem currently to converge on the theme of memory (false and failing), the theme of pleasure (its relation to pain and its regulation), and the theme of death (avoiding and designing it). The convergence of these themes in our own medical times can be understood in part as the persuasive manoeuvrings of baby boomers, who worry publicly about such things; in part as the consequences of new technologies of persuasion—the Internet, for example, which features information over narrative and archive over history, explaining some of our anxiety over memory; and in part as the pervasive persuasive force of late capitalism: Entrepreneurs will repair our desire with one drug and disable it with another.[16]

When persuasions take place in medicine—about diagnosis and nosology and about who is a trusted professional, what is the role of patients in decision making, what is an appropriate institution for a sick person to inhabit, what counts as being sick—those persuasions take their shape from and make sense in the context of a time and a place. The rhetorical ideas then of contingency and fitness-to-situation—in a word, *kairos*—are informing ideas for understanding health and medicine, and it makes sense to deploy kairology in concert with other means of medical historiography.

2 Patient Audience: The Rhetorical Construction of the Migraineur

The patient takes on certain new characteristics when regarded as a speaker and an audience involved in a rhetorical situation. In the physician's office, the patient is not only an ill person or a person with a complaint; he or she is also an interlocutor in a persuasive encounter in which the reward of credibility may be best care, and the price of lack of credibility may be more sickness or pain. Moreover, credibility is not something that the patient can easily carry into the medical rhetorical situation from outside of it; rather, credibility is granted by the situation itself or created by it. In many cases, in order to be positioned to receive the best possible care, the patient must be credible not as an accountant or a sister or a gardener; the patient must be credible as a patient. Furthermore, the role of patient exists primarily in relation to the role of physician; the patient is also the physician's audience and is for that reason also a construct of the physician.

Perhaps more than any other element, the notion of audience defines rhetorical theory. There is no rhetoric without an audience. There is no speech without listeners, no writing without readers. A core principle of rhetorical theory is that discursive encounters are conditioned by speakers' audiences. As Aristotle says, "'Persuasive' means persuasive to a person" (11); the speech is "the joint result of three things—the speaker, his subject matter, and the person addressed" (16).

Twentieth-century rhetorical theory is particularly focused on the idea of audience. Kenneth Burke says that rhetoric is, essentially, *addressed*. Richard M. Weaver refers to the dual obligations of rhetoric: to the "external order of things" and to the audience to which it is addressed ("Language"). Chaim Perelman and Lucie Olbrechts-Tyteca identify three kinds of audience as playing a normative role in argumentation. The first is the *universal audience*, "the whole of mankind, or at least . . . all normal, adult persons." The second is the "single *interlocutor* whom a speaker addresses in a dialogue. The third is the *subject himself* when he deliberates or gives himself reasons for his actions" (30). The audience of contemporary theory is conceptually more expansive than the audience of classical theory; it is also based on a more communal model of rhetoric: the speaker is himself or herself a member of the audience who rises, at least metaphorically, to speak.

In every formulation, the audience inhabits the imagination of the speaker, who, to do his or her job well, composes the speech in light of it. "The writer's audience," says Walter J. Ong, "is always a fiction," the audience-construct in the mind of the rhetor in the act of composition. Maurice Charland takes the idea of a constructed audience further, to talk about the audience as not only imagined by the rhetor but also *constituted by the speech*.

In a way quite helpful for thinking about the patient audience—the patient *as* audience—Charland writes about how a policy paper on Quebec sovereignty, the 1979 "White Paper," addressed primarily to the French-speaking population of the province of Quebec, *interpellated* or called forth an audience, a "peuple Québécois," which did not as a collective preexist the paper itself (Charland cites Louis Althusser on the condition of the subject):

> [T]he White Paper calls on those it has addressed to follow narrative consistency and the motives through which they are constituted as audience members. . . . [A]udiences do not exist outside rhetoric, merely addressed by it, but live inside rhetoric. Indeed, from the moment they enter into the world of language, they are subjects; the very moment of recognition of an address constitutes an entry into a subject position to which inheres a set of motives that render a rhetorical discourse intelligible. (232)

In general, twentieth-century rhetorical theory holds that we are, each of us, made in rhetorical interchange with other people. As we encounter each other in language, we come to be who we are. This view of audience has two levels, at least. We are social beings whose very selves are made in symbolic interaction with other people (see Wayne C. Booth, for example); also, each time we are addressed, we are invited, sometimes irresistibly, to take on the shape of a particular audience.

I am interested in what can be learned about the physician-patient encounter, a central encounter in medical practice, when we think about physician and patient as interlocutors and, in particular, when we think about the patient as an audience, addressed but also interpellated and constituted by the physician.

My example is the migraine patient. In this chapter, I review the history of migraine and of the migraine patient to argue that medical practice includes rhetorical activity that *makes* patients and, even, makes their disorders. Although I do not question the *reality* of migraine and the physiology and biochemistry that account for it, I argue that the migraine patient is among other things rhetorically constructed.[1] My rhetorical-construction claim is not a version of a more general social-construction claim. To say, *migraine is socially constructed* is to enter a debate about the nature and etiology of the disorder. To say *the migraine patient is rhetorically constructed* is only to observe the effects of the inter(textual)play between, at least, medical publication and the physician-patient encounter.[2]

Migraine is a good rhetorical study in part because of its particular ambiguities of both symptom and meaning. Its special problem is that no one really knew and in a sense no one still really knows exactly where migraine comes from. The experts' long-standing focus on the *character* of the migraineur was an attempt both to explain and to diagnose a disease about which until very recently one could only say two things for sure. The first was that there was very little one could say for sure about it,[3] and the second was that it seemed to affect some people and not others. On the matter of the way migraine selects migraineurs, Galen himself had speculated that "certain natures" "may end up suffering from headache if they lead an intemperate life" (Isler 227). It makes sense that where there is medical uncertainty, rhetoric enters to fill gaps of knowledge. Aristotle says, "On matters which admit of no alternative, which necessarily were, or will be, or are, certainties, no one deliberates, at least not on that supposition—for nothing is to be gained by it" (11–12). One of the especially interesting things about migraine is the way that the subject matter for medical rhetoric on migraine so much became the patients themselves.

A note on terms: *Headache* and *migraine* are overlapping terms (some headaches are migraines; most but not all migraines are headaches). I use both terms in this chapter, but the terms are not interchangeable. For example, *migraine personality* does not suggest *headache personality*, and the *headache patient* is not specified in the way the *migraine patient* is. However, I will argue that the patient who complains to his or her doctor of headache will be met, in the rhetorical transaction of the doctor-patient interview, by a physician whose approach to headache has been written in part by his or her reading on migraine. *Headache* is a general term that includes both primary and secondary conditions. In *primary headache*, the clinical diagnosis is headache itself. Often called *functional headache*, to distinguish it from *organic headache*, primary headache has traditionally included migraine, notwithstanding compelling accounts of migraine's organic etiology. *Secondary headache* is a condition that is a symptom of another condition, such as brain tumor or hemorrhage. Migraine is a particular disorder with a number of diagnostic criteria including, for example, the presence of auras, the tendency to unilaterality, and a familial element. Some recent literature suggests the continuity of functional-headache conditions, so muscle-contraction (tension) headache is not seen as categorically different from migraine, which itself is described usually in vascular terms. Very recent literature (see note 1) describes migraine as a specific progressive disorder.

The physician-patient interview is a rhetorical encounter in which the behavior of one interlocutor is determined to a great extent by his or her view of the other. In part because of what has been written about the headache patient as character, the person who enters the doctor's office with chronic headache—an invisible, often benign, and likely to be intractable complaint—is not the same rhetorical partner as one who enters with, for example, a visible tumor or gaping wound. The person complaining to a physician of headache can expect his or her medical interview and course of treatment to be shaped in part by *the headache patient* that exists in the physician's mental cast of characters.

The physician's view of the headache patient is clinically important. Some physicians are reluctant to order expensive diagnostic tests for the headache patient because they believe the tests are not likely to produce physical findings; other physicians initiate a flurry of diagnostic procedures because they believe that the patient will not improve until he or she is reassured against the possibility of brain tumor. In both cases, the course of treatment is influenced by the headache patient in the physician's mind, a patient who may resemble only in certain points of narrative the one actually in the room. My point is not that patients ought to be treated only as individuals in the medical interview and not as instances of kinds. *Kinds* is an essential notion in diagnosis. My point is that a sort of *literature effect* can account for some of the ways the medical general acts on the medical particular. Rhetoric is one way of thinking about this effect, and the keyword in this case is *audience*.[4]

In what follows, I focus on mainstream writing by medical authors, published in English primarily in the United Kingdom and the United States over approximately 130 years, starting in 1873, when Edward Liveing identified migraine ("megrim") as a single disorder and cleared up some problems in the classification of headache to that point. I have selected for attention those texts that were intended for a general medical and medically interested audience (not an audience of specialists), especially texts that were cited by other authors and that seemed from surrounding sources to capture the medical imagination, representing as well as influencing what people thought of headache patients at a time and a place and what headache patients thought or could think of themselves.

The period from 1873 to the start of the twenty-first century has seen the development and persistence and then the decline of a medical wish to describe the migraine patient as a particular sort of person. Tracking medical literature over time reveals some shifts that are particularly telling and are, importantly, rhetorical shifts. For example, clinical interest is diverted from what the migraine patient *does* to who the migraine patient *is*; the migraine patient, first gendered masculine, is later gendered feminine; the migraine *personality* is held accountable for migraine; the warrant in medical literature for claiming the existence of a migraine personality changes, as it would, from professional authority to empirical study; the rhetoric in which the migraine patient is described becomes markedly a rhetoric of science; in the shift in the late twentieth century from psychopathological interest in migraine to primarily pharmaceutical interest, the migraine patient is again reimagined. The underlying question for the study of all this is, "Who is persuading whom of what—and what are the means of persuasion?"

A history of migraine from a rhetorical perspective takes as a topic of special interest the invention and textual reproduction of the migraine personality. The migraine personality was a plausible account of what migraine patients had in common, and its function was both diagnostic and therapeutic. The migraineur could be recognized (literally, in some accounts) by his or her "profile," and treatment would include personality reform. Clinical studies and research projects were ongoing during the period under study—to isolate migraine triggers, to identify the physiology and biochemistry of the disorder, and to test promising treatments, including a range of pharmaceutical ones—but migraine also created a *patient audience*: the overworked man described by William Henry Day, the (f)rigid woman described by Harold G. Wolff, the self-medicating drug seeker described by John Edmeads ("Dark Side"), and so on. Each such patient was an artifact of the medical understanding of its time, embedded in and saturated with culture, and each one existed both as a figure in the medical literature and as the embodied ill person appearing in the doctor's office, suffering.

Liveing's own project was to show that "the maladies commonly known by the names of Megrim, Sick-headache, Blind-headache, Bilious-headache, and some others . . . which have hitherto been considered in too disconnected a way, form a very natural group" (1–2). For causes of the disorder, Liveing turns first to the French physician Samuel Tissot, who reported, in Liveing's words, "the case of a man who suffered from a violent attack of migrim whenever he got into a passion." "It does not seem in fact to matter much," says Liveing, "what the character of the emotion is, provided it be strongly felt" (48–49). Liveing goes on to add "mental exertion" to the accessory causes of migraine.

> Mental exertion, if too close or continuous, and especially if attended with anxiety, will have a like effect. Thus among students—lads at school and young men at college—the malady is often first developed, or very much increased, by close application to books, and by those modern instruments of torture, competitive examinations, coupled with a deficiency of out-door life. The same thing happens in later years to literary and professional men when overworked and over-anxious in business. (59–60)

Liveing's gendering of the migraine patient as male is interesting, partly because the character of the migraine patient as overworked man is short-lived in the literature but also because, by Liveing's own account, "women are slightly more prone to the malady than men." Liveing writes only secondarily about female migraine patients. Migraine is met "in the case of heads of households—wives and mothers—where the nervous system is in danger of breaking down under the accumulating weight of family care" (434).[5]

Writing five years after Liveing, Day notes a behavior in his male patients similar to that described by Liveing, but Day executes a subtle and powerful rhetorical shift. Rhetorical study is a way of thinking about how statements are persuasive even when they are not on the face of things arguments—and Day's choice of words is then precisely material for rhetorical study. In his hands, the "nervo-hyperemic headache" (migraine, if he had been paying attention to Liveing's classification) is still gendered masculine, but the headache is not a result of engaging in particular sorts of activities so much as it is the result of being a particular sort of person. The headache is

> met with in men whose brains are overworked, and whose meals are hurriedly taken, especially if at the same time they indulge freely in wine and spirits, and do not get a full allowance of sleep. . . . *Such persons* go on working against time with an ardour and zeal which they feel to be irresistible. They appear to know that the speed with which they are carried along is detrimental, and that soon they must yield in the contest; and yet, unless they give up work altogether, they have no power of moderation. Control is gone. (186; emphasis added)

Day's description is of a hard-working, usually successful, man, a victim of his own inexorable drive. Day adds that nervous headache is also seen in women "at the change of life."

> The patient complains of flushes of head, and the head and scalp is hot. . . . She sleeps badly, and sees dark spots before her eyes; she cannot concentrate her attention on her household duties; and her children vex her, and easily put her out. She is made jealous and excitable without reason, and magnifies into questions of great moment trifling circumstances, to which at other times she would not pay attention. (188)

Even by 1878, the character of the headache patient is so fully drawn in the literature as surely to be a presence in the diagnostic interview. How could the patient protest, without seeming to protest too much, that he is not working too hard or that she is not easily upset? The headache patient willy-nilly drags into the office with him or her the ghosts of millions of other patients with similar complaints.

An interesting point about the migraine personality is that it often does seem to fit the presenting patient—and not so much in the Procrustean way as in the way of the horoscope.[6] The "truth" of the migraine personality, like the truth of horoscopes, is suggestive, and it is expansive—and never wrong to the extent that it is right. Effectively, the description of the migraine patient accrued so much clinical capital over time because it was so compelling. The description retained its force in part by changing in accordance with cultural norms and stereotypes. That is, the persuasiveness of an account of migraine personality has an important element of *kairos* as might be expected.

43

In Harry Campbell's treatise on headache published in 1894, the patient most susceptible to migraine is, again, the "overstudious" boy: "Those who suffer from [migraine] have always highly strung nervous systems; they do not differ from the generality of people merely in having megrim, but in their entire nervous organization" (316). What Campbell adds to Liveing's and Day's descriptions of the migraineur is, in rhetorical terms, more a matter of emphasis than of substance. Campbell focuses on neurosis; specifically, he suggests a link among migraine, epilepsy, and "insanity":

> If an individual not leading an intellectual or studious life develops megrim in a classical form, he almost certainly has a strong neurotic taint, and I should be greatly surprised if I did not find among his relatives a history of epilepsy, or insanity, or both. (310)

Within six pages, Campbell upgrades his suggestion to the level of fact, making the neurotic nature of migraine an assumption already in place.

> Megrim, as is well-known, occurs in families in which other neuroses, such as epilepsy and insanity, are rife; if a member of such a family has megrim, he is less likely to develop those other neuroses than if he has not. Thus the child of insane parents who suffers from megrim will probably not become insane. (316)

The certainty with which theories of migraine are presented is itself interesting, given widespread acknowledgment that migraine is not actually well understood. In 1956, John R. Graham writes, for example, that theories of migraine have involved such divergent etiological factors as

> autonomic "storms," epileptiform discharges, swelling of the pituitary gland, hormonal imbalance, electrolyte imbalance, allergic reaction, errors of metabolism, psychogenic disturbances, vitamin deficiencies, errors in diet, liver disease, gastrointestinal disorders, cervical and head injury, cervical arthritis and postural deficiencies, and ocular malfunction. (37)

The work of S. Weir Mitchell, contemporary of Day and Campbell, is important to a rhetorical history of migraine because of the culture of personality and diagnosis in which Mitchell worked. While Mitchell did not publish as an expert on headache per se, his work on neurasthenia contributed to the moral-medical world in which patients with headache—especially female patients with headache—of the time existed. Neurasthenia was a general nervous weakness brought on by the pressures of civilized life.

The "Weir Mitchell treatment" was isolation and bed rest, a treatment made somewhat notorious to later generations by Charlotte Perkins Gilman's partially fictionalized account of it in "The Yellow Wallpaper."

Headache was a frequent complaint of Mitchell's patients, and the patient as nervous woman was the focus of his writing:

> There are many kinds of fool, from the mindless fool to the fiend-fool, but for the most entire capacity to make a household wretched there is no more complete human receipt than a silly woman who is to a high degree nervous and feeble, and who craves pity and likes power. (117)

Mitchell helped to form the figure of the female headache patient as neurotic, hysteric, hypochondriac, and fraud. These characterizations are taken up by later authors; increasingly, the material headache patient is an interlocutor with a certain disadvantage.

"Migraine personality" was firmly established by the 1950s, by which time it was thoroughly gendered feminine and had lost most of its earlier association with passion, ambition, and braininess. In 1952, Walter Alvarez comments on his attention specifically to *women* and migraine: "Don't men have migraine? Yes, surely; but they usually have so much easier a time with their headaches that they seldom bother to consult a doctor. Most of them take two aspirin and keep at work" (*How to Live* 5).

Siegmund Auerbach and William H. Robey are headache specialists writing in the first half of the twentieth century, publishing in 1913 and 1931 respectively.[7] Both are important transitional figures for a psychological account of migraine—and migraineurs—that reaches its full expression in the 1950s.

Auerbach is important primarily because his recommended treatments for headache are so straightforwardly behavioral. He understands the patient to be to blame for his or her disorder; the physician's job is to root out the problem and reform the patient:[8]

> [A] thorough investigation into the entire life of the patient is essential, and one must not hesitate to unveil errors with energy and method, although with due tact, and clearly to indicate their dangers to health. The commonest of these errors is the excessive and thoughtless abuse of alcohol and tobacco. . . . Sexual excesses, particularly onanism, are strictly to be forbidden. (72–73)

Robey adds a feature to the character of the headache patient. He describes patients who long for an explanation for their problem in organic disease:

[S]uch patients [those with headaches of unclear etiology] often move from physician to physician, dissatisfied with each no matter how eminent, until one is found who is suspicious that there may be organic disease. His doubtful diagnosis is cherished above all others. (134)

The headache patient Robey describes is not just ill. He or she is seen to have both a problem and a metaproblem. The rhetorical occasion of the migraineur's visit to the physician is, then, complex: The presenting complaint is shadowed with a complaint about the complaint. Even if the patient is, in fact, innocent—just a person in pain seeking help—the rhetorical audience is not simply the patient him- or herself but the patient in the mind of the physician who simply knows too much to be innocent, too.

Robey's disease-seeking headache patient is a figure in contemporary literature on headache as well. Neurologist Hansruedi Isler writes in 1992 of migraine patients who are

highly motivated for attribution, craving for physical causes to explain their disorder, and expecting the physician to furnish explanations lest they should worry about psychological implications of which they are afraid. They are never content with a black box model, will not tolerate declarations of ignorance, and are fully capable of pressurising their physicians to turn hypotheses into positive statements; the need for forced explanations appears almost to be a symptom of the disorder. (233)

Headaches, then, can be blamed on patients, but patients can also be blamed for the sometimes erroneous accounts of headache that doctors may come up with apparently to satisfy them. Edmeads in 1984 mentions the migraine patient's desire for explanation as a peculiarity of these patients that further divides them from their physicians: "Most of *us* . . . would be far more interested in getting rid of our pain than in knowing why we had it" ("Placebos" 343; emphasis added).

Robey is also of interest as the physician-author who enters into headache classification the "headache of convenience." With this move, he adds a significant feature to the circulating portrait of the headache patient:

Years ago the writer knew of a young woman who always had a violent headache whenever she could not have her own way or failed to receive the attention to which she thought she was entitled. On a coasting party, she started out in the best of spirits, but finding that another was receiving more attention from a particular young man than she, a violent headache developed which lasted until the party was over, but the object was attained since she became the centre of sympathy. (129–30)

The headache patient, once officially associated with false complaints, could not easily be recuperated. In fact, Wolff's 1948 case notes take the possibility of the headache patient as liar quite for granted: Wolff mentions in passing that his investigation of a particular patient's complaint only proceeded "after the possibility of malingering had been carefully excluded" (307). The headache patient now has a long history as suspect—and that, of course, could hardly be, rhetorically, more problematic.

Wolff himself is the preeminent headache specialist of the twentieth century, still lavishly cited in the literature,[9] and the first in a generation of headache specialists for whom "migraine personality" is the key to headache etiology, diagnosis, and treatment. This generation of specialists, after Wolff himself, includes, for example, Noah D. Fabricant, Alvarez, Graham, Harold Maxwell, and Seymour Diamond and Donald J. Dalessio. In the late 1970s, migraine personality fell somewhat out of favor, although research efforts continued and still continue to correlate headache findings with psychopathological ones. Currently, the sufferer of chronic pain is sometimes considered to be a particular kind of person or a person having suffered a particular kind of experience.[10]

Several elements of Wolff's account of the migraine patient illustrate the dependence of a pathology of migraine personality on cultural norms and values of the day, notwithstanding the rhetoric of science in which the description of the migraine personality is rendered. One reason that Wolff is still so much cited is the currency of that rhetoric. Whereas the dominant appeals in the literature on headache were, even into the 1940s, appeals from case study, personal observation, and professional authority, Wolff's appeals are largely from measurement and experiment. Indeed, one of his experiments in support of a personality hypothesis is a study whose strategy was "to create in a tense, perfectionist man with migraine headaches a state of inadequacy, lack of energy, and mentation defects [by continued administration of codeine] and then under these circumstances to oblige him to perform according to his own high standard" (343). This is Wolff's argument for migraine personality:

Awareness of the potential importance of the psychobiologic aspects has prompted the study of the personality functions of 46 subjects with migraine. These functions were systematically investigated, although no free association or far-reaching analysis was undertaken. Among the subjects in this group certain features were found to occur with striking frequency. (319)

In its details, Wolff's work on headache provides good examples of the way medical "realities" can be read variously to produce different sorts of medical knowledge. A case in point is the well-documented increase in migraine in some women around the menstrual period. There is currently quite a lot of clinical and experimental evidence for a hormonal effect on migraine, giving a biochemical account for an increase in headache paramenstrually.[11] But Wolff takes the correlation between migraine and menstruation as evidence of the psychological problem of the migrainous woman, whose menstrual discomforts, "added to the burden of domestic routine," precipitated attacks or who was simply afraid of pregnancy, "reluctant to accept and adjust herself to the consequences of maternity" (337).

Wolff's migrainous women are unwilling to accept their female role. They are also "inflexible" and unwilling to "let themselves go." Their "personality problem" is associated with "sexual maladjustment" or "dissatisfaction with sexual experience" (337). Wolff's male patients, in contrast, are reported to be sexually well adjusted except in the cases of "3 migraineur men with vigorous sex drive who were married to sexually indifferent or frigid wives" (336).

Wolff's account includes a few contradictory claims, but these did not, overall, if we take citations of Wolff as evidence, weaken the persuasiveness of his case. "Attacks follow failure," he says, but adds, "but not only failure, since success sometimes precipitated them" (324). Migraineurs are pathologically concerned with neatness—"The women sometimes even sacrificed a degree of attractiveness for austerity or severe neatness" (322)—except when they are pathologically not concerned with neatness: "Apparently, if their major concern had become one of ambition, centered primarily on distinction, money, or power, they were less meticulous or even indifferent about their homes and dress" (329).

The idea of a migraine personality is not simply a fabrication of a misogynist mind or an invention of a paternalist medical profession. It is not "mere rhetoric," either. Indeed, the longevity of the idea in some form argues for at least some truth of co-morbidity: A significant number of people with migraines also exhibit personality traits like those associated with the diagnosis of depression.[12] However, irrespective of the possibility of a migraine-associated personality, migraine personality as a construct is a case of the rhetorical element in medical practice. The shift from a *eulogistic* to a *dyslogistic* account of the features of the patient's character is one to notice. (On the terms: Burke says that "greed" is a dyslogistic covering for "ambition," "ambition" a eulogistic covering for "greed" [see, especially, *Rhetoric of Motives* 92–93].) Migraineurs, as I have noted, were seen by the end of the nineteenth century to be particular sorts of people rather than people doing particular sorts of things. As they became in the literature predominately women, the valuing of the traits that described them also shifted. The studious man (eulogistic) became the overfocussed woman (dyslogistic); the too-diligent patient became the impossible-to-please one. Moreover, what it meant to be a person impossible to please changed with the times; the migraineur, man or woman, above all, was at odds with the world. By the mid-twentieth century, the most maladaptive trait of all was simply to be out of step; and it so happened that the problem was especially acute for women.

Wolff's migraine patients find it "difficult to forgive or accept the foibles of their fellows" (330); their "strong resentments" are linked with "inelasticity" (330); they desire money "as a means to power," with such a strong urge to "have a thing right away" that they might "buy on the installment plan" (332); they are "self-righteous" (333). "More than nine-tenths" of them are "unusually ambitious and preoccupied with success" (340). "Tension" is a common state among them, but they also feature "anxiety, anticipation, and uneasiness" as well as "frustration and resentment" (341). "Most common" in them is "long-sustained and superficial pervasive uneasiness or anticipation of untoward events." "Less common" are "short-lived intensely moving reactions of rage" (341). Feelings of "insecurity and anxiety" stem from in childhood "frank or disguised hatred by the parents, anxiety in the parents, broken or unhappy homes, frequent illness, or the imputation that the child was 'delicate' or unattractive" (342). The migraineur is "cautious about giving affection, yet is resentful when he fails to elicit it" (342–43).

The headache patient entering the doctor's office is helplessly exposed before he or she has said anything at all. Like Wolff's six-hundred-page treatise, the migraine patient is an open book. As Wolff's forty-six migraineurs, the research sample to which Wolff's findings are attached, are absorbed into the texts of Fabricant, Alvarez, and other headache authors, the options available to the patient for self-presentation are increasingly circumscribed. Fabricant's 1949 treatise on migraine corroborates Wolff's description of the patient:[13]

These people are apt to be perfectionists, highly emotional, tense, and overconscientious. They are usually above average in intelligence and often react strongly to criticism. A distinctive feature of the migraine temperament is easy fatigue. . . . The woman who is subject to migraine is apt to be meticulous—neat, orderly, fastidious and overly efficient in her housework. The man who is disposed to migraine is oftentimes exacting and overly ambitious, with an exaggerated sense of responsibility and an inclination to fret and worry. (71–72)

Fabricant also goes further than Wolff on a topic of some significance in the practice of contemporary medicine: psychogenic pain. Fabricant devotes a chapter of his book to psychogenic headaches, and it may not be too strong to say that, at his hands, the headache patient is vilified:

Psychogenic headaches . . . can be both fickle and bizarre. . . . [They] have no pattern as to time, duration of the attack, or location of the pain. Indeed, there is often a tendency for the victim to exaggerate the extent of the headache, to portray it in melodramatic terms, and to boast of the suffering he is compelled to endure. (85)

With no apparent sense of irony, Fabricant follows his description of patients with psychogenic complaints with this: "The cornerstone of the successful treatment of troublesome headaches of emotional origin lies in the patient-physician relationship" (85).

Alvarez is the author of two very successful books on headache—one for an audience of physicians (*The Neuroses: Diagnosis and Management*) and one for an audience of migraineurs (*How to Live with Your Migraine*). Both follow the conventional wisdom of the time and reinscribe it. Migraineurs, Alvarez says, especially migrainous women, can be recognized "at a glance"; the migraine personality is largely to blame for the disorder; treatment must include reform: "If I am really going to straighten her out I must get her to understand, as she never did before, her inborn nature, and the degree to which her emotions and life problems affect her health" (4); and direct medical attention is generally useless: "Many a migrainous woman could be cured only by a legacy which would supply her with a good maid, or set her free from an unpleasant job or an unhappy marriage" (21).

It has been my claim in this chapter not only that headache discourse in general is rhetorical but also that headache discourses in particular—notably, the published accounts of experts on headache patients—have clinical effects. Alvarez provides a special warrant for the second sort of claim. He provides a way to get from the physician's first glance at the headache patient to the advice with which that patient leaves the office. What his account means is that the migraine patient has only to *appear* in her physician's office in order to short-circuit her own treatment—in what amounts to four steps:

1. The physician looks at the patient.

> Every good internist ought to be able to recognize the migrainous woman the minute she walks quickly into his office. Perhaps she starts blinking at the light coming from the window, and he must pull down the shade for her. Usually she is short in stature; she is well and trimly built, and well dressed. She is obviously intelligent, wide awake, alert, quick in her thought and her movements, with bright eyes and social attractiveness. (*Neuroses* 334)

2. The physician associates appearance with personality.

> It is remarkable that migrainous women have not only a certain type of body but also a certain type of temperament. . . . She cannot stand much gabble of conversation about her, and she cannot stand a crowd. She is usually a poor traveler and often a poor sleeper. . . . The migrainous woman often overworks because she wants her house to be spotlessly clean and run just so. . . . If she is to give a dinner party, she has her table set by noon, and perhaps by the time the guests arrive she is too sick to see them. (336)

3. The physician initiates the fewest possible medical procedures.

> If the physician knows from the start that a certain woman is migrainous, then when the results of her tests are negative he will not be puzzled. He can say, "I expected that because few of you people with sick headaches ever have any organic disease." . . . Actually, migrainous persons seem to be largely immune to serious organic disease. (336–37)

4. The physician reforms the patient.

> Every migrainous woman should try for better mental hygiene, with an earlier bedtime; good sleep, obtained with sedatives if necessary; shorter hours of work; less tension in it; the avoidance of conflicts and annoyance; less fussing and fretting and trying to have everything perfect; more acquiescence to things that cannot be changed; less responsibility outside the home and, very important, a nap in the afternoon. (342)

Alvarez's patient is interpellated, called forth, as a particular kind of rhetorical audience—one that is not herself a fully speaking subject. The patient has, through the texts that provide the context in which she enters her doctor's office, been spoken for. The migraine patient is disabled as an interlocutor in part because she can not with her deliberate efforts at description or complaint overcome the salience of her own appearance. And her *ethos* is damaged, in any case, because she is taken to be responsible by bad living of some sort or another for her own condition. In this, the migraine patient is something like the cancer patient as Susan Sontag describes him or her—and the cancer patient is, rhetorically, badly off in something like the same way as the migraine patient. Sontag discusses the clinical and personal consequences of a medical belief in a "cancer-prone character type," "someone unemotional, inhibited, repressed" (39). "The view of cancer," Sontag says, "as a disease of the failure of expressiveness condemns the cancer patient; it evinces pity but also conveys contempt" (*Illness* 48).[14]

Graham's 1956 *Treatment of Migraine* makes clear that patients are responsible for their headaches; he says it is useful to consider the "personal attributes" of the presenting patient to make the diagnosis of migraine in the first place (26). Graham's recommended treatment is to advise patients about their "errors in living." Graham offers a "list of common deviations from hygienic living . . . that are frequently a source of headache to the sufferer of migraine. . . . Behind these errors in living lie attitudes in the patient that serve both to bring them about and to intensify the damage they create" (88–89).

> Migraine patients do not like to admit, even to themselves, that they have any limitations. When given a regimen to follow, they are apt to adhere to the details of drug therapy to the letter but to forget the afternoon rests, reduction of an overactive social or business program and correction of poor dietary, work and sleep habits. (94)

Some of the advice of doctors like Graham was no doubt helpful to headache patients; it is well known that certain lifestyle choices (less wine, more sleep) do promote health and decrease headache in migraineurs. In suggesting a holistic approach to treatment of a disorder, specialists like Graham were ahead of their time. The question is not whether the physicians studied here were ever *right*; certainly they sometimes were. What is at issue is how migraine patients were characterized in order to become, instead of speaking subjects, slates of a particular kind onto which lifestyle could be pre-scribed.

Graham is an important figure because he not only described the migraine patient and suggested treatment, he also sought to explain the migraine patient. The psychopathology of the migraine patient became in the 1950s a studying point: "Certain patients in whom the family physician finds deep-rooted emotional problems playing a prominent part in the production of headache may be referred to a psychiatrist with worthwhile results" (94). The psychopathological turn in headache is itself explicable in terms of *kairos*, with reference to the psychiatry and pharmaceuticals of the 1950s, but I am interested here primarily in indicating the fluidity of the migraine patient as a subject and object of medical treatment.

In 1966, Harold Maxwell turns to the theories of Freud, Jung, and Adler to account for the headache patient's "need to suffer" (25–26). Maxwell calls migraine a "psychologically determined disease," and he renders his account in the rhetoric of science (12). Wolff had reported on inducing migraine experimentally to test a hypothesis of psychological etiology; Alvarez had talked about migraine in statistical terms ("Because marital dissatisfaction is such a common sensitizing cause of migraine, I once asked 178 migrainous women what sort of husband they had" [15]). Maxwell goes further, assembling a literature that shifts the rhetorical ground of migraine to become at once both scientific and psychoanalytic. This is a sample of his literature review:

> Draper and Touraine (1954) investigated 50 migraine subjects, and found what they considered to be a typical constitutional type with a frequent history of an "acidotic" childhood. There emerged evidence of a conflict between excessive dependence on the mother coupled with a desire to be free of her. . . . Knopf (1935) investigated 30 cases of migraine and found 60 per cent of the subjects to be "goody-goody" or self-righteous, noting also shyness, anxiety, timidity, jealousy, ambition, strong temper, and sensitivity; 50 per cent reported indifferent or unsatisfactory marital relations. (12)

Woven into Maxwell's reports of statistical studies are reports of psychoanalytical studies on migraine as an expression of "sexual frigidity," feelings of lowering of prestige, humility, submission, hostility, and other "typical 'neurotic' character patterns" (13). The literature review and his own case studies (as of the homosexual man whose "non-acceptable . . . drives became repressed and the energy emerged as attacks of migraine" [17]) lead Maxwell to conclude that migraine sufferers

> possess unresolved, unconscious conflicts with consequent and ambivalent attitudes towards people with whom they have close relation-

ships. . . . In an unsuccessful effort to resolve these problems, their life patterns show with remarkable regularity that they have a predilection for situations which must inevitably lead to further real-life conflicts and difficulties. (24)

Headache is a nonadaptive means of removing those with a "pattern of failure" from "the threat of [their] situation" (24).

By the 1970s, psychological studies of the migraine patient underwent another shift: The "migraine personality" per se was no longer a focus of significant attention in the literature although it remained a topic of interest. The business of correlating migraine to various co-morbid conditions, such as depression and anxiety, occupied more pages in medical journals. In a 1986 review article, F. N. Schmidt, P. Carney, and G. Fitzsimmons argue against the notion of "migraine personality type" and the standardized personality inventory used to support claims for the existence of such a type. The authors object to this specific construct, and they cite research to suggest ways in which such constructs as "migraine personality," which rely on "subjective clinical judgement," might be suspect in general.[15]

While interest in "migraine personality" was in decline, physicians and researchers in the 1970s continued to write about relations between headache and psychology—between the complaint and the complainer. Warrants for specialists' claims were increasingly empirical and statistical, but the sort of patient that mainstream medical literature reified was a familiar person:

> We have found many but not all migraine sufferers to be obsessive, compulsive and rigid. They keep long lists of their attacks and treatments and medications. . . . The stress situations of life, such as menopause, puberty and change of school or job, seem to paralyze their adapting mechanisms. Their inability to adapt creates anger and resentment and has been described as the repressed hostility of the migraine patient. (Diamond and Dalessio 50)

One of Diamond and Dalessio's illustrations is a patient's list of migraine attacks and treatments. The caption reads, "This migraine patient is a compulsive list-maker." Ironically, perhaps, migraine patients currently seeking medical help are routinely instructed to keep "headache diaries" in which they record headache severity (on a one-to-three-point scale), in four time periods every day, noting medications taken, degree of relief found, and triggers (from a list of thirty common possibilities), all correlated for women with the menstrual cycle.[16] The therapy here is the symptom, while the strong intuition of headache researchers seems, in any case, to be that migraineurs are, at least, neurotic. Schmidt, Carney, and Fitzsimmons, having concluded that migraineurs did *not* report unusually high levels of resentment or anxiety, add that the lack of positive findings might be explained by another finding that says migraineurs sometimes suppress or inadequately express their emotions (195). The authors are, in other words, willing to consider pathologizing the apparent lack of pathology in people with migraine.

Just as, in the 1950s, physicians like Alvarez short-circuited some diagnoses by drawing a straight line from a patient's appearance to the presumption of negative medical findings, in the 1970s, Diamond and Dalessio perform a kind of statistical short-circuiting: "Most patients with chronic headache who are seen in an office practice by an internist or general practitioner, perhaps up to 90%, have a psychogenic basis for their complaint" (81). Three pages later, they add, "The majority of all patients with psychogenic headache suffer from depression" (84). The patient entering the physician's office, then, with a complaint of chronic headache might expect a diagnosis of depression, and, possibly, little else.[17]

Diamond and Dalessio give special attention to the problem of drug abuse:

> Patients with headache may overuse or abuse their medications, although this is not invariably the case. The physician should at least suspect that the situation may occur in cephalalgic patients. If a proper history can be obtained, the diagnosis of analgesic abuse may be made. (94)

The problems of medication "overuse" are significant. Liver disease, kidney disease, and peptic ulcer (at least) may result from excessive intake of analgesics; undesirable vasoconstriction can result from overuse of ergot; addiction is a threat from narcotic treatments; and so on. But Diamond and Dalessio have claims to make not only about drug abuse but also about the drug-abusing patient: "Patients may be secretive and secretly ashamed about ingesting medications and will put the physician off with inexact replies regarding medication use."[18]

The "medication-induced headache" was identified in the 1980s as a serious problem for headache patients and their doctors, with accounts of "rebound headache," the headache triggered when the person habituated to a certain level of medication is deprived of his or her accustomed dose—

the aggravated condition of headache patients who consume medications almost daily and enter a pain-medication-pain cycle, difficult to break. The new medication-addicted headache patients were said to be difficult to treat, many requiring hospitalization (see Hering and Steiner). Moreover, these patients were said typically to be women and, frequently, clinically depressed (Silberstein 405). The very idea of medication abuse placed the headache patient in an even greater position of weakness in clinical contact. Edmeads, like Diamond and Dalessio a major figure in the American Association for the Study of Headache and himself an editor of the association's journal, *Headache*, writes that emergency room physicians should be on guard for "drug-seeking behavior" in suspect migraine patients ("Narcotic" 343). In a later editorial, Edmeads warns physicians to look out for patients who may be selling their medication on the street and recommends a covert procedure for flushing the dealers out ("Dark Side").

The story of the migraine patient takes new direction in the 1990s, when there is a disjunction in this collective biography-across-time. Early in the decade, the pharmaceutical company GlaxoSmithKline (then, Glaxo) began distributing the first "designer drug" for migraine: Imitrex—the firstborn of the triptan family (of which there are currently seven members—suma-, nara-, zolmi-, almo-, riza-, ele-, and frova-). Sumatriptan succinate (Imitrex) is not an analgesic; rather, it acts on migraine biochemistry and physiology; it causes dilated blood vessels to constrict and normal blood flow to be restored. A key distinguishing feature of Imitrex as a treatment for migraine (it does not cure the predisposing condition but aborts a single attack) is that it *works*—by most accounts, depending on dosage, for about 70 to 80 percent of patients.

Imitrex and the other triptans improve the situation of the migraine patient—both materially by relieving pain and rhetorically by rehabilitating the figure of the sufferer. Rhetorically, the triptans act in at least three ways. First, they relieve the physician of the burden of ineffectuality, at the same time obviating some of the need for the diagnostic work of the clinical interview. Since the drug only works on migraine, the patient whose headaches respond to Imitrex *is* a migraine patient. (This is not to say that physicians will set out to diagnose retrospectively. There are serious problems with such a model; for one thing, it is not also true that the patient whose headaches do not respond to Imitrex is *not* a migraine patient. However, diagnoses of migraine are increasingly prevalent, and the best advice currently of researchers is to treat those headaches that seem to be migraine as though they are migraine.[19]) The physician, that is, in general, has something to do and is no longer in the same problematic rhetorical relation to the patient, who is no longer so intransigent. Clearly, in any case, the presence of specific and effective drugs for migraine has dampened interest in the study of migraine psychology although it has not, by any means, removed it.

Second, triptans act rhetorically by making migraine less interesting (in the way that mysterious complaints are interesting, which is the same as the way that "May you live in interesting times" is a curse)—and, so, vindicates the migraine patient. As Elaine Showalter has noted, whenever an organic element becomes salient in a disorder, patients are relieved of some of the guilt and shame of having that disorder. Because triptans act on migraine by altering biochemistry, migraine is seen to be at least partially out of the patient's control. The patient may still by some accounts be to blame for triggering attacks with erroneous thoughts or attitudes or habits, but the effectiveness of triptans confirms that he or she is also a location for misbehaving chemicals.[20]

Third, by putting the migraine patient in charge of his or her own medication, triptans place control in the hands of the patient: Triptans are used as needed in the case of an attack; they are not prescribed prophylactically, and dosing is not on a prescribed schedule. A remarkable feature of Imitrex is that it is available in injectable form.[21] The migraine patient, presented in (then) GlaxoWellcome's promotional videos as a woman whose polished fingernails guide a concealed syringe into a smooth thigh, is, in a sense, more in control than she has ever been.[22] It would not be too much of an exaggeration to say that Imitrex created a new culture of migraine in which the patient audience is re-constituted and re-voiced.

The physician-patient encounter occurs in a textual world, and this discussion of the migraine patient suggests an approach to understanding other patients as well. It suggests, for example, a way of thinking about the construction and interpellation of the *geriatric* patient, whose textual life has really only just begun.

It would be possible also to assemble a rhetorical account of a condition less ambiguous than migraine or old age and of a seemingly straightforward patient audience. How, for example, were physicians persuaded sixty years ago to perform tonsillectomies routinely for "tonsillitis" and then persuaded not to? Even tonsillitis, in other words, is more than simply a diagnosis requiring treatment; it is a description inviting interpretation, and its patients are shifting interlocutors.[23] My family doctor looks admiringly at the "golf-ball tonsils" (as he calls them) of my adolescent son and says, "Look at that immune system go." A rhetorical critic might look at the language of office visits and popular magazines over the twentieth century to consider the cultural work that was done by the routine tonsillectomy of the 1940s, inviting children and families into a world of pathology and surgery—a domestic world, involving ice cream.

3   The Epideictic Rhetoric of Pathography

In recent years, narrative has found a place in health research, not only among social science and humanities researchers but also among some medical researchers[1] as the default opposite of biomedical discourse. Biomedicine is associated with a thinness in descriptions of patient experience, a tendency to measurement and quantification, and an embrace of the mores of Michel Foucault's clinic, where, as I note in chapter 1, the "individual in question was not so much a sick person as the endlessly reproducible pathological fact to be found in all patients suffering in a similar way" (97).

Narrative is a means of balancing the scientific impulse of biomedicine with a humanistic impulse. Certainly, narrative fleshes things out. For example, in her recent work on bipolar disorder and "the measurement of moods," Emily Martin points to patient narrative accounts of mood shifts to illustrate how people who "live under the description" of bipolar disorder may counter the regime of measurement by describing their moods discursively rather than only matching them to numbers on an eleven-point scale ("Monitoring").[2]

Narrative study in health research covers a wide range of subjects, including narrative epistemology (see Kathryn Montgomery Hunter), narrative therapy (James W. Pennebaker), and narrative ethics (Hilde Lindemann Nelson). Prominent objects of narrative scholarship are personal narratives of illness—one's own (Jean-Dominique Bauby) or someone else's (John Bayley on Iris Murdoch).

Anne Hunsaker Hawkins notes there is interest among narrative scholars in what term to use for stories of illness. "Pathography," she says, denotes only written narrative (*Reconstructing* xviii). In his book on the "wounded storyteller," Arthur Frank uses the more general term "illness narrative," used also by Arthur Kleinman, who introduced it to describe the patient's story as constructed by the physician. G. Thomas Couser says personal narratives pertinent to illness may include, as well as illness narratives per se, journals, essays, and "full-life narratives." "*[I]llness narrative* refers to writing about the episode of one's illness, whereas *full-life narrative* refers to a comprehensive account of one's life, including the illness" (6; emphasis in original). Susan Greenhalgh would add "illness auto-ethnography," in which the central topic is not the ill person but, rather, the illness itself and medicine, as illuminated by the study of the ill person as object by the same person as researcher.[3]

Hawkins describes the growth in the latter part of the twentieth century in illness narrative or pathography publication and suggests its rationale: "Pathography returns the voice of the patient to the world of medicine, a world where that voice is too rarely heard, and it does so in such a way as to assert the phenomenological, the subjective, and the experiential side of illness" (*Reconstructing* 12). Hawkins continues: "Pathography restores the person ignored or canceled out in the medical enterprise, and it places that person at the very center. Moreover, it gives that ill person a voice" (12). Pathography, too, is the complementary text of the medical case presentation, which, as a genre itself, is meant, according to Lorelei Lingard and Richard Haber, to include "just the relevant data," "just the pertinent positives" (165). (An interesting question is begged here—that the case presentation is the "fact" part of illness and pathography the "value" part.)

A canon of pathographies includes work by Nancy Mairs (who writes on multiple sclerosis and on depression), Gilda Radner (ovarian cancer), Anatole Broyard (prostate cancer), Audre Lorde (breast cancer), Bonnie Sherr Klein (stroke), Temple Grandin (autism), and others. There are, in addition, countless pathographies by otherwise unknown authors. In the second edition of *Reconstructing Illness: Studies in Pathography*, Hawkins provides a thirty-four-page selected bibliography of pathographies, organized by disease. Instances of the genre continue to multiply. In a review essay, Peter Kramer says the titles "represent niche book selling, a guide for every challenge" ("Anatomy" 27).

A canon of scholarship, descriptive and classificatory, and sometimes critical, too, has developed around narratives of illness. Hawkins, Couser, and Frank are all well known for having written full-length studies of the genre.[4] What work narrative does, narrative study extends. Kenneth J. Gergen says that narrative is a discipline-breaking genre, opening up social science to literary theory, hermeneutics, and phenomenology, rescuing social science from being "strangulated by empirical foundationalism." If narrative discourse itself is the opposite of scientific medical discourse, then narrative research is the opposite of research limited by its own scientific methodologies. Because there is among patients and scholars alike a kind of narrative rebellion going on, it makes sense to look at narrative inquisitively. I wish to suggest there is an epideictic rhetoric of pathography itself and an epideictic rhetoric of pathography study.

Certain sorts of speeches, we know from Aristotle, are notably speeches about values, whether that is their ostensible subject matter or not. We may surmise further that values are present not only in individual speeches but also in speech genres. The rhetorical principle that informs this chapter is that genres determine, to some extent, the rhetoric of their material examples. Not only are patients *heard* in ways guided by textual culture (as chapter 2 has argued) but also patients *speak*—they compose their stories and even live their experience—in ways guided by textual culture. That is, by supplying the shapes in which stories may be told, genres write stories.

Aristotle identifies three occasions for rhetoric: deliberative, forensic, and epideictic. Deliberative rhetoric is speechmaking directed at the future, he says; its business is exhortation and dissuasion, and its exemplary genre is the political speech. Forensic rhetoric is speechmaking trained on the past; its business is accusation and defence, and its exemplary genre is the advocate's summation in a court of law. Epideictic rhetoric is the rhetoric of the present; its business, Aristotle says, is praise and blame, and its exemplary genre is the funeral oration. Epideictic rhetoric is a culture's most telling rhetoric, because, in general, we praise people for embodying what we value, and we blame them for embodying what we deplore. We discover what people's values are by listening to the eulogies they have composed or by reading the letters of recommendation they have written. Some epideictic rhetoric is so conventionalized that its genres themselves formally enact its values. So, for example, winners of Academy Awards (Oscars) not just typically but almost inevitably thank the Academy, their fellow workers, their families, perhaps the other nominees in their category, and, frequently, God. This is the way winners are humble and the way we, all of us, honor humility itself.[5]

What are we doing when we compose and when we study personal narratives of illness? What is it that the work itself honors? What values does the work itself praise?

Clearly, each illness narrative performs an epideictic function. Radner's story of her struggle with ovarian cancer inscribes, among other virtues, the virtue of a sense of humor; it almost goes without saying that her story inscribes the virtue of struggle itself. Mairs's story of quotidian life with multiple sclerosis inscribes the virtue of a sense of irony. Klein's story of slow recovery from stroke inscribes the virtue of a sense of family. And so on.

That individual pathographies would perform an epideictic function in a community is to be expected. Hawkins says that pathographies attend to the cultural "myths, attitudes, and beliefs . . . that a sick person uses to come to terms with illness" (4). Frank says, "People tell stories not just to work out their own changing identities, but also to guide others who follow them." But the genre itself of pathography is epideictic. Its features themselves enact an in-forming set of values: Narratives have protagonists; narratives have conflict; narratives have conclusions; narratives, as a whole, have narrative logic. And while there is not a monolithic scholarship in illness narratives, there is also a way in which the *study* of narrative has itself an epideictic quality. When we study narratives, we certify many of the values that the genre itself certifies. We read narratives with recourse to the same virtues that allow them to count as narratives in the first place. These virtues include the virtue of narrative coherence, preeminently. Hawkins says that "the task of the author of a pathography is not only to describe [the] disordering process but also to restore to reality its lost coherence and to discover, or create, a meaning that can bind it together again" (18). These virtues include also the indirect virtue of illness itself, which has, if nothing else, enabled the narrative.

Three narrators are especially good resources for revealing the epideictic nature of pathography and pathography study. They are good resources because they complicate their own narrations—although, as any postmodern reader would expect, they do not always do this intentionally. Their three narrations showcase the narrative values of pathography and invite us to consider the genre critically and to see the power of the genre to determine both the structure and the substance of narration.

The first complicating narrator is an Internet narrator, with a first name and not a last one, who tells her story in fragments, to Internet readers and interlocutors who are, as she is, really, anonymous. The narrator I have in mind is an eating-disordered narrator found at a pro-Ana Web site. Pro-Ana (Ana, diminutive of anorexia) and Mia (diminutive of bulimia) Web sites are devoted to exchange of information, especially helpful tips (ice cream comes up easy; brushing right after purging is bad for teeth) and support among anorexics and bulimics. The sites celebrate the anorexic body, mixing images of nameless skinny girls and women, with images of skinny celebrities—for example, Calista Flockhart and Mary-Kate Olsen, their images widely reproduced as "thinspiration." Home pages feature disclaimers and warnings to visitors, making clear that these are not sites for the reform of the eating disordered but rather for the support of them *as* eating disordered.[6]

"Illness narratives" at pro-Ana sites (I use both terms *illness* and *narratives* advisedly, but pro-Ana is clear that "[a]norexia is a lifestyle, not a disease"[7]) shaped a question for me that had been forming since I had been introduced through the work of Carl Elliott to another set of problematic Web sites: sites for amputees, the people who love them (for being amputees), and the people who want to be them ("amputee wannabes") ("New Way"). My question was about the authenticity of the Web narrator and his or her narrative: Can we treat *as* personal narratives those stories that may be fabricated by authors who are fictionalizing their lives under cover of anonymity? How much has authenticity of identity to do with the worth of a story or with what can be said about it?[8]

No sooner had I formed the question than it seemed to me naive. We engage with fictional narratives all the time; as literary critics, we certainly take them seriously. Still, I resisted taking seriously "Josie from Iowa," who may or may not *really* have traveled the hard road from disordered to ordered eating; I simply did not feel I could trust her. My problem was not the familiar problem of self-misrepresentation on the Web (the problem summed up by the *New Yorker* cartoon featuring a dog at a computer, saying, "On the Internet, they don't know you're a dog"); it was not the problem of "truth," exactly, either.[9] My problem with the pro-Ana narrators had to do with the ontology of the narrator and the genre of personal narrative.

Elliott says that a feature of pro-amputation Web sites is that they create the conditions under which one might *form* the idea of the attractiveness of surgical amputation or self-mutilation. Elaborating Ian Hacking's notion of "semantic contagion," Elliott suggests this about apotemnophiles (those attracted to the idea of being an amputee)[10]:

> The idea of having one's legs amputated might never even enter the minds of some people until it is suggested to them. Yet once it is suggested, and not just suggested but paired with imagery that a person's

> past may have primed him or her to appreciate, that act becomes
> possible. Give the wish for it a name and a treatment, link it to a set
> of related disorders, give it a medical explanation rooted in childhood
> memory, and you are on the way to setting up just the kind of con-
> ceptual category that makes it a treatable psychiatric disorder. (83)

In other words, amputation Web sites not only provide a forum for people
who already are amputee wannabes, they also *interpellate*—call forth,
hail—such wannabes. The Web sites, in part, constitute the very community that by their address they address.

The process of interpellation is described well for rhetorical theory
by Maurice Charland, and I mentioned it and him in chapter 2 in my discussion of the headache patient. Charland writes about the rhetorical force
of speeches addressed to an audience whose very identity is formed in the
act of address. Rhetoric is constitutive, he says, when it calls into being
those it addresses, rather than in the first instance addressing an audience
that preexists the address.

Charland is interested in, among other things, the "ontological status of those addressed by discourse before their successful interpellation"
(232). I want to introduce into the discussion of illness narratives the
possibility that just as advertisements of certain conditions interpellate
certain people who have them (as Elliott suggests), *so the advertisement
of certain narrative structures interpellates certain sorts of narrators.*

Narrators are made in part in the tyranny of narrative coherence. Not
only do we like to tell and to hear stories of battle, stories of overcoming, or stories of quest (Couser, Hawkins, and Frank all note such repeated
plots and themes in pathographies[11]) but also reports of other experiences
may not quite seem to qualify as stories at all. In Frank's catalogue of
narrative types, the quest narrative is clearly the one to be strived for:

> Realizing who they have always been, truly been, each [quest narra-
> tor] becomes or prepares to become the re-created, moral version of
> that self. In this display of character, memory is revised, interruption
> assimilated, and purpose grasped. "Whatever has happened to me or
> will happen," the storyteller as hero implicitly claims, "the purpose
> remains mine to determine." (131)

"Quest stories meet suffering head on; they accept illness and seek to *use*
it," says Frank (115)—but the chaos narrative is no narrative at all; "Gilda
Radner's story is not a chaos narrative, precisely because it is a narrative"
(100). Coherence is not really optional. It is a feature of acceptable accounts
of lives lived. Hawkins writes that pathography "constructs meaning by

subjecting raw experience to the powerful impulse to make sense of it all, to bind together the events, feelings, thoughts, and sensations that occur during an illness into an integrated whole" (*Reconstructing* 18).

"Kate" posting to the pro-Ana site "Anasway" tells the fear-of-discovery story and the striving-for-anorexia story (anorexics do not eat, whereas bulimics eat and purge; bulimics suspect themselves of having less self-control than anorexics and, moreover, find their eating lifestyle more difficult to conceal):

> I'm scared that somehow my parents or brohter [*sic*—and so for typographical errors throughout] or sister will be able to find out that i am coming to this site, but i need support. I feel like i can't make my goals without it. I also have a problem with pucking. . . . I am desperately wanting to switch to Ana, but everyday i tell myself that i will stop eating, and then i do and get really depressed. Plus, it is getting harder and harder to try and puke when my parents are just downstairs, more than once theyv'e come upstairs while im in the bathroom, but luckily haven't even considered anything.

A survey of profiles, journal entries, and other narrative segments at Ana sites reveals a repertoire of available plots, although many Ana plots are depression plots, with narrative deficits. Narrative itself requires conflict, suspense, aspiration, and struggle—and anorexic narrators, like Kate, do not fail to supply them.

"Amanda's" personal Web site is multifarious. Amanda has many interests. She lists her favorite books, movies, pastimes, and even classes, as she is a university student. But when she links to her own pro-Ana site—"Future Perfect"—Amanda narrates E.D. (eating disorder) and tells a fat-girl-dying-to-be-thin story:

> I've been fat all my life. I've been teased, ridiculed, humiliated. And after every time this happened, I would think, "That's it. I'm just going to stop eating and then I'll be skinny and perfect." I've grown up a little since then. My current regiment [*sic*] pretty much consists of going to the gym 3 times a week and eating between 600 and 1000 calories a day. When I was 18 I decided to try to purge. It was hard, but I eventually got good at it. So now I'm trying to lose 100 pounds and get in shape. Me in a nutshell. Like I would ever fit.

The Web narrator has been formed in part by the invitation to exist in the form in which it is most possible for her to exist as a narrator at all. In this sense, she is a complicating narrator for the study of the epideictic rhetoric of pathography. She makes us think not only about permissible and impermissible stories but also about what counts as a story at all and what does not.[12]

A second complicating narrator is Barbara Ehrenreich, suggesting a second tyranny, a tyranny of cheerfulness, itself a kind of economic tyranny, a tyranny of productivity. Ehrenreich was treated for breast cancer and writes in the November 2001 issue of *Harper's* an essay on the breast cancer "cult of pink kitsch" and the "Darwinian" cult of survivorship. Ehrenreich is the renegade narrator, who refuses to tell a story of battling and enduring and overcoming, refuses to be relentlessly upbeat (as she says, "implacably optimistic"). In particular, Ehrenreich protests the "ultrafemin[ity]" of the "breast cancer marketplace"—its pink ribbons and teddy bears, its wind chimes and trinkets.

The corporate-sponsored infantilization of women with breast cancer perplexes Ehrenreich: "Certainly men diagnosed with prostate cancer do not receive gifts of matchbox cars" (47). Ehrenreich refuses to be, as a person with breast cancer, docile. But, when she goes public with her complaints, she is ostracized by the breast-cancer community, which has embraced, in general, a rosier *ethos*:

> What has grown up around breast cancer . . . resembles a cult . . . perhaps we should say a full-fledged religion. The products—teddy bears, pink-ribbon brooches, and so forth—serve as amulets and talismans, comforting the sufferer and providing visible evidence of faith. The personal narratives serve as testimonials and follow the same general arc as the confessional autobiographies required of seventeenth-century Puritans: first there is a crisis . . . then comes a prolonged ordeal . . . and finally, the blessed certainty of salvation, or its breast-cancer equivalent, survivorhood. ("Welcome" 50)[13]

Ehrenreich is interesting for a rhetorical study of illness narratives because her account of her experience of breast cancer is self-consciously an account of its persuasive and coercive elements—and because her attempt publicly to resist the dominant discourse of her disease is met itself with such resistance. Support groups, according to Ehrenreich, cease to be supportive when one's illness narrative violates the conventions of the sanctioned story. Like an Oscar winner who refuses to perform humility, Ehrenreich refuses to perform cheerfulness. She learns, however, that dissent from cheerfulness is a "kind of treason." When she posts to a Web discussion group a list of her "heartfelt complaints about debilitating treatments, recalcitrant insurance companies, environmental carcinogens, and

. . . 'sappy pink ribbons,'" her post is met, she reports, with a "chorus of rebukes" (50). Those who do not rebuke her pity her: "You need to run, not walk," one respondent says, "to some counseling. . . . Please, get yourself some help and I ask everyone on this site to pray for you so you can enjoy life to the fullest" (50).

Although she is mindful of the history of support groups, especially for women—how the groups for over thirty years have seen women through troubles and triumphs and transformations—Ehrenreich is deeply suspicious now, having noticed, it seems, that support groups can also serve purposes of surveillance and patrol. They do this in part by regulating narratives.

Ehrenreich contributes to the discussion of the rhetoric of pathography a double narrative. There is the series of posts she offered up on the Web in the course of her illness and treatments, the first renegade narrative. But there is a second renegade narrative: the story Ehrenreich tells in the *Harper's* article itself. Noticeably, the sentiments of the first layer of community response are replicated in the second layer of response. Ehrenreich's observations on the cult of pink kitsch are no better received by the readers of *Harper's* than they were by the readers of her cancer postings. In a letter to the editor of *Harper's*, Sharon Yandle writes, "There is life after breast cancer, and there is nothing shallow about wanting life. There is, however, something very superficial about reducing to cult status the desire to reach out to others." Physician Barron H. Lerner writes that most women with breast cancer

> focus on obtaining the best available therapy and then receiving close follow-up for possible recurrences. And although pink ribbons and teddy bears may be infantilizing, many survivors appreciate these touches or at least tolerate them as furthering a worthwhile cause. ("Letter")

In total, four additional letters of response to Ehrenreich are published in *Harper's*, and all are critical of her. Even the letter-writer who seems to share Ehrenreich's view of the need for a more political response to cancers linked to environmental carcinogens blames the author for devoting so much of her essay to "sneering at women for succumbing to the cancer-driven version of positive thinking" (Crowther). Of course, Ehrenreich has the last word, published in *Harper's* a second time with a response to her critics. Other cancer dissenters are just caught in the web.

Ehrenreich's narrative complicates pathography by illustrating the hegemony of certain conventions of illness narration. Hawkins writes about a subgenre of pathographies she calls "angry pathographies," "intended to expose and denounce atrocities in the way illness is treated in America today." Angry pathographies "testify to a medical system seen as out of control, dehumanized, and sometimes brutalizing; and they are written from a sense of outrage over particular and concrete instances of what is perceived to be the failure of medicine to care adequately for the ill" (6). But, like the range of acceptable plots, the range of acceptable antagonists in illness narratives is also a matter of pathographic convention. Doctors and medical institutions are easily railed against. Hawkins cites Martha Weinman Lear's *Heartsounds* as an example of an angry pathography. There is a way in which Margaret Edson's play *Wit* belongs to the subgenre, too. *Wit*'s plot is the demise from cancer of the main character, Vivian Bearing, but the subplot is the war between Bearing's doctor and her cancer cells, Bearing herself being only collateral damage. The villain of the play is the medical system that dismisses Bearing's life in the course of trying to save it.

Multinational corporations are *not* easily railed against. Feature films like *Erin Brockovich* and *A Civil Action* showcase corporate health antagonists; pathographies, in general, do not. It is not that there is genre legislation concerning villains, but stories of "survivorship" are generally stories of *individual* survivorship.[14] A happy ending extends or redeems a single life. In typical pathographies, heroes survive, when they survive, one person at a time. Ehrenreich has more broadly social concerns:

> [O]bedience is the message behind the infantilizing theme in breast cancer culture. . . . [B]y ignoring or underemphasizing the vexing issue of environmental causes, the breast-cancer cult turns women into dupes of what could be called the Cancer Industrial Complex: the multinational corporate enterprise that with the one hand doles out carcinogens and diseases and, with the other, offers expensive, semitoxic pharmaceutical treatments. . . . In the harshest judgment, the breast-cancer cult serves as an accomplice in global poisoning—normalizing cancer, prettying it up, even presenting it, perversely, as a positive and enviable experience. (52–53)

Suggesting the limited helpfulness of individual stories of pain and suffering, Susan Sontag in the face of her own cancer wrote *Illness as Metaphor* instead of writing her own pathography.

> I didn't think it would be useful—and I wanted to be useful—to tell yet one more story in the first person of how someone learned that

she or he had cancer, wept, struggled, was comforted, suffered, took courage . . . though mine was also that story. A narrative, it seemed to me, would be less useful than an idea. (*AIDS* 101)

Pathography is generically epideictic when its repeated gestures enunciate values preferring certain sorts of accounts over others but also, for the same reasons, preferring certain sorts of experience. A reasonable concern about a generic groove for illness narratives, then, is that the genres of pathography invite us not only to report experience in certain sorts of ways—Couser says breast cancer narratives "often involve both a kind of master plot and a series of recurrent scenes and topics" (43)— but also to interpret experience and even to *experience* experience in certain sorts of ways.

One of the remarkable things about the pro-Ana narrators is how they have absorbed and returned the "control" discourse that in popular psychology and popular media explains their behavior. At Ana and Mia sites, there are countless stories of men and women who *see themselves* as controlling their eating in order to control their lives, whereas perhaps twenty years ago, before these explanations circulated, anorexics would only have seen themselves as controlling their eating. What I am suggesting is partly a reiteration of Elaine Showalter's point in *Hystories*—that people are ill in the idiom of a time and a place, influenced by circulating discourse on fashionable illnesses. I am suggesting also something else: that genres write stories. Hawkins talks about how narrative overtakes memory. While memory is fleeting and fluid, narrative is formed, and narrative fixes memory while also sculpting it somewhat, fixing it then as sculpture; we remember experience in the form in which it was storied.[15] Narrative also gives us a repertoire of available responses; we live in the terms of the epideictic rhetoric of the moment. That is why the idea of epideictic rhetoric, a rhetoric of values, has such heuristic usefulness for cultural study and the study of human experience.

A third complicating narrator is Carla Cantor, whose *Phantom Illness: Shattering the Myth of Hypochondria*, published in 1996, is a first-person account of her struggle with the illness of excessive health anxiety (see my chapter 4 for a discussion of hypochondria). Cantor complicates the genre of illness narrative, inadvertently, by being the commercialized subject of her own story. That is, Cantor's account of her illness, rendered in the dialect of contemporary biomedicine and psychopharmacology, likely had as its first effect the movement of Paxil off the shelves of pharmacies, because, more than anything else, her book is an account of hypochondria as a disorder treatable by SSRIs (selective serotonin reuptake inhibitors). In *Phantom Illness*, hypochondria is installed in David Healy's "antidepressant era." This is Healy:

> In the 1950's, estimates of the incidence of depression were fifty people per million; today the estimate is 100,000 per million. What was once defined as "anxiety" and treated with tranquilizers in the wake of the crisis of benzodiazipine dependence and the development of selective serotonin reuptake inhibitors became "depression." And as SSRI's have been shown to be effective for treating other nervous conditions, such as panic disorder, estimates of their frequency have increased markedly as well. Disease increasingly means whatever we have a reimbursable treatment for. ("Good Science" 1)

Cantor's account of her hypochondria, although it is, in the first instance, an account of human suffering, is so conventionalized that it might have been written by a software program for illness narratives. It is the protracted telling of a story told succinctly in the book's foreword by physician Brian Fallon:

> New medical perspectives on hypochondria now suggest that hypochondriacs may in fact be physically ill. However, the illness is a result not of the disease they fear but of a neurochemical imbalance in the brain. . . . This new medical perspective has important treatment implications and provides new hope for the patient with illness fears. (x)

In particular, hypochondria sufficiently resembles obsessive compulsive disorder to make hypochondriacs good candidates for treatment with SSRIs.

In Cantor's own narrative, the conventional tropes of an overpracticed genre somewhere between confession and self-help are lined up like rhetorical soldiers. There is the no-fault trope: "[I]ntrusive thoughts could be related to deeper psychological troubles or biochemical imbalances" (8); the end-the-silence trope: "In living rooms, at parties, we talk . . . about topics like incest, bulimia, and rape. Why is hypochondria something we turn away from?" (8); the statistical-relief-from-shame trope: "[O]ne in ten [patients] continue to be frightened of disease in the face of reassuring information. That meant I had nothing to be ashamed of" (6); the community-of-sufferers trope: "What has probably helped as much as anything is the realization that I am not the only one fighting this battle" (11) (the battle metaphor itself is already so absorbed as not to seem metaphoric); the quest trope: "Share the journey," says Cantor (12); the pain-is-real trope: Hypochondriacs "are not malingering or pretending to be sick"; their pain is "as genuine as it is intense" (18); the hope trope: Ask your doctor for a prescription for Paxil.

A further trope—the superiority trope—deserves additional attention because it appears also in characterizations of patients with migraine (see my chapter 2) where it suggests how tropes turn. Cantor writes, "[M]ost sufferers from hypochondria, a perfectionist bunch, don't 'crack up,' have nervous breakdowns, or end up in mental hospitals. They function, even achieving great things, but often at a cost of happiness and intimacy with the people they most care about" (9). The hypochondriac is drawn as being a little too good for the world, but as in the case of migraine, this narrative trope can turn on the sufferer, and the high-functioning perfectionist can be re-presented as an obsessive prig.

Cantor's story illustrates a blending and homogenization of genres of illness narrative. Her story is the Web-site confession writ long, the infomercial writ large,[16] the pathography writ by numbers. It is also an iteration of a circulating narrative of disease, providing readers with the terms in which to view their own distress. While Cantor's story may be consoling to some, it is also advisory, and this narrator is the anti-Ehrenreich, embracing exactly the corporate world that Ehrenreich rejects.

Cantor is a complicating narrator who invites us to consider what it means for us as scholars to participate in propagating the narrative values that make such a book sell. Cantor's narrative has many features of just the sort of story that Frank praises, when although he announces that he will classify illness narratives, he actually also evaluates them. I said earlier that, for Frank, the quest narrative is the best narrative. Cantor's narrative is just such a narrative—a journey of self-discovery, a story of determination and triumph. "Readers pick up published illness stories," Frank says, "for all sorts of reasons, but the moral purpose of reading is *to witness a change of character through suffering*" (128; emphasis in original). "The quest narrative recognizes ill people as responsible moral agents whose primary action is witness; its stories are necessary to restore the moral agency that other stories sacrifice" (134). Not all illness narrative scholarship is so moralistic—Hawkins and Couser, for example, are less judgmental in their scholarly work—but some narrative scholarship can be read as colluding with some narratives to suggest there are better and worse ways to be ill, better and worse stories to tell.

Cantor is the commercialized subject but a more general problem with illness narratives is the making of the pathographized subject. Deploying a peculiar narrative grammar, pathography can reproduce the very biomedical model of disease that the genre itself sought at first to unsettle. Illness narratives were embraced initially, as I have said, as a means of establishing a patient's voice to compete with the voice of biomedicine, generally considered to be depersonalizing, objectifying, and fragmenting. Couser says, "Personal narrative is an increasingly popular way of resisting or reversing the process of depersonalization that often accompanies illness—the expropriation of experience by an alien and alienating discourse" (29). But pathography in its proliferation has also an effect quite different from the desired one of demedicalizing illness: It diseases biography.

Psychiatrist Neil Scheurich writes against the culture of illness narrative. Patients' stories, he says, "do not originate from some pure well of authentic truth, only to be contaminated by medical ignorance and presumption."

> Many illness stories stem from pernicious sources, such as cultures of disability, hopelessness, and drug use. And due to medicalization, the stories patients tell are increasingly illness-saturated; *illness stories are eclipsing life stories*. Writers such as [Kathryn Montgomery] Hunter and [Howard] Brody . . . have accused physicians of focusing on the patient rather than the person, but the fact is that . . . patients are tending to do the same thing. Physicians and patients often collude in the fostering of illness-saturated stories. (470; emphasis added)

Years ago, as I report in chapter 5, I watched my mother's professional life retreat from her medical chart as her stroke gained distance on her retirement: the longer she lived as a hospitalized, disabled person, the more the story of her illness came to overwrite the story of her life. A genre in pathography routinely reenacts that sort of overwriting. Some of us might prefer to have instead of a pathography a biography-to-the-death.

Not only narrative but also narrative scholarship may endorse the idea that with illness, the story of a life ends, and the story of an illness takes over. Or narrative scholarship may endorse the terms of a particular kind of story. Or it may by the shape of its own interest participate in discrediting narratives that violate the conventions of a narrative community. The scholar's attention to narrative itself may devalue the experience of the ill person who refuses or who is unable to narrate within the ideology of the genre: the disorganized ill person, the aphasic ill person, the silent ill person.

One way for narrative scholarship to escape the possibility of being a kind of critical voyeurism is for it to reflect on the determinist inclinations of *both* narrative and narrative studies. Certain rhetorical principles suggested by Aristotle are helpful to the project of understanding epideictic rhetoric:

> One must consider [. . .] also the audience to whom the praise is addressed; for, as Socrates said . . . , it is not difficult to praise the Athenians to an audience of them. Whatever the quality an audience esteems, the speaker must attribute that quality to the object of his praise. . . . Since we praise men for what they have done, and since the mark of the virtuous person is that he acts after deliberate moral choice, our speaker must try to show that the subject of his praise is a man who does so act. To this end one will find it helpful to make it appear that the man has often acted with moral purpose. . . . There is a specific interrelation between praise and advice; for anything you might suggest in a speech of advice can, by a shift in the expression, be turned into encomium. (51–52)

Illness narrative and illness narrative scholarship each constitutes an epideictic discourse, a discourse of values. Regarded this way, they can be treated critically, and the qualities they praise and blame can be subjected to scrutiny.

4   Hypochondria as a Rhetorical Disorder

If primary headache is the headache that is of interest in itself, not as a symptom of meningitis or brain tumor, then, on analogy, hypochondria is a kind of primary suffering, a suffering in itself, more complete because it takes place at a heightened level of awareness. Indeed, reflection is what ties hypochondria of the eighteenth century to hypochondria of the twenty-first. In the late eighteenth century, James Boswell describes the suffering of the hypochondriac—himself. Boswell's hypochondriac feels ill and is languid, but he suffers not only from his illness and his languor but also from his memory of a time before them; he suffers by comparison with his former state of activity. Yet he is more miserable for not being able to wish to return to his former happiness because he is certain he was deceived in it. Or he desires to be alone, and he despises himself for that desire. While hypochondria is not the same disorder now as it was in Boswell's time—the historical variability of the disorder under hypochondria's name is one of its most interesting features— hypochondria's relentless, ruminative misery endures as its characteristic mode of suffering.

Hypochondria is an irresistible topic for rhetorical study in health because it is *essentially* a rhetorical disorder. Contemporary hypochondriacs are people who have become persuaded in the absence of an organic precipitating cause that they are ill. Often, external agents who publicly advertise diseases and treatments have persuaded them that they are ill; in private, and often in the middle of the night, hypochondriacs have persuaded themselves. Hypochondriacs bear the burden, then, of persuading physicians and others (family members, for example) that they are in need of care. Only rhetorical resources are available to them for this purpose. Hypochondriacs make their case for disease with arguments more reliably left to blood or heartsounds or ultrasounds; the very complaints of the hypochondriac are challenges to belief, lacking demonstrable correlatives in the body. Hypochondriacs, furthermore, make demands on the rhetorical capacities of other people: Physicians, for example, try to persuade them that they are well. Overall, the hypochondriac's interlocutors are unsuccessful; if they were successful, the hypochondriacs in question would not officially be hypochondriacs (hypochondriacs are defined in part by their inability to be persuaded that they are well). Hypochondriacs, finally, inspire other patients to dissociate rhetorically from them. Persons with fibromyalgia, chronic fatigue syndrome, chemical sensitivity, and whiplash and others who understand themselves to be taken as suspect patients seek to persuade other people that they themselves are not hypochondriacs.

So, its myriad persuasions make hypochondria a rhetorical disorder in its own right. Hypochondria is also a rhetorical disorder in relation to the culture in which it appears. As was noted in the chapter on migraine, discourse fills the space that certainty in medicine leaves unoccupied. Much about the medicine of a time and a place is revealed by that discourse. The hypochondriac inhabits a specific illness-discourse universe, but also medicine as a set of terms and practices gives at different times and places different accounts of its suspect patients in general and its hypochondriacal patients in particular. Hypochondria, in other words, is importantly kairotic. In 1912, British physician Frederick Parkes Weber wrote about female patients with a condition he called "hysterical malingering" (a sort of irrepressible impersonation of an ill person). The "tendency to simulation and deception" was not surprising in these patients, for women, in Weber's view, were bred for deception, an "exaggeration . . . of an instinct which is normally greater in women than in men, the greater prominence in woman of the tendency or instinct to deceive constituting a normal psychical sex character" (138). That is, in Britain, in 1912, a reputable physician might proffer a Darwinian, and thoroughly sexist, account of certain complex complaints, finding in the general discourse of the time (Weber was a great collector of newspaper clippings and a dutiful archivist) support for the thesis that hysterical malingering might be associated with a tertiary sex characteristic arising from the natural selection of wily women, their wiles compensating for their deficits in physical strength. And the trait might be weeded out by eugenics.

Hypochondriacs invite theories about themselves in part because they are, overall, medically anomalous.[1] They do not make sense according to the basic precepts of biomedicine: that diseases consist in deviations from measurable biological norms; that diseases have specific and discoverable causes or origins; and that diseases have characteristic features that are universal. Hypochondria is not necessarily inexplicable as a disease entity itself—indeed, it has recently been viewed as a mental disorder with a biochemical etiology (see Fallon)—but the idea that people would experience themselves as having stomach cancer or AIDS or multiple sclerosis when they do not have these diseases at all is what biomedicine is at somewhat of a loss to explain. Rhetoric reframes the problem. Discursive elements of hypochondria are rhetorical, and bodily actions are rhetorical as well. This is Kenneth Burke:

> The accumulating lore on the nature of "psychogenic illnesses" has revealed that something so "practical" as a bodily ailment may be a "symbolic" act on the part of the body which, in this materialization *dances* a corresponding state of mind, reordering the glandular and neural behavior of the organism in obedience to mind-body correspondences, quite as the formal dancer reorders his externally observable gesture to match his attitudes. (*Philosophy* 10–11)

Burke goes on to explain, in support of a rhetoric of the body, that a person who with most external signs persuades others that he is calm may be betrayed by his own salivation as someone who is afraid. His saliva, in this case, is dancing an attitude of fear. The hypochondriacal body may, then, in some literal sense, have a mind of its own. Or perhaps, the protesting body may dance an illness it does not have.

This chapter argues that a rhetorical account complements existing accounts of hypochondria, and it outlines some problems and questions that the rhetorical analyst might consider in studying the disorder. It offers a series of observations about hypochondria, which together suggest possible strategies for ameliorative thinking about it. As a medical problem, hypochondria is intractable; as a psychological problem, it is mysterious; as a psychiatric problem, it is perhaps too easily biologized; as a social problem, it is amorphous. But as a rhetorical problem, hypochondria is bounded, interesting, and suggestive. A rhetorical view turns the hypochondriac into someone who may be re-viewed and re-engaged discursively with promising results. I am not suggesting that rhetoric is a cure for hypochondria (although more than one physician has suggested scripts with which to treat the hypochondriac; see Mead), but I am suggesting that hypochondria's rhetorical element, heretofore underexamined, provides novel ways of thinking about the disorder.

The chapter describes hypochondria in both its medical/psychiatric version and its colloquial version and outlines its history so the kairotic element of the disorder is clear. Certain of hypochondria's special features are then discussed in support of an argument for a new sort of study of hypochondria and hypochondriacs. The principle that shapes the chapter is Burke's observation that the ambiguities themselves of human motive are *resources* for studying human action: "[I]nstead of considering it our task to 'dispose of' any ambiguity by merely disclosing the fact that it is an ambiguity, we rather consider it our task to study and clarify the *resources* of ambiguity" (*Grammar* xix; emphasis in original). Then, hypochondria is not so much a medical mystery to be solved as a mystery of motive to be explored.

Hypochondria refers to some or all of the following: a preoccupation with health; a propensity to self-diagnosis; a tendency to overuse health services; disease phobia; and attention-seeking, worry, and obsession, all with respect to illness. More specifically, the *DSM-IV* (*Diagnostic and Statistical Manual of Mental Disorders*, fourth edition) lists the following criteria for the disorder:

A. Preoccupation with fears of having, or the idea that one has, a serious disease based on the person's misinterpretation of bodily symptoms.

B. The preoccupation persists despite appropriate medical evaluation and reassurance.

C. The belief in Criterion A is not of delusional intensity . . . and is not restricted to a circumscribed concern about appearance. . . .

D. The preoccupation causes clinically significant distress or impairment in social, occupational, or other important areas of functioning.

E. The duration of the disturbance is at least 6 months.

F. The preoccupation is not better accounted for by Generalized Anxiety Disorder, Obsessive-Compulsive Disorder, Panic Disorder, a Major Depressive Episode, Separation Anxiety, or another Somatoform Disorder.[2]

There is a way in which hypochondria *is* its *DSM* definition, for the *DSM* acts to make the disorder and the definition one and the same. The *DSM* gives us reason not to use the term *hypochondriac* promiscuously. But there is a truth, too, of everyday language. When we call someone a hypochondriac, we do not necessarily mean the *DSM* definition, but what we do mean is understood. *Hypochondria*, then, also refers in more general parlance to the problem of people who are both worried and well, ill and

not diseased, seeking a diagnosis and dreading one, and ill-disposed to receive the only diagnosis that may be forthcoming: the diagnosis of hypochondria itself.[3] To borrow a description from novelist Jeffrey Eugenides,
the hypochondriac is a "sick person imprisoned in a healthy body" (20).
We are interested here in both the technical hypochondriac and the non-
technical one.

In the eighteenth century, hypochondria was seen to be a pitiable,
organic distemper, featuring characteristic ills from flatulence and fatigue
to the distress of rumination on these complaints. "The hyp" was at the
time a distemper of men, the counterpart of hysteria in women. That is,
hypochondria and hysteria were alike symptomatically but different etio-
logically—hysteria arising from the uterus and hypochondria from the
upper abdomen (*hypo* meaning *under* and *chondros* meaning *cartilage*).
In the nineteenth century, hypochondria began to take on its current
meaning and suggestion of malingering.[4] Hypochondria today is associated less with a specific gastrointestinal profile and more with false complaints and misinterpreted signs of the body.

Esther Fischer-Homberger is one of a number of social historians of
medicine to be interested in the possibility that a single constellation of
hypochondriacal symptoms was noted over time under different descriptions, appearing in the medical literature as: melancholy, hypochondria,
neurasthenia, and neurosis.[5] In light of such fluidity, it is interesting to
consider that hypochondria, having moved from an organic account to a
psychological one, is currently finding legitimation as an organic disease
redux in the disordered biochemistry of worrying (see Cantor and Fallon's
account of hypochondria discussed in the previous chapter).

Hypochondria is oddly both conventional and anomalous. It can be
represented in a familiar biomedical idiom of suffering—Fallon says,
"New medical perspectives on hypochondria now suggest that hypochondriacs may in fact be physically ill," their illness due to "a neurochemical imbalance in the brain"[6] (x)—but it also doesn't quite fit into the canon
of diseases. Hypochondria also taps into a cultural ambivalence that is
understandable, in part, in Burkean terms: "Put identification and division ambiguously together so that you cannot know for certain just where
one ends and the other begins, and you have the characteristic invitation
to rhetoric" (*Rhetoric of Motives* 25). Hypochondriacs are to some extent *us*—we have all been anxious about our health or preoccupied with
it—but hypochondriacs are also, we may insist, *not us*; typically, we find
hypochondriacs a little loathsome or, at least, ridiculous.

Humor is one way that anomaly, ambivalence, and ambiguity are expressed. It is not surprising that the hypochondriac has long been a figure of general ridicule. Consider Argan of Jean-Baptiste Molière's *Le malade imaginaire*, so preoccupied with his health that he insists that his daughter marry a physician so that one will be close by. Recall the pathetically cautious Mr. Woodhouse in Jane Austen's *Emma*, always avoiding a draft or something worse. Alexander Portnoy's father (Roth) is never out of the grip of his constipation. In the twenty-first century, there is a minor industry in hypochondria humor, featuring books like Wendy Marston's *Hypochondriac's Handbook*, which will tell the reader what diagnoses can be made at home with just a protruded tongue and a mirror, and another is Gene Weingarten's *Hypochondriac's Guide to Life. And Death*:

> The ordinary person will notice a slight spastic tugging on his eyelid, that rhythmic twitching we all feel from time to time, and go, "Hmmm." . . . That doesn't happen with the hypochondriac. A hypochondriac would not go "Hmmm" unless you told him there was a new fatal disease whose first symptom is the inability to say "Hmmm." Then he would say "Hmmm" 1,723 times a day until he got laryngitis and could no longer say "Hmmm," which would of course constitute proof he is dying. (22)

While hypochondria has enduring cultural meaning, and the term persists as a name for something both pathetic and sympathetic, debate over the nature of hypochondria led F. E. Kenyon, over a quarter-century ago, to suggest that the noun *hypochondria* be removed from use entirely in favor of the adjective *hypochondriacal* to denote certain sorts of patient fears and behaviors: "Is there such an entity as primary or essential hypochondria which is not part of another syndrome?" (7). Is hypochondria a distinct medical entity, or is it a feature of our humanity expressed in connection with other medical entities? Or is hypochondria a feature of our humanity expressed in connection with other rhetorical entities?

Elements of the life course of *hypochondria* as a term and a diagnosis point to some of its rhetorical qualities. In his *Essays on Fashionable Diseases*, written in the late eighteenth century, James M. Adair named hypochondria as a kind of disease du jour:

> [A]s people of fashion claim an exclusive privilege of having always some thing to complain of, so the mutual communication of their ailments is often the topic of conversation; the imagination frequently suggests a similarity of disease, though none such really exists; and thus the term becomes soon compleatly fashionable. . . . In the later

end of the last and beginning of this century, *spleen*, vapours, or hyp, was the fashionable disease. (5–6)

According to Adair, hypochondria itself is a somewhat nebulous disorder that enters the public imagination and finds adherents: "Fashion has long influenced the great and opulent in the choice of their physicians, surgeons, apothecaries, and midwives; but it is not so obvious how it has influenced them also in the *choice* of their diseases" (4). Adair prefigures Ian Hacking's theory of the "looping effect" in the social life of kinds. According to Hacking, "new knowledge about 'the criminal' or 'the homosexual' becomes known to the people classified, changes the way these individuals behave, and loops back to force changes in the classifications and knowledge about them" (*Social* 105). The kind in Adair is the hypochondriac. The notion of "fashionable illness" also brings to mind the suggestibility of persons to circulating diagnoses of any sort—a phenomenon amply discussed and, here, provocatively described in Mary McCarthy's 1954 novel *The Group*:

> Polly told [the doctor] her mother's idea: that her father had changed his symptoms when he learned the new name of his disease [manic depression]. The doctor laughed. "That isn't possible, is it?" said Polly. "With these nuts anything is possible, Polly," he declared. "Insanity is a funny thing. We don't really understand anything about it. Why they get sick, why they get well. Changing the name may make a difference. We've noticed that now that we no longer speak of dementia praecox, we get few dementia-praecox patients. It tempts you to think sometimes that all mental illness has a hysterical origin, that they're all copying the latest textbooks. Even the illiterate patients." (296)

The hypochondriac is inter alia someone who is susceptible to the persuasive force of experiences that are by a process of internal rhetoric translated into symptoms of particular diseases (see Wenegrat for an analysis of this process of the model of performance).

Disease is, notwithstanding its public discursive element, a pronouncement of someone authorized to make such a pronouncement. Diagnosis is a particular kind of speech act requiring a particular kind of speaker.[7] Social life requires that this be the case: If one is to take on the "sick role" as Talcott Parsons described it over fifty years ago, then one must not simply be ill or think oneself ill; one must officially be pronounced ill. According to Parsons, illness is not only a *condition* but also a *social role* with special benefits and permissions. Illness exempts persons from the performance of certain social duties, for example, and from some responsibility for their own state; at the same time, it obligates ill persons to cooperate with physicians and therapists and to attempt expeditiously no longer to be ill.

It is important for a rhetorical understanding of hypochondria that the ill person himself or herself is without authority of diagnosis. Hypochondriacs are sometimes reviled in the medical literature, under headings like "the hateful patient,"[8] as people who present themselves to their physicians with a diagnosis instead of with a set of symptoms, complaining of "an ulcer" instead of stomach pain, or "pneumonia" instead of a cough.[9] Because the patient lacks authority of diagnosis, any argument in the course of the doctor-patient interview can compromise the *ethos* or presenting character of the patient, whose attempts at making a case for illness undermine themselves by *being* such attempts.

The persuading hypochondriac is well known for arguing, for example, from the *topos* of uniqueness: He or she may claim to be sick in a way no one has ever been sick before. Yet, nothing is less persuasive than uniqueness to the physician whose own rhetorical task is to find the generic in the idiosyncratic and to return to the patient the idiosyncratic in the form of the generic. According to Arthur Kleinman, "The patient's intuition that the illness is unique and the doctor's counterintuition that the disease is a copy of textbook examples is a conflict not limited to hypochondriasis" (196). In hypochondria, however, the tension produces a rhetorical zero-sum game. The patient's argument from uniqueness is a refutation of itself, an argument that undercuts itself as it is being spoken. Note in the following chapter the ironic tone in which the physician says to the daughter of his patient, "Perhaps [your mother] has something unknown to medicine." To be ill is, in part, to participate in the conventions of illnesses according to their categories.

The idea of the patient who is sick like no other is both rhetorically weak and clinically troubling, not least because the hypochondriac may at any point also be "legitimately" sick. Just as paranoids are sometimes being followed, so hypochondriacs are sometimes very ill. It seems that both parties in the conversation of hypochondriac and physician have some self-doubt. Each interlocutor as a point of persuasion claims certainty, and each one in claiming certainty increases self-doubt. In Kleinman's analysis, "the hypochondriac must maintain the social fiction of not doubting his own doubt, when perhaps the most disturbing part of the experience of hypochondriasis is the patient's intractable doubt that his belief is correct" (195). Meanwhile, "the hypochondriac's doubt has an exact complement in the doubt of the practitioner, who knows at heart that, in spite of trying to convince the hypochondriac to the contrary, he can never be completely certain himself that the patient doesn't have a disease" (197). The hypochondriac, for his or her part, is rhetorically paralyzed by the attempts of the physician to argue that he or she is basically well.[10]

The hypochondriac is well known for being tenacious, for holding on to the idea of illness even when there is no evidence of disease. This is in part because the *absence of evidence* of disease falls short persuasively of *evidence of absence* of disease, and the latter is almost impossible to secure.[11] The medical and psychological literature make much of the fact that patients may qualify as hypochondriacal if they fail in the matter of being reassured that they are not ill. From a rhetorical perspective, one might wonder also why the physician fails to be sufficiently persuasive. The rhetoric of hypochondria is, in that sense, about the burden of proof.

To say that hypochondria is (in part) a rhetorical disease entails that it is a uniquely *human* disease: There are dogs with heart conditions and stomach ulcers, but there are no hypochondriacal dogs. Hypochondria is a disorder requiring an interlocutor, and the first interlocutor in this case, as I have suggested, is the self. An interesting thing about the essentially dialogic nature of hypochondria is how many things one can find to say to oneself when the topic of conversation is the state of one's own health. Where does all this material come from? There is a way in which it does not *simply* come from the body. Immanuel Kant, himself a hypochondriac, gives this account:

> Hypochondria is called *Grillenkrankheit* [cricket illness] from its analogy to listening, in the quiet of the night, to a cricket chirping in the house, which disturbs our mental repose and so prevents us from sleeping. The hypochondriac's illness consists in this: that certain internal physical sensations are not so much symptoms of a real disease present in the body as rather mere causes of anxiety about it; and that human nature has the peculiar characteristic (not found in animals) that paying attention to certain local impressions makes us feel them more intensely or persistently. (82)

The source of the hypochondriac's trouble is not simple—not, in the first instance, only material: Bodily signs are worrisome only as signs *of* something. A cough that would have been unremarkable only days before becomes alarming once SARS (severe acute respiratory syndrome) has arrived on the hypochondriac's radar. In general, hypochondriacs respond most often to ambiguous signs: chest pain, head pain, muscle pain, dizziness, and fatigue. As physician Eric J. Cassell says, what turns pain into suffering is *meaning* (*Nature of Suffering*). Most hypochondriacs suffer from bodily data that falls just short of being information. The hypochondriac, then, is seeker, calculator, claimant, performer, and persuader of an intolerable ambiguity.

To view hypochondria rhetorically includes also noting more precisely the ways in which the hypochondriac is made in public discourse—public discourse constituting, in Burkean terms, a *scene* for hypochondria. "Even before we know what act is to be discussed, we can say with confidence that a rounded discussion of its motives must contain a reference to some kind of background" (Burke, *Grammar* xvi–xvii). Public rhetoric sponsors the hypochondrias of a time and a place and answers at least in part the question posed earlier: Where does all this material come from when we talk about ourselves to ourselves?

Barbara Harrison, in a 1977 issue of *Ms.* magazine, gives an anecdotal account of a key process by which public discourse agitates and feeds the hypochondriacal imagination:

> When I read . . . an article in the *Reader's Digest*, explaining "Your Body's Early Warning Signals," I had every symptom for every killer disease. . . . A bursitis-like pain in one shoulder, according to this scary piece, may presage lung cancer. I developed a bursitis-like pain in one shoulder. Pain in the chest was, of course, mentioned as one of the symptoms of lung cancer. My chest cavity was one massive pain. "A significant enlargement of the area around the nails, called clubbing," was, I read, another symptom of lung cancer. My fingernails became . . . a cause of concern. (85)

The sort of experience Harrison describes is reported very commonly; people who are not hypochondriacs also get captured, if briefly, by symptom lists and health alerts. Richard Ehrlich describes "the healthy hypochondriac" as someone who attends to the body, even worries about it sometimes, but does not become excessively anxious or self-focused in the presence of bodily signs and unwelcome deductions. Another hypochondria researcher reveals that "the highest score of self-report measures of state anxiety have been recorded from people awaiting the results of medical tests" (Rachman xvii). That is, health concerns are the most ordinary things in the world; hypochondria is the condition of those whose health concerns have become unreasonable. In a sense, though, even the unreasonable has its reasons.

What follows is a rhetorical account using the example of depression of part of the process of *making* the hypochondriac—one who becomes attached, in this case, to a diagnosis of mental illness. The story is by now familiar. Diagnostic information, arguably too available, is presented in such a way as to make self-diagnosis almost impossible to resist. You (any you) feel unusually miserable, maybe inexplicably bleak and sad. You read the Zoloft advertisement in *People* magazine and do the checklist for depression; maybe you record the mnemonic that comes with the checklist so you don't forget how you qualify for the diagnosis.[12] Your sadness has been translated by the ad into the language of a disorder with a disease classification. You go to your doctor, as the ad suggests you do, with the diagnosis in hand—in search of confirmation and also a prescription for this disease that is both created and treated by the drug available for it.[13]

A full-length feature article "The Science of Anxiety" (Gorman) in *Time* magazine exemplifies the phenomenon exactly. Under the banner, "Are You Too Anxious," is a sidebar:

> Everybody feels a bit of anxiety from time to time, but a *clinical anxiety disorder* is a different matter. If you suspect you may be suffering from one, *you should consult a professional for a diagnosis.* The psychological diagnostic manual lists 12 anxiety conditions. *Here are the signs of five of the most common ones* [list follows]. (37; emphasis in original)

Another sidebar catalogues seven possible responses to anxiety, under the heading "What You Can Do": behavioral therapy, cognitive therapy, antidepressants, minor tranquilizers, exercise, alternative treatments, and lifestyle changes. However, only the chemical response (the antidepressants and tranquilizers) actually speaks to the neurological/biochemical description of the disorder offered under the heading "The Anatomy of Anxiety." The *clinically anxious person*, then, is not simply addressed by the *Time* article but also interpellated by it—hailed, invited to exist.

The *hypochondriac* is hailed at the same time. The *Time* article invites all of us to regard ourselves as ill. If we were inclined to worry in the first place, who among us would not qualify for a diagnosis of generalized anxiety disorder, for which the definition is "excessive anxiety or worry, occurring more days than not for six months" and whose diagnosis depends only on the presence of three or more of the following: "restlessness; difficulty concentrating or sleeping; irritability; fatigue; muscle tension" (37).

We know that the medicalization of sadness is bound up with advertising for treatments for depression; rhetoric is implicated in both the diagnosis and the experience of the disorder. Its rhetorical element, however, does not mean that depression is not *real*. (Extending his idea of "looping effects," Hacking sets aside the *real* versus *socially constructed* division by recasting the problem of kinds as a division between *indifferent* and *interactive* kinds.[14]) When sorting through the problem of the rhetoric of hypochondria, one might think about how the depression-Zoloft relation is like and not like the erectile dysfunction–Viagra one or the estrogen deficiency–hormone replacement one or the irritable bowel syndrome–Zelnorm one.[15] In each case, people are both persuaded that they are ill and persuaded that they do not need to be ill, at the same time. The second question, of course, begs the first.

Carl Elliott writes about the nature of the disorder one is inducted into when one is inducted by diagnosis into depression—and, indirectly, he suggests where some of depression's rhetorical interest may come from. It may be that what ails the depressive is not an internal state like depression or anxiety but a social state like alienation ("Pursued"). That is, depression may be one sort of syndrome rhetoricized as another.[16] My own main concern, however, is not the persuasive element in depression itself but rather the persuasive element in hypochondria. When we go to the doctor and say, "I am sad, not sleeping, having trouble concentrating," we may be depressed. When we go to the doctor and say, "I am depressed," we may be hypochondriacs.

It is not advertising or even publicity alone or even their ubiquity that invigorates hypochondria as a rhetorical disorder. Advertisements for health pharmaceuticals are nothing new. Amulets and tonics were advertised in eighteenth-century leaflets and cards and then in periodicals and dedicated monographs. Historian Roy Porter describes the process through which "[h]ealing power was crystallised, through some imaginative alchemy, into tangible commodities"—and advertised:

> The sick were more prepared to fork out for medicines than for advice . . . [f]or drugs possessed a reassuring tangibility—solid and substantial, they could be swallowed, applied, or rubbed in. They also suggested speed and convenience—it was less trouble to gulp a pill than to follow an exacting regimen or diet over many months. (*Health* 41)[17]

Drugs, that is, have long had special appeal to the sick and the quasi-sick, and they have long been advertised.[18] In the "great patent medicine era," especially, ill health was so broadly defined, so inclusive, that it was hard as it is today not to qualify as suffering from it. At least, it was hard to refuse the possibility of feeling better.[19]

The scope of health-product advertising has changed in two hundred years along with the media for it. We have newspaper, magazine, billboard, radio, and television advertisements to be sure. But a Google search also turns up (in 2005) over two million hits for Prozac and nearly six million for Viagra (fewer hits in each case, interestingly, than in 2004)—while every person checking e-mail is met with a barrage of advertisements and sales offers for prescription drugs.[20] Also changed in two hundred years is the status of health *information*, packaged for any number of reasons by pharmaceutical companies and by lifestyle-product manufacturers, health-food distributors, health practitioners, and disease-specific fundraisers. Clinical and epidemiological experts on hypochondria say almost in passing, because it is common knowledge, that health anxiety can occur when "the person is exposed to illness-related medical information" (Asmundson, Taylor, and Cox 13). Lewis Thomas wrote in 1983 about an "epidemic of anxiety" caused in part by this nefarious health information. Now, of course, health/illness information is ubiquitous on the Internet; the special hypochondria it fosters has been called *cyberchondria*.

The health consumer is not just health-product consumer; the health consumer is persuaded of the worth of particular goods and services as well as of the worth of health itself as it is advertised. Sometimes, the hypochondriac is a health consumer not so much ill, not even so much impossible to persuade that he or she is well but rather impossible to persuade that he or she is well *enough*. The hypochondriac is a health consumer who can not get enough health to be well.[21]

As Susan Baur suggests, one sort of hypochondriac is the perfectly acceptable "health nut." The health nut is, in general, an unmarked kind. According to Baur, mild hypochondrias can include "irrational health worries that affect so many people that *not* to be preoccupied seems bizarre" (157). The health nut may keep a diary of nutrient and caloric intake, of ministrations of supplements and treatments and enhancers, and of exertions and exercises. Preoccupied with the healthy body, this hypochondriac may produce a sort of documentary *health narrative* on parallel with the *illness narrative* that was the topic of chapter 3, both narratives suggesting a kind of fetishism of the body. Yet, the health nut is seldom viewed as hypochondriacal. (In an unusual twist of reverse pathology, a reformed, self-described "obsessive healthful eater," Steven Bratman, himself a physician, writes *Health Food Junkies: Overcoming the Obsession with Healthful Eating*, revealing his struggle with what he calls "orthorexia nervosa.")

Health fetishism has also sponsored an emerging industry in recreational diagnostics, aimed at the hypochondriac as canny consumer of health services—or, indeed, again, inviting the hypochondriac to exist.

Canadian Diagnostic Centre advertises in *Vancouver Magazine*, for example, that it uses "cutting-edge diagnostic equipment [to] scan your body for heart disease, lung cancer and aortic aneurysms."[22] In another issue of the same magazine, a company named ScanQuest advertises "Ultra-Fast CT scans . . . available without referral." One can enlist for scans for oneself or for somebody else: ScanQuest suggests the full-body scan as the perfect gift for the hard-to-shop-for loved one. Canada's national newspaper the *Globe and Mail* has run a feature article on the diagnostic resort—a getaway with blood work and imaging; and *Esquire* magazine has documented the diagnostic double date, based on "two full-body scans for a cut price of $1600 instead of $850 apiece" (Pesman).

This surprisingly unremarkable, vaguely narcissistic hypochondria may present itself also as *aesthetic hypochondria*: the nagging feeling that one doesn't look as well—or as good—as one should or might. Candidates for various physical, including surgical, interventions are people who are, sometimes to a very great extent, dissatisfied with their appearance. In cases of cosmetic procedures, it can be hard to tell where cure ends and enhancement begins—because cosmetic solutions have long been proffered for psychological problems (Elizabeth Haiken documents the deployment in the 1930s of the "inferiority complex" as the medical-psychiatric rationale for surgery aimed at beautification)[23] and because some treatments themselves have a peculiar destination-ambiguity: Botox treats both wrinkles and migraines; liposuction treats obesity by making the patient *look* healthier.

What I am calling aesthetic hypochondria is a sense of a dis-ease of the surface—which includes both the pathology currently known as "body dysmorphic disorder" and a more pervasive skin-deep version of the sense that things are not right. Cosmetic surgery is one means by which unattractiveness is absorbed into the medical realm and made a treatable condition about which one may worry and obsess. On the reality-television series *Extreme Makeover*, contestants desiring a cure for unattractiveness are subjected to multiple treatments, including surgeries to the eyes, nose, ears, chin, and breasts, which may render them younger-looking and more buxom versions of themselves or may radically conventionalize their appearance, erasing what is idiosyncratic and familial in their faces and surgically engraving an aesthetic norm—itself, somehow, a sign of wellness.[24]

In a rhetorical view of hypochondria, then, we might ask not only what hypochondria *is* but also what it *does*. One of the wonderful things about hypochondria as a topic of research is that there were so many great and articulate hypochondriacs who, given what Anne Hunsaker Hawkins has called "the narcissism of illness" ("Writing"), were only too happy to talk about themselves. So we have, for example, the literary record of Molière, the essays of Boswell, and the diaries of Charles Darwin. From these, we learn about the functions of hypochondria, including the rhetorical functions of it. While a psychological account, according to Baur, explains hypochondriacs as "high strung individuals in 'noisy bodies'" (5), most interesting when considered inside their own skins, a social account says hypochondria is a way that persons act on society and a way that society acts on persons.

Parsons has described illness as a means of social persuasion that endows the person in the sick role with an assortment of exemptions and benefits. *Ideally*, illness does this and more when it is acute than when it is chronic. Hypochondria includes a bid to secure the advantages of the sick role in the absence, perhaps, of illness but seldom in the absence of distress. Even "amputee wannabes" who, sometimes obsessively, desire the removal of one or more of their body parts are persons who genuinely feel themselves not to be well while they are in possession of all their limbs and digits.

It is difficult to separate *hypochondria* as a means of persuasion from *illness* as a means of persuasion. However, what we can say about hypochondria is that because of what must be construed as an element of choice in it, hypochondria is a rhetorical instrument, or agency, in a way that other illness is not. Janet Browne, writing about Charles Darwin's hypochondria, describes his body as a resource of persuasion: "Darwin seems to have put his body under the Victorian spotlight just as concretely as he presented his mind through the *Origin of Species*" (243). Browne notes the uses to which Darwin put his many ailments. If he became ill at eating, he could refuse dinner invitations; if he became ill in social intercourse, he could isolate himself and he could write. (According to some reports, his flatulence already isolated him.) If he were in danger of dying before his work was complete, he could insist on the urgency of publication.[25] Rhetoricians will know from John Angus Campbell that Darwin's ill health is a trope in *The Origin of Species* appealing to readers' sympathy and good will: "[A]s [this work on species] will take me two or three more years to complete, and as my health is far from strong, I have been urged to publish this abstract" (Darwin 1). Much of the circumstantial value of Darwin's disabilities, according to Browne, "lay in their diversity, applicability, and lack of diagnosis. . . . Such illnesses . . . act as a mode of social circulation as well as instruments of domestic tyranny" (248). Darwin's illnesses are integrated well and efficiently into his life, including his intellectual life and his public life, as might be the case for others of us. Illness offers respite and *gravitas* and is at its best kairotic, suited to situation.[26]

Persons use hypochondria to act on society then; also society uses hypochondria to act on persons. Threats of illness, for example, may act as social deterrents of a place and a time. Hypochondrias are responsive to social prohibitions that are themselves expressed as threats to good health. For example, in the nineteenth century, sexual promiscuity was understood to predispose women to reproductive cancers; during Prohibition, whisky was blamed for both insanity and death. My own early searches for articles on the "worried well" in the 1990s turned up primarily reports of patients who feared they had contracted HIV-AIDS (and counted as the "worried well" because they had not).[27] Hypochondria, in other words, in taking different forms at different times reveals itself as a means of social persuasion regulating behavior through the discourse of risk. Indeed, the hypochondriac is someone for whom the discourse of risk has overcome the discourse of desire. Furthermore, the hypochondriac is, in this, a personal location for a more general (cultural) hypochondriacal frame of mind.

Not only, then, is the hypochondriac vulnerable to public persuasion (he or she is perhaps a run-of-the-mill health fetishist who has read the newspaper too closely and taken a turn for the worse) but also the hypochondriac supplies some terms of public persuasion. Continuing the confession quoted earlier from *Anthropology from a Pragmatic Point of View*, Kant writes, "The hypochondriac is a crank . . . of the most pitiful sort: he stubbornly refuses to be talked out of his imaginings and haunts his doctor, who has no end of trouble with him and can calm him only by treating him like a child" (83). The hypochondriac's revenge is that we have no choice but to take this crank seriously—not because he is the worrier in all of us, although he is, but because, in the course of his worries, he produces so much of the rhetoric of everyday life.

So, there are countless addresses and dialogues implicated in hypochondria: The hypochondriac is addressed by mass media; the hypochondriac converses with himself or herself, making interpretations, coming up with arguments for illness, resisting them, being won over; the hypochondriac addresses the physician, arguing overall unpersuasively; the physician addresses the hypochondriac, matching the patient's unpersuasiveness with his or her own; the hypochondriac is left to contend with social life, usually in the absence of a satisfying diagnosis and subject again to media address and self-talk. In a Burkean grammar of motives, hypochondria is an *act* (many acts, really—from the act of coping with uncertainty by performing it broadly, to the act of impersonating an ill person); the hypochondriac is an *agent* acting against a *scene*, having also emerged from that scene, impossible without it; the hypochondriac acts for a *purpose*, which may be unknown even to him or her. The hypochondriac is also *acted upon* (by the forces of self-persuasion and those of mass persuasion in both product advertising and a seemingly innocuous rhetoric of good health and good looks). As just noted, hypochondria is also an *agency*—both a personal instrument by which individuals act on society and a social instrument by which society acts on individuals.

Burke's *dramatism*[28] goes some way to illuminating hypochondria in its humanity, its symbolicity, and its activity. A rhetorical account of hypochondria is deliberately inconclusive; this is the condition of dramatism— for, according to Burke, "what we want is *not terms that avoid ambiguity, but terms that clearly reveal the strategic spots at which ambiguities necessarily arise*" (*Grammar* xviii; emphasis in original). But a rhetorical account begins to disentangle hypochondria by tracing its rhetorical thread.

Hypochondria is a case study in the role of *persuasion* in health. While many other illnesses have a social/rhetorical dimension, most lack the reflexivity that makes this dimension apparent. Furthermore, a rhetorical account of hypochondria suggests a procedure for traversing the rhetoric of science and the rhetoric of everyday life, noting their reciprocity. Health and illness are themselves terministic screens, directing the attention, as Burke says, "to one field rather than to another" (*Language* 46). The hypochondriac is, finally, an agent, a patient, and a scene on which hypochondria is enacted, as well as a user of terms who has come to experience his or her life through the screen of "illness."

In addition, then, to any medical, psychological, or social intervention for hypochondria, I suggest a rhetorical one—an intervention that provides the means of awareness, criticism, and analysis of the terms in which health anxiety takes place.

5   A Rhetoric of Death and Dying

Some of what transpires between health professionals and patients or their family members in conversation at the end of life—and, indeed, some of what is taken to constitute shared decision making or to warrant informed consent—does not meet all of the conditions for rhetoric itself. Chaim Perelman and Lucie Olbrechts-Tyteca say the conditions for rhetoric include conditions for "a contact of minds," and if these conditions are not met, then the people addressed do not properly constitute a rhetorical audience, and what is going on is not really *rhetoric* at all but something else: coercion, perhaps. "The indispensable minimum for argumentation appears to be the existence of a common language" (Perelman and Olbrechts-Tyteca 15). So, two people are not engaged in a properly rhetorical process if only one of them really speaks the language of exchange. Another condition for rhetoric, according to Perelman and Olbrechts-Tyteca, is mutual respect: "To engage in an argument a person must attach importance to gaining the adherence of his interlocutor, to securing his assent, his mental cooperation" (16). Furthermore, "[a]chievement of the conditions preliminary to the contact of minds is facilitated by such factors as membership in the same social class, exchange of visits and other social relations" (17). For Aristotle himself, a proper audience was the relevant judge in a particular case; these were persons to whom appeals could be made because they had the power to act once their minds were made up. For eighteenth-century rhetorician George Campbell, an audience was a body poised to act once the understanding had been informed, and the will, then, moved.[1]

This chapter takes death and dying as its topic. Reporting on complementary research studies, it illustrates the problematic nature of end-of-life conversations between medical professionals and patients/family members. The first study centers on a narrative account of one family facing the nursing-home death of a parent. The second study offers an analysis of transcripts collected in connection with a hospital-based research project aimed at establishing an interview protocol for end-of-life decision making.[2] The relation itself of the two studies suggests something about a trajectory for humanities research in health. The first project is driven by a question that emerges from an individual researcher's personal experience and reflections on experience; the question is then explored for the most part in the library. The work leads to her participation in the second study, which responds to an experimental question and is carried out in a clinical setting by an interdisciplinary team of researchers.

The idea that is specified by both studies is that there are competing discourses of death and dying and that some means of traveling between these discourses is necessary in order for the most productive rhetorical process to take place. As Susan Sontag, Virginia Warren, Howard F. Stein ("Domestic Wars"), and Assya Pascalev have described, death in biomedicine is tied to a war narrative of professional practice. (The metaphor is discussed in more detail in chapter 6.) In biomedicine's story, the body's defence mechanisms resist invading microbes; pharmaceutical magic bullets target enemy cells; and physicians are warriors whose calling is to defeat death and save us to die another day. The metaphor is not evenly distributed through health settings: It holds more sway in hospitals than in hospices, for example. Meanwhile, increasingly, in public discourse, death is quite a different matter. It is a matter, above all, of reluctant inevitability. This difference between biomedical and public discourses on death seems to sustain itself despite the usual power of biomedical thinking in everyday life—its ability, as Pascalev says, to "penetrate the patterns of thinking and the imagination of laymen" (223).[3]

Certainly, we have seen in the past decade or so an increased *quantity* of public discourse on death. The *quality* of public discourse on death has also changed: Death talk has become oddly neutralized. It is not that death is no longer an uncomfortable subject, but we can read in our local newspapers that "smoking is an economic boon because it kills off people before they become a health burden" (Binder) and respond not by recoiling but by doing the math. Public discourse has taken a death turn.

We find, for example, discussions of caskets and memorials in feature articles of newspapers and magazines (see Richards, "Death Becomes You," and Anderssen, "Graveside Manners"). The discussion produces an unexpected intertext: A piece in the *New Yorker* is taken up in the *Canadian Journal of Medicine*; an article in the *Journal of the American Medical Association* is taken up in the *Quarterly Journal of Speech*; a piece from the *Vancouver Sun* is the basis of commentary at a death Web site. The new death invites us to surf DeathNet or in our spare time to consider the economics of designer cremations and knock-offs.

A developing public discourse on death and dying is struggling, often gracelessly, to find its own terms. A television commercial features a cheerful spokesperson, a minor Canadian celebrity, promoting Funeral Coverage Plus. "And if you happen to pass away," he says, "really anywhere in the world"—he rotates his living-room globe—"this plan will pay to have you returned home at no cost to your family." Perhaps Funeral Coverage Plus also covers a kind of denial: It is "you" being flown home (you may be dead, but you want good service). More interesting is the very presence of death in prime time, both in programming (witness the success of *Six Feet Under*) and in the discontinuous reality text of commercials. In Canada, the National Will Kit is sold on radio and television among commercials for soft drinks and tires. At Just for Laughs, the Montreal comedy festival, comedian Robert Schimmel tells non–Hodgkin's lymphoma jokes and laments that there is no Make-a-Wish Foundation for dying adults.[4] The death-themed comic strip is not unheard of.[5] A biomedical rhetoric of death as "medical failure" now competes with an emerging public rhetoric of death-as-a-part-of-life.

As children and parents and siblings and partners, we are, most of us, however, not experienced speakers of the language of death and dying. When we are called upon to speak it, we are often in conversation with people who are more fluent speakers than we are and experts in its topics. Our health-professional interlocutors are, in general, well trained, and they are often generous and kind; however, we are unsure how to speak to them and how to be understood by them and how (and how much) to depend on them. Of course, they can not really tell us. Somehow, although we know so little, we are sometimes enlisted to make or participate in making certain decisions. We seldom pause to consider that we may, as this chapter will illustrate, at the moment of truth be constrained in conversation by the terms and information with which we are supplied by the professionals we are speaking with. The questions we ask the experts are themselves limited by our knowledge of possible questions and the opportunities provided to us for asking them. We may, however, sense that the decision is not really ours to make. In any case, we may not wish to claim the decision at all, because we do not want to take responsibility for a future that has every likelihood of going very badly.

Framed in the problematics of "shared decision making," some issues of physician-patient conversation have been taken up recently in health and social science literature. C. Charles, A. Gafni, and T. Whelan review three models of physician-patient decision making (models they call "paternalistic," "informed choice," and "shared decision making") and note that none of them really describes a process in which *decisions* are shared, no matter how much *information* is shared. For his part, David Silverman says that the idea of physician's "disclosure" of information is itself a token of asymmetry in the physician-patient relationship, but he adds that many patients desire asymmetry, especially where illness is grave. Richard Gwyn and Glyn Elwyn say that there must be equipoise—options must really be options—for shared decision making really to take place. That is, where one of the options presented is actually ill advised and not really an option at all, then a shared decision "would be more accurately described as an informed decision engineered according to doctor preference" (437).[6]

The following studies engage in different ways a single problem: that end-of-life decision making frequently takes place in conversations between people who are medical experts and people who are not. The studies raise questions about the nature of the decision making. What frequently is thought of as "informed," "shared," or even "consensual" decision making is actually when considered rhetorically a process of persuasion in which the parties are not despite appearances fully rhetorical partners. I am not suggesting that in medical matters, family members should know as much as doctors; of course, that is impossible. But this chapter asks, for example, if the medical expertise at the front and center of end-of-life conversations is the most important expertise to have in matters of life and death. In the first study, the single-case report, it is the incommensurability of discourses that is of interest; the case suggests that what seems to be informed decision making really is something else. In the second study, the account based on interviews at a psychiatric hospital, there is clearly a strong professional will to distribute decision making among interested parties—but even in this deliberately "consensual" process, there is some question as to whether the conversations that take place fulfill Perelman and Olbrechts-Tyteca's requirements for rhetoric.

The Single-Case Study

The period of rhetorical interest is the three months leading up to my mother's death. The conversations reported here were memorized rather than mechanically recorded. In other words, this is an unscientific account, based on my own experience, but it is not, therefore, untrue. The conversations are rendered from detailed notes made immediately after each one took place. I wrote down the conversations at the time so that I could recount them fully to my sister and so that I could study in the cold light of my mother's room just what I was being told and what I was being asked to do. Over the course of the following pages, I step outside of and back into the story. I do that intentionally to correct perspective where I can.[7]

My mother died on 20 January 1996 of the complications of pneumonia and starvation and misery. Although her doctors gave no indication they had ever seen anyone die in quite her way before (pressed for an explanation, one of them said, tongue in cheek, "Perhaps she has something unknown to medicine"), I have learned over the time since her death that many people die almost exactly as my mother did—speechless and in a state of post–acute-illness starvation that resembles and may or may not be depression. My mother was as a dying person lost in the space between the rhetoric of her doctors and that of her daughters, and it was, in part, the space between these rhetorics that increased the agony of her final months of life. "Health care" had already increased her number of months in agony.

In October 1995, my mother was seventy-six years old and for the most part over the pneumonia that had been her most recent health crisis in the six years of her residence in a large and well-regarded nursing home. In 1989, she had suffered a stroke that left her paralysed on her right side and aphasic. The paralysis was unremitting, and the speech-impairment worsened over time. Owing to another condition (Ménière's disease), she was also nearly deaf. By the year of this pneumonia, she spoke only a few words, with great difficulty, and not every day. It was part of her aphasia, too, that the words she could speak were seldom the ones she wanted. Even "yes" and "no" came out as their opposites *some* of the time, so one only knew for sure which one she meant when she thought to laugh after saying the other.

The pneumonia or the encounter with it or something else left the patient that October weak and disoriented and almost motionless. She moaned, and sometimes she screamed. She had lost twenty-five pounds, over a fifth of her pre-pneumonia weight, and she was refusing all food and medication. She was never taken from her bed, where she was hydrated intravenously. She was for all but a few minutes a day in a state of sleep or near-sleep. When she emerged into consciousness, she was able to recognize her daughters, and she was able even to display affection.

The first recorded conversation took place outside the patient's room and was initiated by a (my) request for information about her condition. The second conversation took place the following day inside the patient's room, as though the patient were not there, except as a point of reference.

Conversation 1. A daughter speaks with the attending physician.

PHYSICIAN: Your mother has survived the pneumonia, and there is no organic reason, as far as we know, for her to be refusing food. I can tell you, though, that if she doesn't eat, she will die. Not tomorrow, or next week, but she'll die. We're keeping her hydrated with an IV drip, but we can't get food into her that way. There are really only two options here. Your mother is depressed. Who knows, maybe she's trying to commit suicide. We can get her started on a program of ECT—shock therapy—and that should deal with the depression. Or we're going to have to insert a feeding tube. To be honest, the feeding tube won't be pleasant. She might even pull it out—if she's not in restraints. No, the feeding tube should be our last resort. I'm going to send in someone from psychiatry to discuss the shock therapy with you. Don't worry. It's not the way you may remember it from *One Flew Over the Cuckoo's Nest*.

DAUGHTER: Have you done any tests to rule out other causes for her refusing to eat?

PHYSICIAN: No, and I don't think tests are warranted at this time.

DAUGHTER: If she does eat and regain some strength, what can we expect of her quality of life?

PHYSICIAN: We can't expect her even to return to the level of alertness she had before the pneumonia.

DAUGHTER: Then are we talking about shock therapy or a feeding tube more or less to maintain her as she is now?

PHYSICIAN: More or less, yes.

DAUGHTER: If she will spend the rest of her life this way, without moving or speaking, moaning with pains she can't even point to, is it possible to talk about letting her die?

PHYSICIAN: Um, no, that's not an option. She could be weeks, even months, away from dying. The psychiatrist will be here in the morning. He'll talk to you.

Conversation 2. A daughter speaks with the psychiatrist.

PSYCHIATRIST: Hello. [*Shakes hands.*] I'm Dr. Ohmann [not his real name]. Your mother has a condition we call catatonic depression. Luckily, there's a treatment for this condition. It's called ECT, or electroconvulsive therapy, and we could start it right away.

DAUGHTER: Doctor, have you ever spoken to my mother?

PSYCHIATRIST: I've seen her a couple of times, on rounds, but she's, as you know . . . it's not really possible to talk with her.

DAUGHTER: Well, then, I have a question. How do you know she's depressed?

PSYCHIATRIST: That's a very good question. It's true that you can refuse this treatment, but I don't think that would be advisable. If your mother had a broken hip, would you deny her surgery?

This is what transpired after the two conversations: The daughters refused shock therapy, having come over days of observing their mother (in a way that medical staff never can—at her bedside for eight or ten hours at a time) to believe that depression had been diagnosed primarily because there was no other available diagnosis so amenable to treatment. After some time, the physician, without additional family consultation, ordered a feeding tube inserted in the patient, and she was tied to her bed to prevent her from removing it. Somehow, she succeeded in removing it anyway. Tube feeding was stopped at the request of the daughters. The psychiatrist, meanwhile, having been pressed into long conversations with the daughters, took some additional interest in the case. On his recommendation, blood tests were ordered to probe one of those illness cycles that can be missed in medical care: When the patient started refusing her medication, one of the medications she refused was artificial thyroid hormone (Synthroid); the result was a lethargy that made it difficult for her to take her medication. Later, neurological tests were ordered to try to discover if the patient's refusal or inability to eat was in fact a consequence of another stroke. That test was delayed past the point of its results being useful. The patient died before the results were known, and they were never discussed. The time between the reported conversations and the death of the patient was three months.

During these three months, the subject of death in the context of the nursing home was taboo. The staff created no openings for it, and when the daughters broached the topic, they were quickly silenced. Evidently, the patient was too healthy to die, even if she was dying too inevitably for any but the most unimaginative interventions. In Pascalev's terms, the patient was caught between two metaphors: the rescue metaphor, *death is an enemy*, and the impotence metaphor, *dying is torture*. The metaphors, Pascalev says, betray an inconsistency in medical perceptions of death and dying and "engender two conflicting courses of action and two competing concepts of the proper role of medicine in contemporary [North] American society" (233).

When the patient began to experience periods of apnea (interruptions of breathing), and her physician predicted her death within a matter of days, a clearly well-established end-of-life protocol took over, and the status of the daughters in the culture of the nursing home changed. One daughter was led from her mother's room by a nurse who announced that the end was near. She was taken to see a social worker and given an audience with the physician. She was invited to discuss palliation and, finally, withdrawal of intravenous fluids. Even then, when this daughter haltingly asked if anything could be done to hasten her mother's now certain and apparently (from the evidence of vocalizations and facial expressions) difficult death, the social worker looked at her with that I-understand-you're-going-through-a-hard-time-so-I'll-let-that-pass look and said, "Dr. Kevorkian doesn't work here."

This conversation notwithstanding, the patient died that night following one of those shots of morphine that are given to relieve pain with the knowledge that they will kill, while everyone maintains for the record that death is an unpleasant side-effect of pain relief and not the main event.[8]

It is important to note that it was not our mother's right to die that my sister and I wanted to insist on. I wish we could have insisted on it to help our mother not to continue a life that had by her own report become intolerable for her some time before, but that is a different story. A Kevorkian intervention, treatment by death, would still have been an intervention on biomedicine's terms—not unlike the morphine intervention that finally ended her life, only more timely.[9] Rather, what we sought was the possibility of talking about the process and meaning of our mother's dying, perhaps properly to make a decision, perhaps to learn the code in which a decision would have to be rendered to have any effect, perhaps only to understand that a decision that looked like it was ours to make was not really ours to make at all. Sherwin B. Nuland writes that "every life is different from any that has gone before it, and so is every death" (3). It was the opportunity to consider on its own terms this death, our mother's death, that we missed.

What seemed to happen in this case was that each of us, daughters and health professionals, was trapped inside the discourse that moved each of us to speak. When a stalemate was reached—the medical staff strongly recommending invasive treatment and the two of us refusing it—we the daughters were offered a meeting of the ethics committee to help us decide on a course of action, our decision having been determined, even by us, not to be tenable. But ethics committees do not in any important sense mediate among discourses; rather, they are representatives of biomedicine, too. That is, to convene a meeting of an ethics committee is not to step outside the dominant model but to deepen it, to add to the psychiatric protocol and the neurological protocol the ethics protocol.

I remember that in the weeks before my mother died, I paused to wonder what my mother's doctors were reading, because it seemed clear to me that they were not reading much of the recent literature on end-of-life decision making, communication with families, and so on. It was an odd thing, in the midst of events, to be able to think about my situation theoretically (and theory left me only insignificantly less helpless in the face of things).[10] I have since read additional medical literature on death and dying, and I have discovered evidence of some distance between what health professionals say and what they think, some distance between theory and practice, and some distance between what looks structurally like conversation and what might actually count as conversation of any useful sort. These disjunctions contribute to a larger disjunction, between a biomedical rhetoric on the one hand and a public, very human one on the other.[11]

In a study reported by Merrijoy J. Kelner and Ivy L. Bourgeault, researchers interviewed twenty physicians and twenty nurses about their views on patients' desires to exert more control over the circumstances of their dying. The physicians and nurses were first asked their personal views on patient control over the dying process. Later, they were asked more specific questions involving particular cases and circumstances. In response to the first, general question, nineteen physicians and all twenty nurses said they believed that patients should control the circumstances of their own dying. In response to more specific questions, however, almost every one of the health professionals withdrew from this position and identified circumstances that would affect the extent of the control "they were prepared to *give* a patient over dying" (759; emphasis added).

Kelner and Bourgeault offer this explanation:

> [P]atient control represents *a challenge to [the physicians' and nurses']*
> *clinical judgement.* They are reluctant to give up the right to use their
> clinical discretion in the face of a patient's wish to make a final deci-
> sion about their own fate. . . . When patients request that their lives

be terminated, it almost seems to be an affront to their core task of healing and comforting; in other words, a failure. (763; emphasis in original)

A typical physician comment in the Kelner and Bourgeault study was, "I have no problem with [patient control] whatsoever, provided the patient has a *legitimate* and *realistic* appreciation of what it is they're going through" (760; emphasis in original). This doctor's response takes for granted what a legitimate appreciation *is*. The problem, however subtle, is crucial. The opportunity to control one's own death is given by the physician, and the giving is based on an understanding that is both derived from the physician and returned to the physician for evaluation.

The problem of death talk is, then, in part, a problem of rhetorical control. Yet, it is seldom viewed that way. Rather, there is a notion in liberal medicine that "communication" between doctors and patients/families needs to be *increased*, apparently on the principle that more talk of any kind is better than less.

The real nature of the communication problem is made clear by the results of another study of the care of seriously ill hospital patients: the widely publicized SUPPORT study reported in the *Journal of the American Medical Association*. SUPPORT is an acronym for the Study to Understand Prognoses and Preferences for Outcomes and Risks of Treatment). In this large-scale (over nine thousand subjects), multisite study, researchers hypothesized that "increased communication" between patients/families and medical professionals would improve the end-of-life experience on a number of scales.[12] Improving the experience meant, for example, decreasing the number of days the patient spent in an "undesirable state" or increasing the percentage of patient-family-professional agreement on do-not-resuscitate orders; other experimental "targets" were median time until the DNR order was written, severity of pain, and use of hospital resources.

SUPPORT researchers designed a two-part "intervention": Physicians were provided with prognostic information about patients as well as reports of patients' and family members' perceptions of end-of-life experience, while specially trained nurses prepared patients and family members to engage in "informed" and "collaborative" decision making with physicians. Despite the extensive work of the experiment, the intervention produced no significant improvements in measurable patient outcomes. Researchers concluded that success with respect to outcomes would "require examination of our individual and collective commitment to [the] goals [of improving care at the end of life], more creative efforts at shaping the treatment process, and, perhaps, more proactive and force-ful attempts at change" (1597).

As results of the SUPPORT study were released, Bernard Lo, editor of the *Journal of the American Medical Association*, speculated that more, and more profound, changes would be needed to produce the desired effects: "Physicians will need to change hospital culture and practices and our own behavior" (1636). That is, it seems that *increasing* communication of the existing sort is a less promising idea for end-of-life care than *changing* the very terms and structure of communication—changing, that is, the usual discourse of the hospital.

It seems also be the case that outside of clinical experiments, end-of-life care can involve very little patient/family and health-practitioner communication of any kind. A *New York Times* article corroborates that the most common kind of hospital death is death without death-talk. One physician quoted in the article said he very rarely discusses death with any of his patients even when the absence of discussion complicates patient care: "As a practicing physician, you'd think I'd have learned . . . [b]ut I'm still lazy on the subject" (Fein). One question arising from the newspaper report is whether practice can be brought into line with research. Another question is whether health professionals will be willing to look critically at death-talk in use or if the talk itself will be viewed uncritically, while there is a call for more of it.

End-of-life conversations between health professionals and patients/family members may fail to meet the conditions for rhetoric as Perelman and Olbrechts-Tyteca have described them. The Kelner and Bourgeault study, for example, which shows almost every practitioner retreating from an initial liberalism on patient control over dying, reveals a problem of rhetorical pretense. A real rhetorical situation, according to Perelman and Olbrechts-Tyteca, is one in which interlocutors speaking the same language use persuasive strategies to arrive at the best course of action. If that is the case, then, in the months before my mother's death, I was engaged in a false rhetorical situation, and it left me powerless except when I stepped outside of it or flouted it. If two people can not have a real conversation when only one of them speaks the language they are using to converse in and if two people can not have a real conversation when only one of them knows what they are talking about (and the other one knows only what the first one divulges), then my conversation with my mother's physician was not a real conversation, and it was not about real choice. Where did the options of ECT and a feeding tube come from, anyway? When the psychiatrist was making his argument—saying, for example,

"If your mother had a broken hip, would you deny her surgery?"—he was not really being persuasive but, rather, coercive. The biomedical thinking that made the hip analogy possible also made it possible to name my mother's problem in such a way that the only solution it required was also the only action the model could provide.

The way medical decision making works, in part, even when it appears in the world as shared decision making, is by the expert foreclosure of certain courses of action. Moreover, that foreclosure takes place in a context that is already, by the terms of its operation, somewhat determined. Not medicine (or health) but *bio*medicine is the context in which the notion of the patient's control over the circumstances of dying is itself constructed. For example, just months before the onset of her pneumonia, it would have been possible to elicit from my mother an advance directive, a guide to her treatment in exactly the kind of situation she was finally in.[13] But the option was never made available because my mother was simply not taken seriously enough as an agent of her own care. Her stated wish to die was taken as a summons to music- and pet-therapists. I witnessed dialogues like this:

MY MOTHER: I want to die.
THE SOCIAL WORKER: You don't really mean that, Mrs. Segal.
MY MOTHER: I do. I don't want to live like this.
THE SOCIAL WORKER: Don't talk like that, Mrs. Segal.

I am not suggesting that a patient's statement of his or her wish to die should be taken by caregivers at face value. In the Netherlands, for example, where cases of legitimate euthanasia are not prosecuted, the following are necessary conditions for physician involvement in a patient's death: The patient must request euthanasia consistently and freely; the patient's illness must be unbearable, and recovery impossible; and the physician must consult a colleague on matters of diagnosis, prognosis, procedure, and legality. My objection to the response of my mother's caregivers to her statement of her wish to die is not that it was not acted upon, but that it was not, in any useful sense, even heard.[14]

The night my mother died, my conversations with the nursing staff took place over the sounds of tabloid news coming from the television in the nursing station. The nurse's last words to me, shouted over the sounds of a commercial, admonished me to take off my mother's wedding ring before it was too late to remove it except by cutting. We were, all of us, family and staff, upset by my mother's dying; any of us might have acted a little badly; I suppose no one knew what to say.

The Riverview Project, described next, attempts directly to engage family members in end-of-life decision making for loved ones.

The Riverview Project

In this section, questions of the rhetoric of end-of-life decision making are taken up again but with different "data" and a different method of analysis. In the first section, a rhetorical view of conversations revealed certain problems of shared decision making on matters of the end of life. The case study suggested that morally shared decision making does not require that everyone knows the same things; rather, it requires recognition of a pluralism of expertise, allowing a properly rhetorical exchange among parties sharing respect and an agreed-upon language for decision making.

I am reporting here on a research project at Riverview Hospital in Port Coquitlam, British Columbia, the goal of which was to establish a protocol for interviews involving health professionals and family members, aimed at consensual decision making on advance directives for hospital residents who were both seriously ill and cognitively impaired. Advance directives in this case pertain to two sorts of instructions to medical staff: The first concerns resuscitation orders (in the event, for example, of cardiac arrest, should the patient be resuscitated?); the second concerns "levels of intervention" (four levels at Riverview, ranging from interventions aimed at providing palliative care to extreme interventions aimed at prolonging life).

The clinicians involved in the Riverview project entered the study with the expressed goal of improving the conditions for consensual decision making. That is, there was a belief from the start that the best decisions about DNR orders and levels of care came from shared decision making and shared responsibility. I was invited onto the research team as an expert in matters of language and communication. (I was part of the research team but not part of the *clinical* team, which consisted of a psychologist as principal investigator, a nurse, a social worker, a physician, and a chaplain.)[15] It was clear that while I was interested in helping to improve communication between family members and professionals, I was interested also in taking a critical step back from the clinical interview. The purpose of my own research, in other words, was not only to *facilitate* the AD interview but also to *understand* it. My questions were "How could this process go more smoothly?" and "How does this process work?"[16]

The Riverview study itself included the conduct of consensual decision-making interviews experimentally. Family members of qualifying residents were contacted by letter and phone and invited to participate in the study. The project's objectives and the procedures of consensual decision making were described to them, and resuscitation orders and levels of intervention were explained. Family members, many of whom were already well acquainted with hospital staff, were asked to meet before the decision-making interview with the team psychologist. Then, each decision-making interview took approximately one hour and involved one or more family members and all five members of the clinical team. After the interview, a summary of the discussion was sent to family members for signature, and they were advised that the AD could be changed at any time. Where family members granted permission, interviews were video-taped, and conversations were transcribed. Transcripts of nine of about thirty interviews are the material for my analysis.

Several elements of the AD interview were relatively constant over all of the transcripts (and the project as a whole). One common element was the shape of the interview itself. Interviews began, after introductions and formalities and after family questions and comments were invited, with a report by the physician on the medical and psychiatric condition of the patient. The nursing perspective, with its focus on "quality of life" issues, came later in the interviews. And certain interview elements, notably the following four, were routine. Transcripts are numbered one to nine; page numbers are indicated.[17] Interview participants are identified as follows:

R = resident/patient
FM = family member (numbered as necessary)
MD = physician
P = psychologist
N = nurse
SW = social worker
C = chaplain

Element 1. The structure of the interview was described. Transcript 5:

SW: So the way we're going to do this meeting we'll keep it informal but we have a bit of a structure. MD is going to give us the most current medical and psychiatric condition of R. N will talk about sort of the behaviours on the ward, abilities, deficits, sort of quality-of-life matters that are important to this decision. P will take us through the form that we'll be completing as a result of this meeting and go through it step by step with you as he's probably already done. A little bit. And

C and I are here to . . . C is here for, I guess, spiritual questions in a matter like this. And I'm here just to sort of facilitate and make sure that you're understanding and that we're all understanding the essence of what we're discussing here. (2–3)

Element 2. Family members, having been encouraged to do so, drew on knowledge of what the patient would have wanted for end-of-life care.
Transcript 7:

FM: In 1990, R had the pacemaker put in him. He was very ill with the heart problem. And they rushed him to [the hospital], and they installed the pacemaker. And when he woke, he said, why did you bother doing that to me, he said, I'm eighty years old. And he said, these old bones just don't want to carry me no further. And there's more room for other people in this world. So he felt in his mind that, even at that time, that prolonging his life wasn't necessary. So it's his wishes as well. (9)

Element 3. Where there was no clear knowledge of what the patient would have wanted, family members were urged to empathize with the patient.
Transcript 6:

MD: One way of making it easier to think of is put yourself in her position . . . and where you can make a decision, what you would want. (9)

Element 4. Family members were reminded that the decision making was consensual with the clinical team and that hospital staff would not act on any advice with which they did not feel comfortable.
Transcript 6:

P: Let me also add that in this process of discussion and giving you different options, we wouldn't carry out and follow an instruction which we didn't feel we were comfortable with. So we're working within a range here that we feel comfortable with, with whatever you decide. And the options of somebody—if a family member came and gave us options which we felt were totally unreasonable, we would say that. We would not go along with it. (12)

What follows are descriptions (with transcript support) of five of what might be called my "rhetorical findings." Later, I report on conversations in which I shared my findings with my coresearchers.

Finding 1. The placement of the physician's report in the initial position in the interview itself has rhetorical force.

While issues of quality of life are at the center of AD decision making, the interview routinely begins with medical rather than quality-of-life concerns. Of course, medical concerns and quality-of-life ones are related; however, beginning with the medical report gives a particular importance to medical information in decision making. The initial place of the medical report in the interview as a whole also underlines the expert–nonexpert division—or, perhaps, privileges one kind of expertise over another. Family members clearly are aware of their own limitations in conversations about the end of life.

Transcript 3:

FM: Well, when you talk about the vascular [dementia], does that mean she's had some of these small strokes or not? . . . The reason I wondered was that one time when she was living with me, she started to get up off the chesterfield . . . and she was dizzy . . . it seemed as though she might have had a small stroke. What I know. Not being a doctor or a nurse or anything else. But it gave me that feeling that maybe that's what was happening. (3–4)

Transcript 7:

FM: I think that move, that short move up the hill [to another hospital ward] affected him. So taking him out of hospital, he would not survive. In my opinion. And I'm, certainly, I'm not a doctor. Or anything. But, yeah. (11)

A further significant feature of the physician's initial medical account is its monologic quality. That is, because consensual decision making is necessarily a dialogic process, the medical account itself is *generically* out of phase with the interview. The medical account does count as a conversational turn, although an inordinately long one. The MD is receptive to interruptions and requests for information and clarification but clearly has the floor for several minutes once the meeting is under way.

Finding 2. The terms that family members bring to an AD interview can be terms that are cultural conventions for end-of-life talk and, for that reason, unexamined.

It is certainly the case that some terms circulate in a culture for end-of-life talk. The same terms circulate in an AD interview and themselves play a role in decision making.

Transcript 4:

FM: We don't believe that she should be kept on a machine just to be kept alive and be a vegetable. (6)

Transcript 5:

FM: Oh, if he could talk, he would say he'd be the first one to pull the plug. I know that. (21)

Transcript 3:

FM: It's this keeping a person alive with tubes and things just for the sake of keeping them alive, no. I have never wanted that. Wouldn't want it for myself so why would I want it for anybody else? (8)

In some cases, as illustrated below, team members sometimes push at the terms, asking family members to think about their assumptions. However, phrases like "pull the plug" and "die in peace" (transcript 4) were not examined.

Transcript 1:

P: What did you understand by code blue when you initially instructed us that you didn't want a code blue? (7)

Transcript 7:

P: And that's part of the discussion really, to clarify what people mean by palliative care when they say that. That's why we're going through this to really ensure that what we're saying is the same as what you're saying and the same as what [other FM] is saying. (12)

Finding 3. The ways in which choices are framed and articulated by clinical team members may seem to foreclose some options.

In general, the central choice presented to family members in the AD interview is a version of this: "to decide are we going to intervene and treat the person or allow nature to take its course" (transcript 1, p. 3). That is, the decision not to treat is portrayed as "natural"; conversely, the decision to treat is usually termed "aggressive."

Transcript 1:

P: So the level one, the goal would be primarily and almost only to keep the person comfortable, . . . not do anything to stop nature from taking its course. . . . The second level would be a little more aggressive than that. We'd say—and each level up includes everything you would do below, so we'd, naturally we'd keep the person comfortable, pain free, under all circumstances, anyway. (3)

Transcript 4:

MD: We want to try to establish something with your help, trying to figure out what R would have wanted for herself in the future should she
become critically ill. What she would want the doctors here and the
medical staff to do. How to treat her more generally—aggressively
treat an illness or back off a little bit and let nature take its course. (1)

Transcript 5:

MD: We should differentiate transferring within the hospital, like to the
medical unit, where they can do more aggressive interventions than
we can do on the ward, and then transferring out of the hospital, which
in a way is, you know it can be, it can be necessary for even more
aggressive treatment. (14)

While it is clear that the clinical team means to leave choice in the
hands of family members providing them with information, it is also true
that options are charged rhetorically and that some terms, like "natural,"
are eulogistic while others, like "aggressive," are dyslogistic.

Transcript 6:

P: The question is do we feel, if something natural occurred, it's time now
to let nature take its course, or if we fairly without a lot of intrusion
return her to the current level of function that she's now at, should
we do that?

FM: Well, as far as an antibiotic or penicillin, say an injection of penicillin that was to clear up some infection and that would work? Certainly,
we would give her that. We wouldn't just let her—that part, yes.

P: Right, so the things we can do on the ward (FM://Umm hmm, exactly,
yes.) At least, we should try and do that. Okay, . . . what about if it
required a transfer to our medical surgery ward which would be where
she'd have to be treated more aggressively with certain intravenous
injections or intravenous . . . ? (10–11)

The clinical team members by their own report do not intend to lead
the decision, and, indeed, they do want to press for specificity, precision, and
clarification because their goal is to have directions that will become orders
on a patient's chart. My observation is about the valence of terms. Although
aggressive has, like *heroic*, a particular meaning in a medical context, it is
also the case that the term carries weight, even metaphoric weight, in use.

Furthermore, family members in many cases seem to wish to comply
with what they assume are the wishes of medical professionals; they may

seek the approval of professionals and make assertions with respect to end-of-life care that will find approval.

Transcript 1:

FM: Not that I think R is going to get better. You know there's some people keep saying to me, don't you want him to get better, of course, I do but I mean, I have to face reality. . . . (7)

Moreover, professionals sensing the need for approval may offer it readily:

Transcript 1:

FM1: I know, Mom, this is an emotional thing, and it's very emotional for me. . . . I'd like my dad to go.

N: I respect that. I respect that. (10)

Some family members respond to the importance of the medical element of the occasion by adopting a medical-sounding language themselves.

Transcript 1:

FM1: What is R's time to live?

FM2: Expected life span.

FM1 (later): He absolutely does not believe in suicide.

FM2: Or assisted, or assisted suicide. . . . I know that it's, there's part of the disease I understand is psychotic and it can also be . . . a suicidal tendency as a part of it. (9)

Finding 4. Family members make moves to claim authority in the rhetorical situation.

Family members assert authority primarily in two ways: first, by claiming knowledge of the patient and, especially, knowledge of his or her current institutional life (the family member who visits the patient regularly or speaks to him or her frequently on the telephone is one who is in the best position to state preferences) and by assuming the ability to praise or blame—they usually praise—hospital staff (for example, Transcript 7, p. 10: FM: "I think it's a good, good system you're devising"). Sometimes, the two claims to authority are merged:

Transcript 3:

FM: [My sister] really responded to music . . . you know what I mean. Um, and I don't know. I'm not saying—I'm not blaming anybody for it, don't get me wrong in that, but, um, I've always felt that it would have done a lot for her earlier. (10)

Transcript 4:

FM: I hope you understand I'm not complaining about this here, I'm just bringing it, make you, make you aware of it. . . . Well, myself personally, I know she's in the best of care . . . because I talk to nurses over here and, uh, we pretty well leave it to the doctors here and to the nurses because their judgment be a lot better. And we realize that the mood she is at times, it makes it very hard for the nurses over here. Because physically she is a strong woman. I know because I've had to manhandle her. (5)

Finding 5. While the primary goal of the AD meeting is to arrive at decisions regarding end-of-life care, another important purpose of the meeting is to provide a context within which decisions already made can be aired and made less fraught.

Providing support to family members is certainly an element of the AD project. The videotapes and transcripts show an interesting movement between the patient (although absent) at the center of attention and family member(s) at the center of attention. In a sense, while the physician and nurse take the patient as their primary focus, the psychologist, social worker, and chaplain take the family member(s) as their primary focus. When, as in the case of one interview, the resident patient is a schizophrenic who has been institutionalized for forty years and now has dementia, what family members need is not so much a way of making decisions about the end of life as a way of coping with decisions that are sadly too easy to make:

Transcript 6:

FM: . . . the way she's deteriorated, I mean, she, I can see it, I mean, she's, uh, incapable of, you know, doing her own bodily functions, and, uh, as you say the dementia started so I mean—it's—I know it sounds maybe hard or cruel but if—

MD: No, I mean it's not a matter of—there was a light at the end of the tunnel I would say. . . . No, if you think that what she would want, then it's not cruel. (12)

An important element of the interview, in other words, is to deal with feelings of guilt that family members might have, having decided that they would want an advance directive featuring a DNR order and the lowest level of intervention:

Transcript 5:

FM1: . . . Like it's hard. (P://It is hard.) It's still that guilt. I would agree I'm really laying guilt on myself. So that's why I'm afraid to mention too much of that. I don't want [wife of R] to feel that. Because I'm glad she feels good. But I'm, I'm—

N: But she knows him the best.

FM1: She does.

N: She knows him the best.

P: Well, guilt is also—

N: And if that's his wish, then that's his wish.

P: Guilt is also in two directions. One is prolonging suffering.

FM1: Yeah I know.

P: You know as well. (FM2://That's the part that . . .) And that's what I'm hearing for somebody—

FM1: But, you see, I'm, I'm at the other end, too, where my dad, should be, have died by now. And I'm feeling guilty and wish he would almost . . . (22)

The goal of members of the clinical team was to arrive at the best guidelines for care of resident patients. A rhetorical analysis was one means of understanding how the AD interviews met or did not meet the objective of securing a truly *consensual* basis for providing instructions to hospital staff for patient care at the end of life. The findings of my rhetorical analysis were discussed at a research-group meeting where we considered their practical, clinical implications.[18]

Members of the team were willing to reconsider the structure of the AD meetings, particularly the possibility of leading off interviews with something other than information giving by the physician. We discussed the extent to which positioning the medical information at the beginning of the interview gives primary importance to a medical perspective on the patient (as opposed to a quality-of-life perspective or, perhaps, a spiritual one). We noted, too, that the knowledge of family members might seem to be more valued if the matter first discussed in the interview were not the medical condition but, for example, a day in the life of the patient, a matter in which family members are often expert. We noted, too, the advantage of opening a dialogue with a dialogue and not what must amount to a monologue.[19]

Team members were interested in matters of the language of the meetings. We discussed the advantages of treatment options being presented in the most neutral possible terms—so not "aggressive" treatment as opposed to "letting nature take its course" but rather, for example, "If R were to contract pneumonia, would you want her moved to a different ward for intravenous antibiotics?" The change is not a simple one to effect, though. Such specific choices are offered already, as is evident even from the transcript fragments reproduced here, and, in many cases, the more value-laden terms serve an important summary function, clarifying issues of general intention. Team members said they would be more aware of the force of their terms and particularly of the special radiance of a term like "aggressive." None of us, however, could suggest any ready solution to problems of terminology.

Terms used by family members were also discussed. On the matter of the mobilization of unexamined terms ("pulling the plug" and so on), team members were interested in taking opportunities to help family members examine their assumptions about end-of-life care and procedures. As the transcripts show, team members already do this to some extent. It was noted that much popular discourse about the end of life comes from television and the Internet. That such preconceptions would have a role to play in an AD interview is a matter of some concern and is relatively straightforward to address by calling attention to it.

Family members' imitation of medical discourse (also related to television and the Internet, possibly—concerning if used unreflectively) is of additional interest because it provides one way into the question of interpretation of the data of the study in general. My own first reaction upon noting the tendency among some family members to adopt terms from biomedicine was to see it as evidence of an imbalance of power: Nonmedical people would employ medical terms as a way of claiming an authority of which they felt deprived.[20] However, the clinical-team psychologist and lead investigator, Maurice Bloch, saw the same phenomenon differently. According to Bloch, the process itself of consensual decision making both invites and requires linguistic adjustment by all parties: Family members speak more medically as a means of making contact with the medical staff, and the medical staff make an effort to speak in the ordinary language of experience. Over the course of the investigation, Bloch wrote the following to me:

> The efforts of the clinicians to use everyday language and of the family members to use medical jargon are indicators of the efforts of each

to try and reach the other. On one level one may think that as the patient becomes more sophisticated and is able to speak in the language of the physician and as the physician is humanised and comes to speak to the person in his/her (the patient's) own language so the barriers will disappear. But language is only part of the story—a bigger part is for the physician to be in touch with the possibilities of the subjective experience of the patient.

Bloch's is a hopeful view of the AD interview and a corrective to my outsider's view. While my explanation of family members using the language of biomedicine is not necessarily wrong, it does leave out the account from empathy that Bloch provides as a matter of course. Similarly, while I have noted what I take to be approval-seeking moves by family members, Bloch finds that clinical team members, no less than family members, seek approval of their attitudes and actions.

Finally, the clinical team and I discussed the question of whom the interview seeks at any point to assist and noted the usefulness of acknowledging when the focus of clinical attention moves from the patient whose life and death are being discussed to the family member who is seeking understanding for the choice he or she is making or has made with respect to the patient:

Transcript 4:

FM: Ever since [incident], I have never taken R out [of the hospital] again. . . . I want to make it clear, as to the reason why. With me not feeling too too well with these ribs of mine with chronic pain, we haven't come down and seen her as much as we'd like to but we talk to her well pretty well every week except for January when we went south, there was a spell where we didn't communicate.

My second study is one sort of answer to questions raised by my first. It suggests that some health professionals are willing to look at end-of-life conversation as an important problem to be solved, even a problem of incommensurability, and it suggests that structural changes can be made to conversations such that they will be more properly rhetorical, better designed to lead to the best course of action. Like the first study, the second one makes clear that the terms of a predominately biomedical rhetoric of death and dying are not sufficient to provide a framework in which human beings can engage satisfactorily in a conversation about the end of life.

The rhetorical critic can play a role in the negotiation of disparate discourses. My mother's death was a death in silence—her silence the result of stroke and institutionalization, mine the result of a well-meaning censorship by experts. The Riverview project offers an approach to improving the structure of decision making at the end of life by seeking actively to redress the "contact of minds" deficits of perhaps more typical institutional end-of-life decision making.

End-of-life decision making is one occasion of medical discourse that is illuminated by the rhetorical principle "Two people are not fully engaged in a rhetorical process if only one of them really knows what they are talking about." Like other rhetorical principles we have considered, this one can be applied to an understanding of discursive encounters in health and medicine more generally.

Postscript. In March 2005, the case of Terry Schiavo altered the landscape of death discourse in North America. Ms. Schiavo had suffered severe brain damage from lack of oxygen when, for unknown reasons, her heart stopped in 1990. Ms. Schiavo's husband fought for years to have her feeding tube removed, arguing that, although she had not prepared an advance directive, his wife had made clear when she was well that she would not want to be kept alive in a persistent vegetative state—and this, according to her doctors, was her condition, certainly by 2005. Ms. Schiavo's parents disagreed, and their efforts to keep their daughter's feeding tube in place brought interventions on their behalf from the governor of the state of Florida, Jeb Bush, and the president of the United States, George W. Bush. The courts, which had considered the medical view and prognosis and decided in favor of the understood proxy wishes of the patient, prevailed, and Ms. Schiavo's feeding tube was removed. Terry Schiavo died, nearly two weeks later, on 31 March 2005 (see Grady).

The case imported medical discourse into public discourse—and vice versa—and made life-and-death decision making itself a topic of widespread discussion: medical, moral, legal, practical, and religious. Such decisions became the stuff of general conversation; advance directives entered public discourse on a large scale. A question commonly asked in the course of things was, "Would you yourself want to be kept alive if you had Terry Schiavo's quality of life?"

6   Values, Metaphors, and Health Policy

Metaphor is the most rhetorical of figures, and its ubiquity is the best evidence that we are, each of us, everyday rhetorical beings. Metaphor operates lavishly in health and medicine, but it operates, at the same time, somewhat under cover; such is the way of metaphor.

Sometimes, metaphors are easily recognizable *as* metaphors. The person who says, "my love is a rose" is not taken literally to have a disorder involving flowers—rather, to have more fully realized the sentiment of the simile "my love is like a rose." But even our most ordinary conversation is full of metaphors that cause us to think along certain lines, while we believe that we are just thinking. Indeed, "along certain lines" is a usually unnoticeable spatial metaphor for how we think. Laurence J. Kirmayer writes (and his topic is biomedicine), "When values are explicit, they may be openly debated but rhetoric uses metaphor to smuggle values into discourse that proclaims itself rational, even-handed and value-free" (57). While some of the terms we use in debate clearly represent values (when someone calls a foetus a "pre-born child," we know where we stand), some terms that seem neutral, or even like the only terms available for debate, represent values also, so there is good reason to be most interested in the terms we notice least.

The purpose of this chapter is to bring metaphors of health and medicine to light and consider how they behave, especially in the realm of health policy. The chapter points to specific metaphors—some well established (*medicine is war*), some still emerging (*the person is genes*). It teases out and mines and also proves a rhetorical principle: that the terms of a discourse constrain not only the outcomes of debate but also what it is possible to argue at all.[1]

As I write this, I am waiting for the results of a diagnostic ultrasound. The ultrasound technician, who cautioned me, as she studied her monitor, not to draw any conclusions from her grimaces ("It's not that I'm finding anything; I'm just looking very hard; you can't find anything if you don't look very hard") told me in the end that "something did show up." She said I should get in touch with my doctor to discuss the results of my test. Of course, the technician did not say *what* showed up. I do not know if I am due to receive another diagnosis to add to the list of annoying but basically benign conditions that clutter the lives of healthy people past a certain age, or if I am due to receive a diagnosis the very speaking of which, tomorrow morning, will change my life for a time or forever. I can say, though, that I was willing enough to have the test.

I report the event because it indicates a way in which diagnosis is a metaphor, an idea in which we have invested a series of meanings transferred from another medical idea, the idea of health itself. We crave diagnoses, most of us, and not just those who are hypochondriacs or who "long for organicity."[2] We visit health professionals in search of diagnoses (as chapter 7 notes, we sometimes desire the diagnosis even more than the relief from symptoms). Given the opportunity, we request all available diagnostic tests and may feel unsatisfied with the medical consultation if we do not get them.[3] In our homes, we complete checklists aimed at diagnosis—for depression or premenstrual dysphoric disorder or irritable bowel syndrome—and carry these checklists to our physicians and request specific prescriptions. Recently, we have gone further and fetishized diagnosis: We step out to be diagnosed—at diagnostic centers that have encouraged us to bypass our physicians and at diagnostic resorts (see chapter 4); we equip our homes with the technologies of home diagnostics. *Newsweek* reports on the availability for home use of both monitoring devices (for glucose levels, cholesterol levels, ovulation, etc.) and diagnostic devices. A company called Home Access Health offers for HIV and hepatitis C, for example, tests in which bodily fluids are collected at home and sent by mail, anonymously, to a laboratory for analysis (Carmichael 67–68). It should go without saying that accurate diagnosis is typically antecedent to appropriate medical treatment—this is certainly true for HIV and hepatitis C—but it is the metaphor, in which diagnosis is health, that accounts for much of the persuasive appeal of diagnosis itself.

The metaphorical ability of diagnosis in public discourse outstrips the ability of diagnosis to perform medically. Recently, cancer specialists have reported that *early detection*, the idea that has structured the bulk of cancer information campaigns and cancer protocols for decades, does not always benefit patients and, indeed, may harm them. The early-detection idea is that if cancer is discovered early, the chances of curing it are increased, so alertness to the possibility of cancer is necessarily a good thing: *Diagnosis is health*. The problem, these researchers say, is that certain aggressive cancers will already have spread by the time they are detectable by current means, while very slow-growing cancers may better go undetected, obviating treatment that would be more harmful than the cancer itself would ever have been.[4] (Should, then, diagnostic screening routinely be performed for cancers about which current tests cannot say reliably whether they need intervention or they do not?)

As a person awaiting the result of a diagnostic test, I am in a rhetorical quandary; of what shall I persuade myself? There is something counterintuitive about hoping for a diagnosis of anything at all—really, I want a diagnosis of "nothing"—but the force of the metaphor is strong. Does no diagnosis now mean a worse one later? (After all, I do have symptoms.) Shall I hope for a diagnosis that being timely is actually health, only, perhaps, health delayed? The *Vancouver Sun* reported recently that heart attacks were missed in 5.3 percent of cases of people reporting to Vancouver hospital emergency rooms with chest pain. These patients were simply discharged. In these cases, the hoped-for diagnosis, "nothing serious," turned out to be problematic, because it was wrong (see Fayerman, "Two City Hospitals").

Health policy is made in language in which the metaphor *diagnosis is health* has quite a lot of currency—certainly, a great deal of health care is actually the administration of diagnostic tests—even though most of us understand that diagnosis is not *literally* health. To apply, on a large scale, a critical view of early diagnosis is to strip diagnosis of some of its metaphorical value and recirculate it as a more neutral term of praxis. From a rhetorical perspective, the economy of values, with trade in metaphors, should be a branch of the study of health policy.

Authors from many disciplines—sociologists, anthropologists, historians, physicians, nurses, ethicists, and others—have studied the production and perpetuation of values in health and medicine by studying specific metaphors in medical discourse. In general, these authors have extracted embedded figures from medical discourse and exposed their meaning.[5] This chapter reverses the process, returning a few salient medical metaphors to the discourse from which they have been withdrawn for scrutiny, to argue that because biomedicine supplies the terms in which health-policy debate takes place, its metaphors not only reflect medicine as it is but also stage medicine as it will be.

A rhetorical view of the relation between a medical model (biomedicine) and health policy invites us, for example, to turn attention away from a fiscal construction of a health-care crisis to the terms of a debate that *relies already* on the assumption of such a crisis. The rhetorical view is suggested by Kenneth Burke when he argues that observations are not free but are constrained by the terms we use to make the observations in.

> Not only does the nature of our terms affect the nature of our observations, in the sense that the terms direct the *at*tention to one field rather than to another. . . . Also, *many of the "observations" are but implications of the particular terminology in terms of which the observations are made.* In brief, much that we take as observations about "reality" may be but the spinning out of possibilities implicit in our particular choice of terms. (*Language* 46; emphasis in original)

A Burkean view of terms is all the more pertinent for metaphor, where values are transferred from one thing to another, and the value-ladenness of terms is even harder to see. Moreover, metaphor, as George Lakoff and Mark Johnson argue, "is not just a matter of language . . . [rather] human *thought processes* are largely metaphorical" (6; emphasis in original). Lakoff and Johnson's perhaps most famous example of "metaphors we live by" is the metaphor, *argument is war*, which itself underlies metaphorical statements such as, "Your claims are *indefensible*," "I *demolished* his argument," and "He *shot down* all of my arguments" (4). The metaphor, Lakoff and Johnson say, is intimately connected to the concept of argument. Our culture, in the grip of that metaphor, is different conceptually and actively and not just linguistically from a culture in the grip of the metaphor, say, *argument is dance* (5).[6] Multiplying examples, Lakoff and Johnson alert us to the resident values of the most innocent-seeming locutions.

Thus is Emily Martin's project of waking up sleeping metaphors so compelling.[7] Writing, for example, about textbook descriptions of reproduction, Martin notes that sperm production is typically described as a kind of irrepressible activity producing felicitous excess, while egg production is described as simply "wasteful." ("So many eggs are formed only to die in the ovaries," she quotes a biology textbook as saying.) "How is it," Martin asks, "that positive images are denied to the bodies of women?" ("Egg" 489). Martin finds that textbook accounts of the biology of reproduction also reproduce, at the same time as they are derived from, stereotypical images of the masculine and the feminine. The egg as feminine is irredeemable: If it is not utterly passive in its encounter with sperm (typically, the egg is "transported," or it "drifts" along), then the abrasive zona is aggressive and sets a trap (as one textbooks says, to "capture the sperm with a single bond"). But Martin's purpose is not simply to set the record straight on reproduction:

> Although the literary convention is to call such metaphors "dead," they are not so much dead as sleeping, hidden within the scientific content of texts—and all the more powerful for it. Waking up such metaphors, by becoming aware of when we are projecting cultural imagery onto what we study, will improve our ability to investigate and understand nature. (501)[8]

Metaphor is a means, then, by which thought is structured and a means by which debate is, to some extent, determined.[9] That is the principle that impels us to track the metaphors of biomedicine into the realm of health policy. The terms that construct and constrain the debate on health policy in North America belong to biomedicine. Metaphor is one means by which biomedicine controls the debate about health care.[10] Examining metaphor is one way of shifting the ground of the debate— from the values we think *about* to the values we think *with*.

In the United States and in Canada, problems in health care are typically framed in public discourse as, in the first instance, economic problems: We can not afford all the health care we need. Large-scale responses to health-care problems, then, tend either to address financial concerns directly (the closing of hospital sites in Canada is an example) or to address financial concerns represented as human concerns (the introduction of managed health care in the United States is an example). In the course of both responses, health care is further commodified, and the interpretation of the problem as fundamentally economic is reinforced. In 2003, health spending in the United States reached $1.7 trillion, representing an average of $5,635 per person and 15 percent of the gross domestic product (*Organization*). In Canada, the total is Can$123 billion—an average expenditure of Can$3,885 per person—10 percent of the GDP (*Canadian*). The widely held view is that health costs simply can not continue to increase at present rates. An aging population and increasingly expensive procedures and pharmaceuticals, along with a growing sense of entitlement to ever better health, threaten to raise health-care costs beyond the ability of national economies to cope. But the fact that the "health care crisis" is most often represented in public discourse as a crisis of money itself forecloses, by its own terms, the very policy debate it promises to engage.

A short list of health-policy questions suggests what we usually mean when we talk about health policy—although, as I will argue later, the list is itself a strategy for controlling the debate.

- Who should be assured health care?
- How should health care be funded?
- What kinds of personnel should provide what kinds of care?
- Which diseases should be given research funding priority?
- How should health care be geographically distributed?
- How should the efficacy of services be ascertained?
- What should be the role of the state in the administration and regulation of health services, including the licensing of insurance programs?
- How should the health-care industry be regulated, and how should health professionals self-regulate?
- What body(ies) should make and enforce policy—and should these bodies be centralized?
- Who should govern admission of patients to hospitals?
- How should access to health care be decided and administered?
- What should be the role of hospitals in the provision of health care?
- How should physicians be paid (fee-for-service, salary, "capitation")?
- How should medical services be valued?
- How should technology be endorsed? distributed? allocated? contained?[11]

These questions are pertinent to both American and Canadian health-care systems, for although the structural differences between the systems are considerable, a single biomedical *model* organizes health care and health-care policy in both countries. In respect of that model, the differences between American and Canadian health-care systems are managerial rather than conceptual. This is evident in the possibility of borrowings between systems. For example, the American left advocates single-payer insurance, in part, to minimize the bureaucratic costs of health care; the Canadian right looks to private clinics and user fees to relieve the cost burden of health care on government and improve access to services for those who can afford to pay directly for them.

Three primary metaphors have been most widely associated with biomedical theory and practice in the West. These are *the body is a machine*, *medicine is war*, and *medicine is a business*. In recent years, a fourth metaphor—*the person is genes*—has taken hold. Gene metaphors are interesting to study in part because their emergence suggests something about the life course of metaphors themselves. A military and, arguably, xenophobic view of medicine recedes, as will be noted later in the chapter, as the "enemy" is understood more to be within us and less, as is the case with "invading" microbes, to be outside of us. Medical metaphors, in any case, can be followed into health policy.

A dominant metaphor of biomedicine is *the body is a machine.* That the body is viewed in the West as a collection of working and nonworking parts is well documented (see, for example, Osherson and AmaraSingham), and the rhetoric of everyday life offers ample evidence of the continuing hold of the metaphor. We are diagnosed with mechanical problems—from "machinery murmurs" to the host of "biomechanical" faults identified by sports-medicine specialists. We are treated with procedures (transplants, for example) and pharmaceuticals (hormones, for example) to replace our parts and change our fluids. Erectile dysfunction, insofar as it is a diagnosis at all and not simply a description, is a diagnosis that depends, overall, on the assumption that parts ought to work for the life of the machine. We adopt mechanical self-descriptions; like the worst of our pre-electronic watches, we are "wound up," "run-down," and "worn out."[12]

Computer metaphors are an extension of our postindustrial repertoire of machine metaphors. In daily life, we are exhausted when our "hard drives" are full (too much "interfacing," maybe); memory loss is construed as "data loss." According to Evelyn Fox Keller,

> It is not only that we now have different ways of talking of the body (for example, as a computer, an information-processing network, or a multiple input–multiple output transducer) but that, because of the advent of the modern computer (and other new technologies), we now have dramatically new ways of experiencing and interacting with that body. (xvii)

Deficiencies assigned to "software" (demands on the system, overload) are considered more remediable than ones assigned to "hard-wiring."[13] The computer metaphor has enormous popular appeal, even if it somewhat misses the mark, as Kenneth Burke notes (in 1966!):

> If man is the symbol-using animal, some motives must derive from his animality, some from his symbolicity, and some from mixtures of the two. The computer can't serve as our model (or "terministic screen"). For it is not an animal, but an artifact. And it can't truly be said to

"act." Its operations are but a complex set of sheerly physical *motions*. Thus, we must if possible distinguish between the symbolic action of a *person* and the behavior of such a mere *thing*. (*Language* 63)

Some of our elements, like prostheses, are literally, rather than figuratively, inhuman.[14]

The metaphor *the body is a machine* is tied to a series of other assumptions entrenched in the biomedical language most of us use unselfconsciously to describe our own states of health and illness. One of these is mind-body dualism. The body is a machine operated by the executive, the mind.

Kirmayer says that the "Cartesian division of [the person] into a soulless mortal machine . . . and a bodyless soul" has been replaced in contemporary science by a "monistic materialism" in which the person is in toto a "physiochemical machine, all of whose functions can be described in biological terms and rationalized for efficiency" (59). In fact, however, in our quotidian conceptions of health and illness, a dualism persists so powerful that it makes alternatives to itself almost impossible to imagine. Even some putative holistic models of health do not so much establish a unity of self as they strive to have the mind exert a finer control over the body (this is a peculiarly Western holism). As noted in chapter 1, Barbara Duden asks, when we talk about the body we *have*, who is it that is doing the having (*Woman* 45)? Similarly, Keller writes,

> [I]t is the computer that dominates our imagination, and it has liberated us from that odd locution "man has a body." In its place we have an even odder set of locutions. Today, it might be more correct to say that the body—in the sense that the word has now acquired—has man. (118)

When Burke talks about the inaptitude of the computer as a terministic screen, he is talking about the inaptitude of it on analogy with *humans*, not on analogy with *bodies*, per se. That human bodies and human beings are not one and the same is a conundrum tied to both available metaphors and thinkable health policies.

The relation of machine metaphors and of mind-body dualism to health strategies and health policy is not difficult to establish. Ivan Illich noted almost thirty years ago the economic causes and effects of the notion that the body is the possession of a consumer who is able to purchase "repairs" for it. Inevitably, a mechanical notion of the body produces a mechanical notion of health care. A society working with a mechanical model of medicine will prefer the sorts of interventions that are observable and measurable. Diseases themselves have been described as "a means of coordinating phenomena for the purposes of prognosis, diagnosis, and therapy" (Engelhardt 136). Indeed, the development of the nosology was coeval with the maturation of mechanistic thinking.

Robert G. Evans and Gregory L. Stoddart maintain that the policy that results from a mechanical view of medicine is *health-care policy* rather than *health policy*. They argue that while research demonstrates the relevance to health of a variety of "determinants of health" (social class, housing, income, education, exposure to environmental agents, etc.), health (care) policy takes almost no account of such elements. Health (care) policy is, on the other hand, acutely sensitive to even the possibility that some new drug or piece of equipment or diagnostic procedure may contribute to health. Evans and Stoddart argue for "a somewhat more complex framework" for health policy, representing a wider range of relationships among determinants of health (1349).

In view of determinants of health, the policy questions I listed earlier reveal themselves to be neither innocent nor disinterested. Indeed, the list deconstructs itself as an answer to the question, "What do we usually mean when we talk about health care?" by illustrating the limits of health policy conceived as health-*care* policy. The machine metaphor has slowed the ability of policy makers to think about injections of affordable housing as health interventions. Other biomedical metaphors are also implicated in policy.

The metaphor *medicine is war* still informs a great deal of common parlance about medicine. *Invading* microbes are resisted by the body's *defence* mechanisms or by pharmaceutical *magic bullets*; in the *battle* with cancer, we *bombard foreign* cells, and we *fight* for our lives. Howard F. Stein records this excerpt from a physician's lecture on soft-tissue infection: "With a patient in septic shock, you go on a witch hunt for the bacteria or the patient dies. . . . We often have one shot left, and if we lose, we belong to the bacteria" (*American Medicine* 68). Susan Sontag writes,

> [C]ancer cells do not simply multiply; they are "invasive." . . . Cancer cells "colonize" from the original tumor to far sites in the body, first setting up tiny outposts (micrometastases) whose presence is assumed, though they cannot be detected. Rarely are the body's "defenses" vigorous enough to obliterate a tumor that has established its own blood supply. . . . Treatment also has a military flavor. Radiotherapy uses the metaphors of aerial warfare; patients are "bombarded"

with toxic rays. And chemotherapy is chemical warfare, using poisons. (*Illness* 64–65)[15]

So-called *heroic* medicine is the highly visible intervention of the Western practitioner—the bleeding of a hundred years ago, the coronary bypass surgery of today. In the tradition of heroics, a direct effect of the war metaphor on health policy is the preference for the high-technology counterattack: the blasts of radiation, the calling in of the artificial heart.[16] As Edward S. Golub and others have noted, however, this orientation is ill suited to contemporary medical practice, much of which revolves around complex diseases, many of them chronic, with multiple etiologies and no simple causative agent susceptible to "attack."

The war metaphor has other effects on health policy as well. In medicine's field of combat, it can be difficult to isolate the enemy. In many battles—from the rescue of the extremely premature infant to the maintenance on life support of the dissipated adult—death itself is the enemy, which must be kept at bay at any cost. Physicians are recently, with the introduction of hospice care and with attempts to initiate and respect advance directives, coming to find in the medical narrative a place for death as something other than defeat or failure. However, the shift in thinking represents a resistance to the metaphor and is extremely slow in coming (see chapter 5). Overall, health-care professionals continue aggressively to patrol the border between life and death. Health policy concerning care of the terminally ill, pain relief at the end of life, euthanasia, and assisted suicide is conceived in an arena of war.

In the language of the health-care debate, a metaphor so successful as an instrument of thought that it seems not to be a metaphor at all is *medicine is a business*.[17] Although the business metaphor is not derived from biomedicine per se, it is sponsored by the biomedical model. That is, a positivist medical model, focusing on the delivery of quantifiable units of care, ideally with observable and measurable effects, is easily mapped onto the discursive realm of economics.

In an article that first appeared in *Nursing Forum* in 1968, registered nurse Marjorie A. Moore writes, "It is time for nursing educators to stop verbalizing meaningless platitudes about the 'whole patient' or the 'total relationship between the nurse and the patient'" (29). Nurses should instead, she says, support "an investigative, analytical, and scientific approach" to nursing. When Moore's article was reprinted in 1993 in the same journal, her sentiments were endorsed by another nurse-author, Carol A. Wong:

We live in an era of accountability—accountability to the public for the outcomes of our care and the structure, processes, and resources that produce them. . . . In exchange for the cost of nursing care, consumers and government legislators expect clear evidence of the effectiveness of our clinical practice as well as accountability. (32)

Accountability is about more than accounting, of course. But Wong's essay represents the values of what is called in the nursing literature "nursing process"—nursing as a cost-effective, problem-solving enterprise, with measurable outcomes and irreproachable balance sheets.

In Canada, the Canadian Hospital Association has called for "market-style competition for hospital patients" (Mickleburgh), and private clinics have begun to compete for "consumers" who can afford to bypass hospital waiting lists for certain publicly funded surgeries or diagnostic tests. A 2005 ruling of the Supreme Court of Canada approved a significant measure of privatization of health care in the province of Quebec by lifting a ban on private insurance for procedures covered under the public health plan. Margaret Lock reports that Myriad Genetics in Colorado, a private genetic testing firm, will, for $2,400, test women for breast-cancer genes once they have been diagnosed with the disease so that those who carry the gene may encourage family members also to be tested.

The notion of the health "consumer" has a great deal of currency in the health-care debate generally, even though the term may be out of phase with the experience of users of health care who may not at the moment of use see themselves as consumers as much as they see themselves as sick people (or, in the case of genetic testing, about-to-be-sick people). Granted, they may have seen themselves as consumers when, perhaps, they were choosing their HMO, but then, the product they were buying was insurance, not health care.[18] The "consumption" of health care is, in large part, in any case, the consumption of diagnostic-test products; here *medicine is a business* meets the metaphor *diagnosis is health*.

Overall, the rhetoric of health *business* is more pervasive and less veiled in the United States than it is in Canada. American health-care "providers" within HMOs are "managed care vendors," and provider publications compare managed-care firms to "manufacturing companies" (Freeman). American journals of "health-care marketing" report that "urgi-centers" and "surgicenters" are creating a condition of "acute competition" in the medical "marketplace," where the contents of the "medical market basket" have expanded to require rethinking of the "product line" (France and Grover; Goldsmith). An American journal of demographics reports that infertility is a "2 billion dollar a year industry" with a "growing . . . market opportunity," "very attractive if successfully targeted" (Grashof). In Canada, an entrepreneurial medical rhetoric is still, overall, suppressed by a rhetoric of equality of access to health goods and services—the rhetoric of universal health care. The contrast of Canadian and American discourses of reproduction, for example, is marked. In 1991, under the directorship of geneticist Patricia Baird, a Canada Royal Commission was established to investigate and report on new reproductive technologies, in part to protect Canadians against the forces of reproductive business. The tone of the commission's report remains a feature of Canadian public debate on matters of reproductive and associated technologies, including debate on stem-cell research.

In spite of the sometimes obvious fit of the business metaphor for medicine, the goals of business are at odds with the goals of health care. Richard Melito explains that business is, indeed, no *more* than a metaphor for health care: "[A]lthough there may be business-like transactions involved in the delivery of human services, business and service organizations are conceptually different entities" (43). The "prime beneficiaries" of human-service organizations, Melito says, for example, are those who use its services, whereas the prime beneficiaries of business organizations are understood to be their owners.

We seem intuitively to know that health care is not per se a business, which is why we are uncomfortable, for example, with the physician who owns a share of the clinic to which he or she refers patients for X rays; it is why "Root Canals and Retailing" strikes us as an unfortunate title for an article in a professional journal (Grove and Pickett). It is why we feel upset when an infertile woman is redesignated as a market opportunity. The attempt to subsume health care fully within the discourse of business produces absurd results. The truth is that good health care is *un*economical for the same reason that it is good business: People who are saved from early deaths live to spend more money on health care or have more money spent for them. As Willard Gaylin points out, "[P]reventive medicine drives up the ultimate cost of health care to society by enlarging the population of the elderly and infirm" (59). That is, considered individually, the cheapest medical consumer is not the healthy person but the dead one. A health-care system can not then be *motivated* by the desire to save money any more than it can be motivated by the desire to make it.

From a rhetorical perspective, the problem posed by the salience of the business metaphor is that a health-care debate conducted in the language of business has several of its outcomes already determined. To frame the condition of health care as a cost crisis, for example, is necessarily to beg the question of the nature of the problem and therefore to constrain the possibilities for solutions. Writing in the *Journal of Health Politics, Policy, and Law,* David M. Frankford illustrates the point as he critiques the growth industry in "health services sciences," the branch of economics that seeks to analyze the health-care system by counting "the products of biomedicine, the number of tests, the days of care, the dollars spent," and so on (774). Frankford says that the system of analysis acts to reinforce the system it analyzes. In other words, if one uses a positivist model to study a positivist system, the very efforts to analyze the system reproduce it:

> A dilemma perceived from a purely scientistic perspective generates scientistic responses to the particular ills diagnosed by science. These scientistic fixes, however, only reinforce and exacerbate the original scientistic perception of crisis at the expense of alternative [humanistic] perspectives. Because we depend on science for solutions, and because scientific solutions can only reinforce our dependence on science, we are on a treadmill constituted in scientism. (774)

The business rhetoric of the public debate on health care is working in the same kind of loop.

In September 1993, shortly after President Bill Clinton unveiled his (later to be rejected) health-care-reform package, Gaylin, writing in *Harper's,* predicted its demise. Gaylin said, basically, that the two goals of health-care reform, as Clinton had articulated them, contradicted each other: The government could not democratize health care and reduce spending at the same time. Gaylin said that it was not the inefficiency of the health-care system that was to blame for the problem, although the system was inefficient; rather, he said, in the context of increasing technology and an everexpanding definition of what it means to be healthy, it is simply not possible for Americans to have all the health care they need or want. Gaylin then offered his own proposal—that Americans dare to have the conversation about health policy they really need to have: the one about "the goals of medicine, the meaning of 'health,' who shall live and who shall die (and who shall decide)" (57). That is the kind of conversation that a waking up of sleeping metaphors facilitates: the conversation about the values we are using to have the other conversation in.

A metaphor that had already, at the time of Gaylin's writing, begun to occupy the public imagination for medicine is *the person is (the sum of his/her) genes.* The gene trope creates an equivalence of persons and

127

their genes. While genetic action is real, that equivalence is a figurative relation. The gene is, inter alia, a metaphor, and in that sense, it has a metaphor's biography. Keller explains, "The conception of genes as autonomous actors—endowed with the authority and the capacity to direct the future course of organismic development—dates to the mid [nineteen] twenties." In the 1940s the "notion of the chromosome as 'code-script'" arrives (45).

Keller is herself interested in the metaphoric appeal of the gene. "If the ways in which we talk about scientific objects are not simply determined by empirical evidence but rather actively influence the kind of evidence we seek (and hence are more likely to find)," then it makes sense to understand the "strength and persistence of the discourse of gene action" (35). That discourse has a critical effect on the course of biological research.

The gene as metaphor for a certain rationality of life is significant to public perceptions of health and illness and significant to health policy debate.[19] If genes are understood to make people sick, then policy makers may be inclined to neglect other factors in disease causation.[20] I mentioned in chapter 3 Barbara Ehrenreich's objection to the way "thinking pink" depoliticizes breast cancer; the very idea of the breast-cancer gene depoliticizes breast cancer in a similar way.

The genes BRCA1 and BRCA2 are associated with some breast cancers, but the genes are *not* implicated in over 90 percent of cases. Yet the idea of the determinism of the gene is so powerful that it has created worry in those who know they have the gene and complacency in some who know they do not—and it has diverted attention from environmental and social factors connected to the disease. Lock writes, when we focus on genetics, "other factors that contribute to cancer—environmental, social, and political—are eclipsed, allowing us to understand this disease as though it were entirely an individual misfortune" (8). She says:

> Although scientific knowledge about breast cancer genes is without doubt of great significance, there is a great danger that these remarkable "breakthroughs" are deflecting attention away from the major contributing causes of breast cancer: those associated with social and environmental variables. (15)

Gene metaphors affect health policy by steering our thinking about etiologies in some directions rather than others; they also affect policy by causing us to think in particular ways about our bodies and what it means to be ill. Under the influence of a germ theory of disease, in which healthy bodies are infected by invading microbes, we are better or worse fortresses, attacked from without. Under the influence of a gene theory, in which disease arises from features of our genetic make-up, we are better or worse organisms, attacked from within, in a kind of horrible betrayal. Celeste M. Condit writes,

> According to the [gene] model, foreign invaders don't cause diseases, but failures in the body's own constitution do. In other words, viruses can invade and cause damage only if an individual's genetic configuration is such that the individual is unable to resist the viral invasion. ("Women's" 126)

"A genetically ill body is different from a body invaded by germs" (130), and it needs to be treated differently. The war metaphor may be inappropriate to the task at hand.

While Condit sees the move from germ to gene theory as a kind of paradigm shift—"a move from one ideological terrain to another" (126)—and notes the conditions for the weakening of the hold of the war metaphor,[21] Peter Conrad sees gene theory as rather more continuous with germ theory ("Mirage"). He suggests that the machine metaphor, so much a part of the first theory, is intact in the second:

> Genes are often pictured as the blueprint for the body as machine. We can see the mechanistic metaphor when genes are depicted as the coding device which determines how some bodily feature or function will be manifested. . . . The metaphor is evidenced when we talk about gene therapy in terms of replacing faulty genes or selecting particular genes for human enhancement. Change the gene and fix the problem. (232)[22]

Conrad points out the limitations of the machine metaphor in genetic accounts. The machine metaphor is too simple to represent genetic reality: "[G]enetic influences are usually polygenic—traits are determined by many genes acting together—or epigenetic, which involves single-gene or multiple-gene interaction with the environment" (235). Still, the machine metaphor has imaginative force, especially in public discourse. So, while genetic explanation may weaken the hold of the war metaphor, the machine metaphor may have some life in it yet. That is, something that scholars can do with metaphors, in addition to waking them up, is follow their life courses as a cultural study.

What scholars can probably not do is *replace* metaphors. Still, in a short essay in the *New England Journal of Medicine*, physician George J. Annas suggests doing exactly that: "I believe the first necessary step [in reframing the debate on health-care reform] is to devise a new metaphor to frame our discussion of public policy and to help us develop a new conception of health care" (744–45). Annas develops a case for adopting an ecologic metaphor, highlighting "integrity," "balance," "diversity," and "conservation." He makes a good point about the appeal of "ecology," and he is certainly right about the importance of metaphor to policy debate. However, he is naive about the behavior of tropes: Metaphors acquire power over time and in use; they arise from a culture and are not readily inserted into it.

Even if it were possible to order up new metaphors, metaphor replacement would not necessarily be desirable. The same metaphors that seem somehow reprehensible may, at times, serve a positive function in medical research and practice. For example, in a Canadian Broadcast Corporation radio interview, Geoffrey Hoffman, a microbiologist and immunologist at the University of British Columbia, described his AIDS research by talking about "targeting" cells in order to "knock them out"; the war metaphor seemed actually to assist Hoffman's research. (In the course of the interview, interviewer Mark Forsythe asked, "If healthy cells are also zapped, is that collateral damage?" And so it went.) The metaphor of battle can also be therapeutic. Barbara F. Sharf says of writer-poet Deena Metzger, who was the subject of a post-mastectomy photographic portrait, that she "represents a modern Amazon psychologically fighting the stealthy enemy and challenging viewers to look beyond her wound as stigma." "Love is a battle I can win," Metzger is quoted as saying (77).

Biomedical metaphors, moreover, express the values of the biomedical model, itself not easily displaced. If the model were rejected in favor of, for example, a *biopsychosocial* model (George L. Engel is credited with the neologism) with more attention to the psychosocial features of illness, the resulting model would not be new so much as it would be the obverse of the old model, having been produced by it. The term *biopsychosocial* betrays assumptions about three discrete realms of life; they are announced seriatim, and the biological first. There is no easy exchange of terms.

Metaphors highlight some things and hide others and render some things obvious and some things unthinkable. Implications of this insight for health policy run in many different directions and suggest many avenues of research.

The most innocent-sounding terms are not innocent of value. *Caregiving*, for example, both describes and conceals an economics of care. *Care* in the first half of the word is commodified by *giving* in the second half; *giving* also points to care flowing in a single direction. The term establishes a traffic in care: One person gives care, and the other person gets it. A question that is suppressed by this characterization of the care relationship is "What does the care *receiver* give?" (The care receiver with late-stage Alzheimer's may have very little to give, and a model of reciprocity here would be misplaced. However, that only *some* care receivers have such limited resources is itself hidden by the terms and the categories in use.) *Eldercare* as a category makes the age of the person being cared for the most salient feature of him or her.[23] It aligns caring for the unresponsive old person with caring for the responsive old person rather than, as might make more sense experientially, with caring for the unresponsive young person.

In his article on medical language in *Annals of Internal Medicine,* physician William Donnelly draws the attention of physicians to "maladies" in the language of their profession.

> The language of medical case histories uses its users as much as its users use it. It constrains what its users are permitted to say not just in case presentations and the pages of the medical record but in the day-to-day conversations of students, residents, and attending physicians. (1047)

From time to time, consciousness-raising articles such as Donnelly's appear in the professional literature (Annas's is another such article), but language is not frequently a topic in medical journals or in health-policy ones. Yet, careful and systematic analysis of terms and metaphors is not off to the side of issues of health care but essential to deciding what counts as health care in the first place.

That returns us to the metaphor of diagnosis. A current recurring form of medical information (found frequently, but not only, in advertisements for prescription pharmaceuticals) is this: "You thought you were just ————, but maybe you have ————." So, you thought you were just feeling "blah," but maybe you have depression (Zoloft Web site). You thought you just had heartburn, but maybe you have acid reflux disease (Nexium advertisement).[24] You thought you were just bloated and constipated, but maybe you have irritable bowel syndrome (Novartis-sponsored "Talk IBS" advertisement). You thought you were just forgetting names and places, but maybe you have Alzheimer's disease (Aricept advertisement). The message is "See your doctor; get your diagnosis; your diagnosis is your health."[25]

This sort of advertisement is in contrast with an advertisement of the fairly recent past with a very different orientation: "Thank heavens I saw my doctor. I thought I had an ulcer. He said it was only acid indigestion." This slightly vintage antacid advertisement sends us to our physician to find out what we do *not* have. In the absence of a special diagnosis, we can treat what we feel, not what we have (this is how nonprescription drugs are often sold)—while the trend is now to have something that can be treated (this is how prescription drugs are typically sold). These new advertisements belong to a culture of diagnosis, which is the scene in which health policy is composed.

Classifications and nomenclatures themselves can be metaphorical and more value-laden for that reason. They constitute an undergirding rhetoric, a set of constraints in terms of which a higher-level rhetoric takes place. Analysis of terms—for example, both "diagnosis" and the terms of the nosology itself—is a wedge into taken-for-granted talk about health, health care, and health policy.

7   The Problem of Patient "Noncompliance": Paternalism, Expertise, and the *Ethos* of the Physician

Billions of health-care dollars are spent each year because patients do not follow the instructions and advice of their doctors. One authority estimates the cost of medication noncompliance alone, in the United States alone, at $100 billion per annum (Gerbino). Medical and social-science literature counts patients' rebellions and misdemeanors:

- In a study of patients' recall of interviews with rheumatologists within two weeks of visit, 11 percent had forgotten almost everything, including the names of prescribed drugs, tests ordered, and the diagnosis; 33 percent recalled most of the information given; 56 percent recalled some of the information and forgot some (Donovan).
- In a study of seropositive patients at twelve English HIV units, where adequate adherence was defined as taking more than 95 percent of prescribed doses of antiretroviral therapy, 27 percent of patients were found to be inadequately adherent (Brook et al.).
- Only 61.7 percent of travelers to East Africa (97.1 percent of whom were aware of the risk of infection) used regular chemoprophylaxis and two or more antimosquito measures to protect themselves from malaria (Lobel et al.).

A literature search turns up thousands of books and articles on noncomplying patients. Jenny Donovan counts eight thousand English-language articles listed on MEDLINE to 1990 and six thousand more to mid-1994. "Patient compliance" is a subject heading for over sixteen thousand MEDLINE-indexed articles published between 1994 and 2005. Most of these are measurement studies.

This chapter argues that measurement studies in general reinstantiate the terms of the problem that they are measuring. It further argues that recent moves in the medical literature to reconfigure the "compliance" question as a "concordance" question, a question of doctor and patient collaboration and agreement, do not so much improve adherence rates to doctor-recommended treatments as they confound issues of who is qualified to give advice and what are the warrants for taking it. The chapter outlines a rhetorical approach to questions of patient adherence to physicians' advice, noting that patients do in most cases make decisions about their own care, and it is best if they are persuaded to make good ones.

First, a word on terms. *Noncompliance* came into use in the 1960s, with the work of sociologist Milton Davis (see Davis and Eichhorn). Professional interest in noncompliance was established in the 1970s with publications by David L. Sackett and R. Brian Haynes following a 1974 symposium at McMaster University in Hamilton, Ontario. Sackett and Haynes used the term to include all studies of patient cooperation performed since the 1940s. The term *adherence* gained popularity in the professional literature after Sackett and Haynes; compared to *compliance*, it "reduc[ed] attribution of greater power to the doctor in the doctor-patient relationship" (see Vermeire et al. 333; Greene). More recently, the term *concordance* has been suggested by the Pharmaceutical Society of Great Britain to denote agreement between patients and physicians (see Marinker, *From Compliance*).

Patients do not always fill their prescriptions for medication; if they fill prescriptions, they do not always take the medications; if they take the medications, they do not always take them correctly. Donald Meichenbaum and Dennis C. Turk reported in 1987 that with an estimated 750 million new prescriptions written in the United States and England each year, over 520 million cases of partial or total nonadherence are expected. Every year, 230–250 million prescribed medications are not taken at all; as many are taken only partially as prescribed (26).[1] Moreover, doctors tell their patients to quit smoking, and they do not. They tell them to do daily repetitions of a therapeutic exercise or avoid eating fatty foods or change the dressing on a wound or return to the office for a follow-up appointment—and they do not. Sometimes, noncomplying patients improve anyway, because they had some condition that would get better eventually on its own, but sometimes they do not improve. When nonimproving patients return to their physicians, if they do, they may be candidates for tests for a new diagnosis, on the mistaken idea that illness did not abate with treatment for the original one. Physicians, according to D. Dante DiNicola and M. Robin DiMatteo, assume that patients have complied with their instructions; even if they are aware of the extent of occurrence of noncompliance generally, physicians tend to overestimate the degree to which *their* patients adhere to *their* advice (56–58).

Unnecessary testing is only one sort of expense that attends noncompliance. Noncompliance is also responsible for, among other things, increased hospital admissions and increased length of hospital stays. In 1982, Judith Rodin and Irving L. Janis wrote that "it is probably safe to say that patients' failure to adhere to prescribed medical regimens is one of the most serious problems in health care today" (33). There is no significant improvement in the situation well over twenty years later. In 1979, in *Compliance and Health Care*, Haynes, Sackett, and D. Wayne Taylor reported that 20 to 30 percent of patients fail to follow curative medication regimes, the number climbing to 50 percent for long-term medications. In 2001, in a chapter in *Compliance in Healthcare and Research*, Haynes reports, "Once assessed and prescribed therapy, over a third of patients may drop out of care entirely. . . . While in care, patients frequently do not take all of their medication, the average consumption rate being reported as about 50 percent" (5). Review articles note there is no "gold standard" in compliance research (Vermeire et al.), and "[e]stimates of compliance range from 30 percent to 90 percent in the published literature" (Bowen, Helmes, and Lease 25), but there is no question that compliance remains a problem that three decades of research has not done much to solve. A meta-analysis of studies evaluating the effectiveness of interventions to improve compliance concludes, "No single intervention strategy appeared consistently stronger than any other" (Roter et al. 1152). "To date [2001], none of the suggested explanations has accounted for more than a modest part of the observed variations in compliance" (Vermeire et al. 334).

Patients' refusal or failure to follow physicians' instructions or advice has many causes. Patients may not have enough money to fill prescriptions; they may be confused about dosing schedules; or they may find themselves unable to tolerate drug side effects. But a good part of the problem of noncompliance is discursive and relational and amenable to rhetorical interpretation.[2] One reason that patients do not comply is that they are, effectively, not *persuaded* to comply. That is, even if they are *convinced* that a particular course of drugs or diet or exercise regimen would benefit them, if they do not act on this conviction, then, by definition, they have not been *persuaded*. A great deal of rhetorical theory pivots on this distinction between conviction and persuasion:[3] The mind, in its faculty of understanding, may recognize the merit of a particular idea, but to be persuaded is to be moved to action. In some cases, then, noncompliance reflects a rhetorical failure. While noncompliance is often thought to be a failing of patients—who are recalcitrant, neglectful, self-indulgent, or simply disobedient—it can be considered also a failing of physicians, who have not themselves been persuasive enough (like the physicians noted in chapter 4 who are not able to win over hypochondriacs completely to the idea that they are well).

A number of rhetorical principles might be invoked to account for such a remarkably intractable problem. One is the principle of communalism and identification. Chaim Perelman and Lucie Olbrechts-Tyteca write, "For argumentation [that is, rhetoric] to exist, an effective community of minds must be realized at a given moment" (14). The conditions for such a community include a common language, mutual respect, and a sense in the speaker of the importance of gaining the adherence of the interlocutor (17). In a similar vein, Kenneth Burke writes, "You persuade a man only insofar as you can talk his language by speech, gesture, tonality, order, image, attitude, idea, *identifying* your ways with his" (*Rhetoric of Motives* 55; emphasis in original). Indeed, the old term for rhetoric is "persuasion," and the new one is "identification" (*Rhetoric of Motives* xiv). Physicians, for their part, do not, in general, identify with their patients. Howard F. Stein explains that the physician is, importantly, "not a patient" (31): "To be sanctioned to 'repair' another (active) is to remove oneself from the intolerable condition of patienthood (passive)" (*American Medicine* 34). According to Kathryn Montgomery Hunter, the physician, far from identifying with patients, is necessarily "concerned with a disease in its human manifestation rather than with a person who is ill" (84). Nor is this, in Hunter's view, a bad thing; rather, it is a feature of the physician's "egalitarian disinterestedness." By the same token, patients are "guaranteed acceptance and care no matter who they are or what their lives have been, no matter how tired the physician may be or how horrible the malady" (133).[4]

So, although some of the psychology literature on the doctor-patient relationship suggests that physicians "identify" with patients, perhaps pointing to their own foibles and shortcomings in order to win compliance, the suggestion is anything but a suggestion *really* to identify with patients. It is rather a suggestion to feign identification in order to set an example. DiMatteo and DiNicola, for example, recommend the following script for the physician faced with the patient who overeats: "'Oh, I really have trouble resisting desserts too. It's tough isn't it? But I figure it's worth it to resist them and to work toward normal weight'" (106). The authors explain, "Self-disclosure from practitioner to patient should portray the practitioner as strong and able to deal persistently with uncertainty. The disclosure should show the practitioner as a model for the patient's behavior" (106–7). What appears at first to be an argument from *pathos* (identification: the physician and patient share the experience of staring down temptation) is, in fact, as DiMatteo and DiNicola arrange it, an argument from *ethos* (the speaker is exemplary). The authors do not suggest real physician self-disclosure but its opposite. Their advice is not meant to recalibrate power in the physician-patient relationship but to trade on it. Here the compliance intervention reenacts the compliance problem: The contact necessary for genuine persuasion is missing. True, not all successful rhetoric begins with *sincere* identification—Burke includes in identification the politician's declaration, "I was a farmboy myself" (*Rhetoric of Motives* xiv)—but DiMatteo and DiNicola are coaching the physician not in empathy but in moralism.

I first suggested a rhetorical account of noncompliance based on a theory of identification in an article that appeared in the journal *Rhetoric Society Quarterly* in 1994 (see "Patient Compliance"). In that essay, I said that literature in medicine and psychology insistently draws attention to noncompliance and insistently measures it, but the literature as a whole fails to acknowledge that the medical model that produced the problem of noncompliance is limited in its ability to solve it. Even where compliance authors suggest the importance to compliance outcomes of the doctor-patient dialogue, they do not apply *rhetorical theory* to the study of persuasion. Rather, they apply a less complex theory more readily compatible with the terms of the biomedical model: *persuasion theory*. In general, compliance authors' definition of persuasion is David J. Stang and Lawrence S. Wrightsman's definition in the *Dictionary of Social Behavior and Social Research Methods*: Persuasion is "a form of social influence in which one individual attempts to effect a change in the behavior or positions of another." The terms of persuasion theory (as opposed to rhetorical theory) are "source, message, and receiver" (O'Keefe); its model is typically cognitive (Petty et al.); its concerns include "variables that affect message production" (O'Keefe); its successful practitioners are persuasion "professionals" (Cialdini); its authority is, pretty well, Dale Carnegie (actually cited in DiMatteo and DiNicola 183). Although persuasion theory has its uses, it is too instrumental a theory, too much a theory of "influencers" and "targets" to apply to complex interactions in health and medicine, where humans have so much invested and where they must be considered in all their humanity.

In 1994, I argued for a more fully theorized rhetorical address to the problem of noncompliance—on the idea that rhetorical theory so clearly predicts the failure of physician-patient persuasion within the current medical model that the more interesting question is perhaps not why so many do not comply with medical advice, but why so many do. Rhetorical theory suggests that noncompliance is an endogenous feature of Western medicine. Most attempts to improve compliance figures can be expected to yield, as they indeed do yield, only minimal benefit, in part because the biomedical model denies the preliminary conditions that are necessary for persuasion to take place.

Over ten years after the publication of that article, the dynamics of the physician-patient interview have changed somewhat, at least in theory, as a reaction against paternalism in medical practice, but there has been, as I have indicated, no real improvement in the numbers of patients adhering to physicians' advice (advice that, we must imagine, is still mostly good). The delinquent patient has been recast as the independent-minded client, but it is not clear that health outcomes have by that recasting been improved. A rhetorical analysis of current conditions suggests that what may be, in part, a problem stemming from weakness of identification between patient and physician is also understandable, in part, as a problem of weakness of the physician's *ethos*.

By 1994, compliance experts had already established that the physician-patient relationship was central to an explanation of nonadherence. DiMatteo and DiNicola had said that patient adherence relies on the patient's trust in the good will of the physician. Meichenbaum and Turk had said that "other adherence enhancement procedures . . . will work only in the context of a concerned, compassionate relationship wherein the patient is viewed as a knowledgeable ally who must actively participate in the treatment process" (76).

Over the past ten-plus years, the professional literature on noncompliance has both rehearsed measurement studies (both incidence of noncompliance and efficacy of compliance interventions) and taken another direction with respect to analysis of the doctor-patient relationship. The recent literature has a new regard for the patient, overall promoting the idea of the patient as an equal partner with the physician and a rational decision maker in matters of treatment. Much of the literature has claimed that the problem with the typical doctor-patient relationship is that the doctor is paternalistic, and the patient is expected to *comply* with (as in passively obey) "doctor's orders," while it would be better if the patient were a collaborator in health who would *adhere* to agreed-upon regimens, having reached *concordance* with the physician (see Vermeire et al.).

There is much to be interested in when a professional literature embraces a conceptual and terminological shift. But the move from compliance to concordance, from deviance to conscientious objection, from vertical physician-patient relationships to horizontal ones[5] is not as promising as it may seem as a solution to problems of follow-through on best treatment options. Indeed, the move bears features of the problem-of-the-obverse that I mentioned in chapter 6 in relation to the term *biopsychosocial*: The "new" coin is just the other side of the old one. The egalitarian model for physician-patient relationships at best reconfigures the problem of noncompliance; at worst, it aggravates it. The new noncompliance is bound up with a problem of trust.

That the idea of compliance is loaded with value and hierarchy is an argument of, among others, James A. Trostle, writing in 1988, and Søren Holm, writing in 1993. Trostle says that medical compliance is an "ideology of physician control" (1299), supporting the authority of medical professionals: "The concern for compliance is a cultural phenomenon intimately connected with the self-image of physicians, and with their organized (and often successful attempts) to define the limits of their own discipline" (1303). Noncompliance, according to Holm,

> points to a radically paternalistic conception of the doctor-patient relationship, where the doctor decides and the patient complies. As we (slowly) move away from the paternalistic conception of the doctor-patient relationship, to a form of relationship where the patient's autonomy and fundamental right to self-determination is acknowledged, we should also abandon the present conception of compliance. If it is ultimately the patient who has to decide, after being duly informed and advised, then he cannot be non-compliant. He may be non-collaborative, obstructive, foolish or stupid if he blatantly disregards the decisions to which he is a party, but since they are his decisions and not the doctor's orders, this does not imply non-compliance. (108)

Trostle and Holm both articulate an argument that had begun to be made in the medical and social science literature in the 1970s—against the idea of compliance and in favor of the idea of adherence (see Barofsky). The keyword invoked by Holm for the old compliance thinking is "paternalism."

Mildred H. B. Roberson points out in 1992 that the standard medical definition of compliance assumes that medical advice is good for patients and that rational patients follow medical advice precisely. "Compliance," she says, implies that patients who do not follow medical advice are deviant, unreliable, irrational, and/or uncooperative.[6] Roberson's own research is with patients with chronic conditions who "[b]y synthesizing the knowledge gained through all sources with their own beliefs and understandings of their health conditions and their own personal life circumstances [made] what they considered to be the best decisions for them" (23). Roberson concludes that health professionals should learn more about "clients' perspectives" on health problems and treatments: "Ultimately, patients' choices about compliance are theirs to make" (24).

Much of the professional literature had, then, by the early 1990s turned away from "noncompliance" as *irrational* behavior toward "nonadherence" as *rational* behavior. But the biggest shift in thinking came in 1997 with the report of the Royal Pharmaceutical Society of Great Britain: *From Compliance to Concordance*. Marshall Marinker, lead author of the report, summarizes the group's findings, which suggest a "different and more robust model of the relationships between doctors and patients."[7]

> The clinical encounter is concerned with two sets of contrasted but equally cogent health beliefs—those of the patient and those of the doctor. The patient's task is to tell the doctor his or her health beliefs and the doctor's task is to enable this to happen. The doctor must also convey his or her (professionally informed) health beliefs to the patient. The intention is to form a therapeutic alliance—to help the patient make as informed a choice as possible about the diagnosis and treatment. Although this alliance is reciprocal, the most important determinations are made by the patient. ("Personal" 747–48)

The report of the pharmaceutical society argues that what was formerly known as "noncompliance" is actually a person's informed decision not to adhere to a therapeutic regimen. The patient is a responsible decision maker in full partnership with medical professionals.[8] Rejecting both "compliance" and "adherence," the report introduces "concordance" as a term for the arrival by agreement and harmony at medication and other treatment regimens.

[T]he working party now advocates the concept of "concordance."
... In doing so we are not simply offering an alternative, more politically acceptable way of talking about a technically difficult, and
morally complex, problem. Rather, we wish to introduce and urge a
distinct change in culture, in researching and teaching about the relationship between prescribing and medicine-taking, between patient
and prescriber. (*From Compliance* 2)

There are at least five good reasons to concur with the pharmaceutical society and prefer the idea of collaboration and concordance to some
more vertical structuring of the physician-patient relation.

1. Patients deserve more respect than they are typically afforded in a
compliance model. Barron H. Lerner's essay on the historical construction of noncompliance makes clear the extent to which today's "recalcitrant patient" is descended from the "careless consumptive" of the early
twentieth century ("From Careless"). The tuberculous man who might
also be homeless and alcoholic and pose a threat to public health by refusing to be quarantined got no respect at all, and neither, says Lerner,
does the recalcitrant patient.[9]

2. Physicians and patients often think differently about and have different preferences in medical outcomes and the means of achieving them.
Patients, it is said, tend to prefer more conservative and less invasive treatment strategies than their physicians do; similarly, when faced with end-
of-life decisions, patients tend more than their physicians to value quality over quantity of life (see DiMatteo and Lepper 77). It is best then if
both sets of preferences and values are taken into account.

3. Patients are often well informed about medical matters in general
and knowledgeable about their own health in particular. They have access, not least through the Internet, to a great deal of information about
health and health care and about pharmaceutical and other treatments.
They, therefore, may be well-qualified partners in decision making.

4. While physicians alone for decades had powers of prescription, now
patients, increasingly subject to direct-to-consumer advertising for prescription pharmaceuticals, can and do order prescription medications
directly over the Internet. Even in Canada, where direct sale of prescription drugs is illegal, consumers are successful at buying drugs online from
non-Canadian suppliers.[10] Patients, that is, are capable of acting without
the authority of their physicians.

5. *Compliance* denotes obedience to someone else's wishes. When we
follow through on decisions we have made ourselves, complying is not

what we are doing. As Holm says, "It has no meaning to talk about a person who is noncompliant with respect to herself" (108). (Similarly, a person is noncompliant when he or she redeems a prescription but does not take the medication—but not when he or she orders a pizza and does not eat it.) *Compliance* is a bad fit with the idea of patient as client.

While a concordance model of doctor-patient decision making has a great deal of appeal, the fact is that adherence-to-recommended-treatment numbers have not improved since the appearance of Marinker's report in 1997, and publications on "noncompliance" (by that name) continue to appear in great numbers. Moreover, perusal of the index of a 2001 collection of essays on compliance (see Burke and Ockene) turns up no entry for *concordance* at all, the term seeming to have no place on the map of at least some noted researchers in the field. The concordance model, it seems, is a pretty good idea that may include the conditions of its own failure.

A rhetorical view of the renovation of compliance as concordance suggests one element of the problem: the problem of *ethos*, as I mentioned, and of trust—specifically, the introduction of a new ambiguity into the role of the physician. On the release of the report of the Royal Pharmaceutical Society, a piece in the *British Medical Journal*, glossed "concordance": "Doctors and patients are equals. It is not for patients to submit to doctors. Rather doctors have their health beliefs, and patients have theirs. They are all equally valid" (Cuthbertson and Noble 690). Marinker himself says,

> [C]oncordance does not imply an abandonment of the evidence from science. Rather, we wanted to convey mutual respect for the different perspectives of both doctor and patient without predicating that the differences between them should be resolved on the grounds of "superior" medical evidence. ("Personal" 748)

Why does Marinker place "superior" in quotation marks? Physicians must have genuinely superior knowledge in medical matters. Otherwise, on what basis would they be qualified to practice medicine? The truth is, doctors and patients may *not* have "equally valid" health beliefs—just as, for example, professors and students may not have equally valid things to say on matters about which the professors have been thinking for thirty years and the students for thirty minutes. We may all be equally entitled to our opinions, but our opinions are not necessarily of equal value.

Equality rhetoric reclassifies behavior inconsistent with medical advice and solves the problem of "noncompliance" by making the concept, in effect, cease to exist for medicine. It does not make it more likely that a patient will be persuaded to follow a doctor's advice. Equality rhetoric belongs to consumerist rhetoric and is a rhetoric of rights that may be inappropriate to questions of health and illness. Where medical expertise is called for, it will sometimes be best, after all, to defer to the physician. The problem is that medical expertise has often expressed itself as paternalism and now, after some time, is seen to be paternalistic. But expertise itself is not a problem; it is a resource. In order for it to be most effective as a resource, it has to be *trusted expertise*.[11]

The relation of expertise and compliance might be considered historically. I noted in chapter 1 Barbara Duden's account of eighteenth-century German women who knew their bodies in their own terms as carefully and as correctly as their doctors knew these women's bodies in the medical terms of the day. I quoted Duden saying that her Dr. Storch took his patients at their word. *But so did his patients take him at his.* Charles Rosenberg writes that, following its publication in 1769, William Buchan's *Domestic Medicine* was, arguably, the most widely read nonreligious book in England and the United States, its pages illustrating "with particular clarity the shared knowledge and assumptions that bound professionals and lay people together in a community of ideas and healing practices" (32). In the nineteenth century, "common sense" medical guides *cum* advertisements, like R. V. Pierce's *People's Common Sense Medical Adviser in Plain English*, were found in most households; medical knowledge was well distributed through the population. Meanwhile, as Lerner points out, physicians, as records have it from Hippocrates on, were concerned that patients follow their advice ("Recalcitrant"). *That is, shared knowledge of the body and the giving and taking of expert advice are not mutually exclusive.* That expert advice has been construed as paternalistic and coercive in the compliance literature of the past thirty years is attributable to a sort of practice and an *ethos* of the profession that are problematic beyond the terms of the compliance problem itself. A rhetorical view of nonadherence queries the relations among *ethos*, expertise, and trust.

In a 1976 collection of his essays, sociologist Robert K. Merton introduces the idea of "sociological ambivalence," adding sociological inquiry to existing psychological inquiry on the problem of being pulled in two directions at once. Merton is interested in the ambivalence built into the structure of social statuses and roles—especially professional roles.

In its most extended sense, sociological ambivalence refers to incompatible normative expectations of attitudes, beliefs, and behavior assigned to a status (i.e., a social position) or to a set of statuses in society. *In its most restricted sense*, sociological ambivalence refers to incompatible normative expectations incorporated into a *single* role of a *single* social status. (6–7; emphasis in original)

Merton's "sociological ambivalence" can be extended to suggest an account of a structural problem in a concordance model of care. Merton says that contradiction—the tension between norms and counternorms *for a single role*—is an essential feature of physician status. Physicians, he says, for example, must be disciplined in appraising medical evidence, BUT they must be decisive and not postpone decisions (67); physicians must collaborate with other professionals, BUT they must have final responsibility for the work of their team (67); physicians must be emotionally detached from patients, BUT they must not become callous (68); physicians must recognize the provisional nature of diagnoses, BUT they must merit the confidence of patients who want to know what really is wrong (68).

We might conjecture that physicians inherit an additional burden of ambivalence with a concordance model of patient care. *They are experts, BUT they are just people with opinions*. In the rhetoric of physician-patient equality, the physician must say, "Here's my advice, but feel free to think it isn't any good." This ambivalence of physicians is mirrored in the ambivalence of patients. The concordance model charges patients both to seek advice and to decide whether to take it, while the resources to make the decision may be locked inside the advice itself—because, in fact, in most medical situations, an expertise is called for that physicians have and patients do not.

This problem of who gives advice and who takes it, how knowledges compete, and whether they are equal is illuminated by a rhetorical view of physician-patient dialogue on treatment and care. When physicians and patients discuss a course of treatment, who is persuading whom of what? What counts as a good argument for any course of action? (A concordance model, for example, gives more weight than a compliance one to the argument that the pleasure of smoking now warrants the risk of lung cancer later.) What is the *act* around which inducements and cooperations take place (Is the act maintaining health, curing disease, living as long as possible without undue restrictions)? Given different acts—and different motives—can physician and patient be, in Burkean terms, consubstantial agents, agents who act together?

A rhetorical view of concordance includes prior questions, too. What, for example, does it mean to talk about "informed patients" at all? In the

1990s, American health-policy reformers imagined a population of informed health consumers. The reformers suggested creating an additional tier in the health-care system to provide disinterested information to system users, solving the problem of asymmetry of information between physicians and patients. But information itself is not disinterested. As Pauline Vaillancourt Rosenau points out, to empower patients, where empowerment is seen as divulgence of information, presupposes the coherence and validity of the information divulged.[12]

The very idea of "informed consent" presumes that physicians who otherwise continue to work in an old paradigm are able to equip patients as decision makers in a new one. How free are lay choices between or among medical options? As I noted in chapter 5, Richard Gwyn and Glyn Elwyn say that in the absence of equipoise—a situation "in which options really *are* options"—decisions are not really shared at all; rather, physicians attempt to induce patients to arrive at decisions "commensurable with their own [the patients' own] best interests" (446). Even in the presence of equipoise, it is usually the physician who determines what the options are. Yet, how could things really be otherwise? There are some decisions that patients are not plausibly able to make because they are not decisions at all so much as expert judgments: Is this infection likely to clear without antibiotics? Can this child's asthma safely go untreated? Is the evidence of a hysteroscopy sufficient to resolve the question of the presence of uterine tumors?

Weighing in on the concordance debate, Fiona A. Stevenson et al. maintain that

> the concordance model fits with the increasing influence of ideas such as shared decision making, patient participation and patient autonomy . . . together with the increasing availability of information and the reported movement towards a consumerist society. These changes are based on a shift from the notion of a "paternalistic" practitioner to a position in which it is advocated that patients have an important contribution to make in decisions about their own health and that their contribution has a legitimate place in the consultation. (89)

Stevenson et al.'s own purpose is to unpack the notion of "legitimacy" of physician's advice. The authors note the extent to which patients perceive prescriptions as legitimate when they concord with their existing health beliefs. In the course of their article, however, Stevenson et al. reproduce from transcripts some of the things that their informants said about their own adherence behaviors—and the transcripts are more revealing than

Stevenson et al. acknowledge. One patient said she was avoiding seeing a doctor about her child's illness because "I didn't see the point. I knew at that stage that I'd probably be offered antibiotics and I didn't really want to give him antibiotics . . . because they lower the immune system, don't they?" (95). Another said he planned to go off his prescribed pain-killers before his next doctor's appointment "so I can get my pains in my joints, so when I go to the . . . arthritis specialist then he could s- suss out what my joints are like." A third unfolded a plan to take a prescribed treatment for indigestion, only because "if I turn round and go back to [the doctor] and say well the problem's not cleared up and then he turns round and says them tablets didn't work, I can't turn round and say I didn't take them" (99). The transcripts exhibit at least two things about these patients. The first is they seem not really to trust their doctors; the second is that their informing ideas about their own health, while they are sometimes sensible, are not always sound.

One problem, then, with concordance theory is its tendency, for the sake of the concordance model itself, to overgeneralize the situation of the doctor-patient collaboration. A person with a chronic arthritis condition she has had for years, and on which she has become, by research and experience, expert may be invited by her doctor if she is also equipped to make sense of the medical literature to "read up" on a particular course of treatment and see if she thinks it's worth trying. (Furthermore, one might assume that if she does decide it is worth trying, she will fill her prescription and take the drug as recommended.) On the other hand, there are parents who are convinced, despite impressive evidence to the contrary, that immunizing their children against measles, mumps, and rubella exposes them to a significant risk of developing autism; some of these parents are refusing, therefore, against their physicians' advice, to immunize their children, meanwhile creating the possibility of a resurgence of diseases statistically much more likely than immunization itself to cause brain damage. These are proxy-patients whose participation in decision making is, according to the current state of knowledge, to the detriment of their children and the community at large. *Current* is the operative term. This issue remains controversial (see Kennedy). A single model for participatory decision making does not take divergent cases properly into account.[13]

Over fifty years ago, Talcott Parsons wrote about the "competence gap" between physicians and patients, noting that physicians hold more technical information about medicine than their patients do (*Social System*).[14] The gap still exists, of course, and is greater than ever. How its distance is traversed is of some rhetorical interest. Rhetorician Carolyn

Miller suggests that, in the age of technoscience, expertise (acknowledged access to specialized knowledge) stands in for *ethos* (the character of the speaker) as a warrant for belief. This seems to be true. We believe, on certain points, total strangers who we have reason to believe know things that we cannot directly know ourselves. That expertise has such diminished status in a concordance model of patient care is somewhat illogical but can be understood as a backlash, where expertise has been construed as paternalism. Expertise as paternalism gives up its moral claim to authority.[15]

A rhetorical view of advice and adherence suggests the usefulness of a negotiation of expertise. In a general view, the physician is expert in disease, and the patient in illness; the physician in nosology, the patient in experience. Patient expertise is not an imitation of medical expertise; it is a different expertise (as, in chapter 5, family members might have special knowledge of a patient's quality of life to complement the physician's special knowledge of the patient's medical facts).

Like the scientists whom Harry M. Collins and Trevor J. Pinch write about, physicians are "neither Gods nor charlatans; they are merely experts" (143). Physicians should not be apotheosized for having expert knowledge but neither should they be vilified when they seek to act on it. Paternalism in biomedicine is an interesting problem, and compliance statistics may bespeak an anomaly in biomedicine, betraying a paradigmatic problem.

When researchers repetitively measure compliance rates, they do little thereby to increase the chances of patients taking good advice. Quantitative compliance studies run in a groove of understanding and are notable for their lack of criticality.[16] On the other hand, when researchers just reject the concept of noncompliance itself as wrongheaded, they also do not increase the chances of patients taking good advice. A concordance model does not, in the first instance, solve or even attempt to solve the problem of noncompliance. It sidesteps noncompliance with a new protocol in which physicians deploy strategies for achieving harmony and agreement with patients while respecting patients' decisions not to adhere to their advice. The only thing we know for sure about the new protocol is that it is incommensurable with the old one.

This problem remains: Some patients are unconvinced that their doctor's "opinion" is worth heeding; others are convinced it is worth heeding but do not heed it anyway (are not persuaded). "How might patients be persuaded to act on good advice?" is a question that presents itself for rhetorical study.[17]

The rhetorician would say, for example, that arguments with a hypothetical structure—"If . . . then . . ." arguments—are, as a class, not especially persuasive. Perhaps because of the limits of our imaginations or the salience of the present moment, most of us seem not to be moved by arguments that invite us to imagine things in the future. These medical arguments have been notoriously slow to take hold, although they are, potentially, good arguments: "If you expose your unprotected skin to the sun, then you will be at greater risk for skin cancer"; "If you smoke, then you will be at greater risk for lung cancer." Arguments from more immediate consequences fare better but not as well as one might hope: "Under certain conditions, if you have unprotected sex, you may become infected with HIV."[18]

Some arguments pertinent to compliance are rhetorically weak not because they are hypothetical but because they are counterintuitive. Once an infection has seemed to clear after forty-eight hours, why take antibiotics for eight more days? If we feel perfectly fine, why, really, do we need that colonoscopy? In the case of the patients quoted in Stevenson et al.'s article, common sense seemed to fly in the face of doctors' prescriptions, but common sense was sometimes misleading.

Meanwhile, there are other obstacles to adherence. Patients may resist physicians' advice because they are relying on their own experience or the experience of friends or family to guide their behavior.[19] This is the one-two punch of Aristotle's argument from "past fact" and the argument from analogy. However, these patients may not be well enough informed to identify truly analogous situations. In some cases, patients may perceive a choice about treatment reductively, as a choice between only two courses of action (crafting an argument of "opposites") when, in fact, the decision to be made is more complex.[20] A further obstacle to physicians' persuasion may be the one I mentioned earlier: a lack of the identification that is a preliminary condition for persuasion to occur.

A rhetorical view of the compliance problem might furthermore draw on the observations of critical thinkers like Trostle who suggest there are conceptual problems in research on "non-compliers":

> Researchers could hypothesize that all patients are potential non-compliers and that particular kinds of situations cause non-compliance. Instead most of the research hypothesizes that there are non-compliant types of people, and that with sufficient ingenuity their traits can be identified. (1306)

Trostle's point about the misdirection of research is just right. We need only to consult our own experience to know we are all of us noncompliers in some situations. As patients, we are assigned appointments, kept waiting, called by our first names, told to undress, asked personal questions, probed and palpated, and so on. The compliancy of the patient role notwithstanding, we do not always adhere to, or even remember, the instructions that normally signal the end of our medical visit. This may be because we sought from our physicians, in the first instance, not relief from symptoms so much as relief from the fear that they were symptoms of some dread disease. Many of us will opt not to take the suggested medication, do the suggested exercises, and/or make the suggested appointment for the follow-up visit because we can tolerate our symptoms well enough once we do not have to worry about what they mean.

Most of the time we do make our own decisions about treatments and care. We have not, after all, (absent legal injunctions or submission to care as a condition of hospitalization) really received *orders* from our doctors; we have received *advice*. We stand, then, needing to be persuaded. In some cases, we cooperate with our doctors and persuade ourselves to fill a prescription, to take a medication as prescribed, and so on. In other cases, we do not cooperate with them. We may cooperate more readily when we participate in decision making and when prescriptions accord with our health beliefs. That makes sense, but it does not itself turn the compliance question into a concordance question. Rather, it suggests that research attention, as Marinker and his colleagues themselves have observed, is well placed on persuasion.

Two exemplary cases shed some light on the matter of how people are induced to cooperate with their physicians and how adherence might be most usefully understood. They are cases in the public rhetoric and the politics of treatment adherence.

On 1 December 2001, physician Frederick Ross, in Winnipeg, Canada, delivered an ultimatum to his patients, warning the smokers among them (5 to 10 percent of patients) that if they did not stop smoking within three months, they could no longer count him as their physician. Ross is reported to have said, "I got fed up with wasting my time treating people with smoking-related diseases. People who continue to smoke are obviously not interested in maintaining their health" (Love 6). Newspapers all over Canada and some in the United States took the story as an opportunity to debate such topics as the responsibility of physicians to treat all comers, the slippery slope leading to physicians refusing to treat overeaters and underexercisers, the obligations of persons to safeguard their own health, the burden on taxpayers of managing the illness of people delinquent in this regard, the undesirability of the curtailment of freedoms, the evils of prohibition, the genetics of addiction, and the responsibility of governments to enact new anti-smoking legislation and to cover the costs of smoking cessation therapies.[21]

News sources report that many of Dr. Ross's patients took his ultimatum as an incentive to quit smoking and that, at least initially, fewer than a dozen patients quit Dr. Ross instead (see B. Brown). Compliance researchers may be interested in this case in part because of what it suggests about coercion as a means of securing compliance. The case also draws out a neglected politics of compliance and suggests that, finally, what matters most to *the health-care system* about physicians' advice is not that it is agreed to but that it is taken.

Except when there is the impression, retrospectively, that the advice was wrong—and then the noncomplier is, retroactively, a hero. On 10 July 2002, the story broke in the public media that a longitudinal study of the effects of hormone replacement therapy (HRT) was being halted before completion because results were statistically so significant on dangers to women's health of long-term use that continuing the study posed a risk to some participants. The media coverage of the report (the report itself was published in the *Journal of the American Medical Association*) was not coverage of matters of compliance, directly; in many ways, however, compliance is very much what the coverage was about. In the *Globe and Mail*, columns on the HRT story had titles like "Trouble with What the Doctor Ordered" (editorial) and "Who's a Woman to Trust?" (Wente). The research study itself primarily counted the incidence in HRT–treated women of those diseases against which HRT was once thought to offer protection (like heart disease) and other diseases in which HRT had already been implicated (like breast cancer). The focus of more than one newspaper article, however, was not the medical findings themselves, which, after all, were not dramatic but rather the idea that doctors had been seduced by pharmaceutical companies into believing that menopause was a disease needing treatment, and women had been seduced by their doctors into diseasing their own experience. Those doctors and those women who had not been captured were praised in the process and those who had been were blamed and shamed. Women should have known better; *they should not have followed doctors' orders.*[22]

This was the thrust of the coverage in the *New York Times*:

Until recently, medical authorities were telling doctors to encourage almost every woman who had not had a hysterectomy to start taking the drugs when she reached menopause and to take them for years, even for life. Now the growing consensus seems to be that women should carefully consider whether they want to start the drugs at all. (Kolata and Petersen)

The story under the headlines might have been that research produces conflicting findings and must be read carefully and critically and even provisionally. But the story the *Times* told instead was this: In 1966, physician Robert Wilson wrote a best-selling book *Feminine Forever* in which he hailed hormone replacement as a panacea for aging. In 1972, in the *Journal of the American Geriatrics Society*, Wilson wrote that, with HRT, "Breasts and genital organs will not shrivel. [Menopausal] women will be much more pleasant to live with and will not become dull and unattractive" (qtd. in Kolata and Peterson). Furthermore, the pharmaceutical company Wyeth-Ayerst paid all the expenses of writing the book and financed the Wilson Research Foundation and its offices on Park Avenue in Manhattan. By 1975, the Wyeth product Premarin had become the fifth-leading prescription drug in the United States (Kolata and Petersen).

The story confirms suspicions we should all have had about pharmaceutical companies already, but it also belittles both the prescribers and the prescribed to. Even the *Journal of the American Medical Association* is now calling HRT a "vogue" (Fletcher and Colditz 366). Importantly vindicated are the *noncompliers*—people like Cynthia Pearson, executive director of the National Women's Health Network, who is reported to have said all along that the HRT message—"Stay young. Stay healthy. Stay sexually vital. Be less of a pain to your husband"—was "sexist and ageist" (Kolata and Petersen).

The lesson of the HRT revelations for the rhetoric of compliance is not only that the good advice of a place and a time is not necessarily always good advice; it is also that noncompliers can be the heroes of medical stories when the advice they didn't adhere to turns out to have been not that good after all. Physicians and patients are not the only candidates for sociological ambivalence, then. We are, each of us, every day, influenced by norms and counternorms: We should take good advice, BUT we should think independently; we should trust experts, BUT we should not trust them too much. These ambivalences, which operate privately and publicly, medically and politically, make patient adherence to physician advice a complex problem. Noncompliance does not need to be obsessively measured, and it does not, as a concept, need to be rejigged out of existence. The actions of patients need to be studied not mechanistically but with an appropriately complex theory of human persuasion and human judgment: a theory of rhetoric.

In general, we should trust physicians themselves to act on their best knowledge, and we should act on our best knowledge, too, which includes knowledge of what a good idea it often is to take the advice of experts. We all do well to know as much as we can; we cannot all know what doctors know. When the best course of action is discerned, then the question is how to induce patients actually to follow that course of action.

Rhetoric is a discipline whose raison d'etre has been for twenty-five hundred years to have knowledge of the available means of persuasion. Rhetorical theory suggests that when the goal is inducement to action—in this case, inducement to action on a matter of health—some good topics of study are: rhetorical terms (What are the changes in stance, motive, behavior, and reciprocity that attend on the shift from "compliance" to "concordance"?); identification (in this case, identification between physician and patient); *ethos* (the persuasiveness of the physician); warrants of belief (What counts as a good reason for following a particular course of treatment?); structure of argumentation (How are good reasons best represented in physician-patient dialogue?); and rhetorical situation (including the relation between private and public discourse on health topics, the status of professional knowledge, and the politics of assent). In addition, the study of persuasion includes looking to other disciplines, such as, sociology, and science studies more generally, for trade in theory to illuminate questions of expertise and trust.

Conclusion: The Usefulness
of a Rhetoric of Medicine

Each of the foregoing chapters has used a rhetorical principle as a means of probing something puzzling or problematic in health and medicine. Each chapter was meant to be useful in a variety of ways and for a variety of readers. A historian, for example, might be interested in a rhetorical account of recent medical history for what the principle of fitness-to-situation, *kairos*, suggests for a history of patienthood. A physician might be interested in a critical view of "compliance" for what the principle of trust in the speaker, rhetorical *ethos*, suggests for treatment adherence in clinical practice. These are sample pairings of disciplinary positions and chapter occupations. A case could be made for a philosopher and the topic of death, approached through the principle of preconditions for rhetoric—or for a health-policy analyst and the topic of public debate, approached through the principle of metaphor. We are, in any case, all of us, patients or were or will be, and we are the family members and friends of patients. We do not have to be sick to be patients, either: We are patients when we appear for cosmetic surgery, for example, and we are patients when, sometimes healthy as can be, we present ourselves for diagnostic or, increasingly, predictive tests.

The analyses were purposeful individually, but one purpose of them collectively was to indicate some ways in which rhetorical theory can be mobilized to increase understanding in the realm of health and medicine.

While there is no single way that rhetorical criticism does its work (as my introduction sought to explain), a "principled" approach has, I hope, shown itself to be productive. Three tasks remain in conclusion: to indicate, retrospectively, the scope of the usefulness of rhetorical criticism in health and medicine; to suggest some further research questions for the rhetorical critic working among other disciplinary and interdisciplinary scholars; and to say something in general about rhetoric as a strategy for studying and for living with complexity.

Rhetoric is useful as a means of studying health and medicine as a *discourse-in-use*. Consider the complex tropology of hospital life, of treatments "withheld" and "withdrawn" and "refused," of people said to be in "vegetative states," a phrase that evokes nothing so much as cauliflower or broccoli. We converse in this discourse and are persuaded by it into some things and out of others. The discourse, too, captures us; there is a way in which it is sexy, because it is a language of power. But "withdrawing" treatments can offend by seeming a little mean-spirited; "pulling the plug" makes death sound like it happens at an electrical outlet. Rhetorical study helps us attend to what language does.

Rhetoric is useful as a means of studying health and medicine as a *public discourse*, remarkable for its ubiquity and its increasing daring. Following closely the life course of baby boomers, the public was interested in birth control in the 1960s, then pregnancy and childbirth in the 1970s; now we are interested in menopause, sexual dysfunction, eldercare—and death. We care about the quality of our deaths and, perhaps reluctantly, about euthanasia and assisted suicide, not least as alternatives to the high cost of end-stage health care. While differences in laws concerning death options in different jurisdictions threaten to create an industry in death tourism (suggesting the possibility of Club Dead[1] and other last resorts), one thing we know is that how we frame death talk now will be important to how we actually die later, just as how we framed birth control gave us an inescapable politics of pregnancy.

Rhetoric is useful as a means of studying health and medicine as a *commercial discourse*. I have logged over the course of these chapters cases of health and medical advertising for products from eighteenth-century amulets and nineteenth-century nostrums to twentieth-century "designer drugs" and twenty-first century body-scan packages, and I have cited many authors and critics who have applied themselves to the study of these products and their marketing. Roy Porter (*Health*), for example, gives us an account of quackery; Barbara Mintzes ("For and Against") holds direct-to-consumer advertising responsible in part for "medicalising normal human experience" (908). As chapter 6 suggests, *health is a business* is an idea of enormous scope, including more than what is *essentially* entrepreneurial. Rhetorical study is a good, critical way into the commerce of health and medicine.

Rhetoric is useful as a means of studying health and medicine as a *professional discourse*. For example, one of the bewildering things about medical journal articles is their tireless rehearsal of epidemiological facts. Repetitively, headache articles cite headache statistics: number of people affected, number of people by gender affected, number of workdays missed, number of dollars spent, and so on. Repetitively, compliance articles cite delinquency statistics: number of cases of noncompliance recorded by disease, number of prescriptions unfilled, number of appointments missed, and number of dollars spent. When medical researchers gather at scientific meetings, they hear the numbers recited again in the conventionalized introductions of research presentations. The numbers constitute an appeal through the Aristotelian *topos* of degree, but what is their persuasive purpose? If the goal is to indicate the importance of the problem at hand, then what is their purpose for an audience of people who already know?[2] A view of medical journal articles as epideictic rhetoric, a rhetoric of praise and blame, sheds some light on values of medical research, practice, and care.

Rhetoric is useful as a means of studying health and medicine as a *discourse of service*. The features and acts of the physician-patient interaction have been a central topic of five of the foregoing chapters. Chapter 1 considered the doctor-patient relationship over time; chapter 2, for migraine patients; and chapter 3, for hypochondriacs. Chapter 5 considered professional-patient/family conversations on matters of end-of-life care, and chapter 7 considered professional–patient/family conversations on regimens of treatment. The questions "Who is persuading whom of what?" and "What are the means of persuasion?" highlight and make visible for scrutiny the ways in which medicine is inter alia the performance of a human service.

Rhetoric is both discipline-based and, by nature, interdisciplinary (it is always, at least, rhetoric *of* something); it is also complementary to a view from other disciplines. Sociologists (for example, Peter Conrad), anthropologists (Margaret Lock), historians (Barbara Duden), philosophers (Ian Hacking), physicians (Eric Cassell), health economists (Robert Evans and Gregory Stoddart), and others, who have no specific intimacy with methods of rhetorical criticism, offer analyses that border on, enrich, and even resemble it.

Interdisciplinary research on health and medicine includes a number of questions that rhetoricians are particularly well poised to consider: How is disease risk represented as something from which medical testing protects us? What are the risks against which "health insurance" protects us? What counts as good health? What sorts of medical procedures and prescriptions most aid health under a particular description? Is physical attractiveness a sort of kairotic state of health, beauty being a contingent thing?[3] What sort of metaphor is "enhancement"? Is health, like wealth, something that can be accumulated (can we be "unbelievably healthy")? Can a commodity exist that can not be purchased or exchanged?[4] Rhetoricians bring to such questions critical procedures that are both theoretically rich and historically informed.

I said, in my introduction, that rhetorical critics proceed with a sense of the ought, even if they can say only that things ought to be better (but not how); the ameliorative motive is a feature of their criticism. Although I am sure that one can have a sense of the ought and be agnostic on specific points at the same time, I am certain that my own preferences have emerged in my analysis, and so my final comments are about complexity itself in health and medicine.

At the same time that some of us demonize Wyeth Pharmaceuticals for medicalizing menopause in order to sell hormone replacement therapy, we, some of the same ones of us, line up for Prozac, overall not thinking too much about the medicalization of misery.[5] But that is not the most confounding thing for the demonization of pharmaceutical companies. Arguably, the most confounding thing is that Prozac often helps (just as Imitrex is a good antimigraine drug, and HRT can seem to make sagging skin jump back onto an aging face). That pharmaceutical companies are in business to make money and that some drugs are extremely helpful to us are both true.[6] I noted in chapter 7 that the real story about HRT is not simply that pharmaceutical companies want our money or that physicians advised us badly, though both those things may be true, but rather that knowledge is provisional, and medical knowledge certainly is (we are not using leeches so much any more, for example, although we use them a little). The handling of outbreaks in Toronto in 2003 of severe acute respiratory syndrome suggests that we may not be able to trust experts to know everything, but we deeply want to trust them to know what they are doing.[7] Rhetorical study assumes and begins from complexity. A rhetorical analysis may not itself yield good medical advice, but it suggests a means of living with the fact that a revisable knowledge is medicine's only possible currency.

Rhetorical study suggests countless opportunities to reflect on health and medicine's complexity. For example, physician *paternalism* is no virtue, and we may disapprove of the way medicine's condescensions can be sent even through those who dispense the drugs that physicians prescribe—but physician *expertise* is more complex. Expertise does seem to be a virtue, and yet, if we have read all the reports about the dangers of HRT and considered all the risks and benefits, and we decide, in light of our family history, our state of health, and even our preferences for how to die,[8] that we *want* HRT, are we simply noncompliant when we resist the physician who advises us against it? If we go in search of a physician who will write us a prescription for HRT, how should we be characterized? As hypochondriacs, perhaps? As superficial? Questions of hypochondria (see chapter 4), compliance (chapter 7), and the patient audience (chapter 2) are rhetorically related. We deserve respect from our doctors and often do not get it; at the same time, we rely on them for at least some of our health, and, when we seriously disagree with them, there is a good chance that we are wrong.

We make better decisions about our own care when we are well informed and better ones the more we are knowledgeable (and smart, although that is seldom mentioned),[9] but our relation to our own health and medical care is complex in a way that rhetorical sophistication helps us manage. In chapter 7, I quoted Harry M. Collins and Trevor J. Pinch and drew an analogy between my physicians and their scientists: "[They] are neither Gods nor charlatans; they are merely experts, like every other expert on the political stage." Here is the rest of the passage by Collins and Pinch:

> They have, of course, their special area of expertise . . . but their knowledge is no more immaculate than that of economists, health policy makers, police officers, legal advocates, weather forecasters, travel agents, care mechanics, or plumbers. The expertise that *we* need to deal with them is the well developed expertise of everyday life; it is what we use when we deal with plumbers and the rest. Plumbers are not perfect—far from it—but society is not beset with anti-plumbers because anti-plumbing is not a choice available to us. It is not a choice because the counter-choice, plumbing as immaculately conceived, is likewise not on widespread offer. (143; emphasis in original)

Finally, then, in the case of health and medicine, to supply a portion of "the expertise that *we* need . . . the well developed expertise of everyday life" (since the "immaculately conceived" version of health and medicine is not on offer, either), I suggest rhetoric.

Conclusion

In 1974, in *Modern Dogma and the Rhetoric of Assent*, rhetorical theorist and critic Wayne C. Booth made the case for a rhetorical mode of being in the world: We should attend to the good reasons of others, and to do so, we must study to know the difference between a good reason and a bad one and to be able to recognize a good person when we see one. Booth's advice would equip us with the sort of expertise we need for our lives lived increasingly in the idiom of health and illness. To take his advice, I think, is the best thing we can do.

Notes / Works Cited / Index

Notes

Introduction: The What, Why, and How of a Rhetoric of Medicine

1. Aristotle defines rhetoric as "the faculty of discovering in the particular case what are the available means of persuasion" (7). His definition draws attention to rhetoric's element of invention or discovery of arguments. Later, Francis Bacon specifies the "duty and office" of rhetoric as "to apply reason to imagination for the better moving of the will" (149).

2. Observations on persuasion in medical discourse are not exclusive to rhetorical critics. For example, historian of medicine Howard Kushner writes about something like persuasion when he talks about patient credibility in cases of "psychogenic pain"; psychologist M. Robin DiMatteo is concerned with questions of influence when he studies noncompliance with doctors' instructions; psychopharmacologist and historian David Healy writes about the discursive reciprocity of psychiatric diagnosis and psychopharmaceutical treatment; philosopher Ian Hacking is interested in campaigns for household products aimed at purification ("Risk and Dirt"); cultural critic Susan Sontag has alerted a generation to metaphors of illness. But persuasion is typically not central to these accounts, whereas *rhetoric* is a discipline of the study of human action where the *keyword* is *persuasion*.

3. The articles appeared on the same day—Picard's in the Canadian national newspaper the *Globe and Mail* and Fayerman's in the local newspaper, the *Vancouver Sun*. Both are reports on the findings of the study "Evaluations of Surgical Indications and Outcomes," by the Vancouver-based Centre for Clinical Epidemiology and Evaluation.

4. There is a range of approaches in studies of rhetoric of medicine specifically. For example, in 2000, Barbara Heifferon and Stuart Brown guest-edited an issue of *Technical Communication Quarterly* on "Medical Rhetoric"; in 2001, John Lyne guest-edited an issue of *Journal of Medical Humanities* on "Rhetoric and Biomedicine." The contributions to these journal issues and the characters of the issues themselves indicate the variety of rhetorical-critical studies of medicine.

5. Internet searches of book and article titles including the term *rhetoric* turn up prominently the opposition of rhetoric and reality, as in D. R. Silverman, "Narrowing the Gap Between the Rhetoric and the Reality of Medical Ethics."

6. This is debatable anyway. For a discussion of the social nature of criticism and the place of the rhetorical tradition on this question, see the final chapter of Terry Eagleton's *Literary Theory: An Introduction*.

7. In his introduction to *Landmark Essays on the Rhetoric of Science*, Randy Allen Harris offers a compatible description of the rhetorical critic working in the realm of science.

> [R]hetoric of science is the analysis of scientific discourse by scholars whose primary allegiances are to the guiding notions of rhetorical theory, and who

place their work in the tradition of others with those allegiances, some of whom invented those allegiances (a case prominently including such folks as Protagoras, Aristotle, Cicero, Vico, Burke, and Perelman). (xxvii–xxviii)

8. Rhetorical criticism is typically defined by example. Other collections of illustrative essays of rhetorical analysis (with Benson's and Foss's) are Bernard L. Brock, Robert L. Scott, and James W. Chesebro's *Methods of Rhetorical Criticism* and James R. Andrews's *Practice of Rhetorical Criticism*.

9. Foss's categories raise questions of classification. Criticism is not *feminist* in the same way that it is *metaphoric*; *ideological* criticism is no more a form of rhetorical criticism than rhetorical criticism is a form of ideological criticism; the *pentad* is a construct of rhetorical theory, but *narrative* is not, and so on.

10. A summary and a critical deployment of Aristotelian rhetoric are provided by Edward P. J. Corbett (*Classical Rhetoric* and *Rhetorical Analyses*, respectively). A history of rhetorical criticism is in Charles J. Stewart.

11. Rhetorical criticism is not the only criticism identifiable more by a kind of attention than by a procedure per se. For example, this is Jonathan Culler on structuralist criticism:

There is no structuralist method such that by applying it to a text one automatically discovers its structure. But there is a kind of attention which one might call structuralist: a desire to isolate codes, to name the various languages with and among which the text plays, to go beyond manifest content to a series of forms and then to make these forms, or oppositions or modes of signification, the burden of the text. (259)

12. These terms are explained especially in *A Grammar of Motives*, *A Rhetoric of Motives*, and *Language as Symbolic Action*.

13. Nichols's quotations of Burke are from his "Rhetoric of Hitler's 'Battle'" (*Philosophy*).

14. Kuhn's "scientific community" evokes Burke's "tribe." This is Burke: "The human animal, as we know it, *emerges into personality* by first mastering whatever tribal speech happens to be its particular symbolic environment" (*Language* 53; emphasis in original). "[O]nce an animal comes into being that [has an aptitude for language] the various tribal idioms are unquestionably *developed* by their use as instruments in the tribe's way of living" (*Language* 44; emphasis in original).

15. Kuhn's term *paradigm* has been a topic of debate in philosophy of science—especially because Kuhn defines the term in different ways, even in the course of *Structure*. His meaning, however, is not mysterious, despite the relative elasticity of the term:

By choosing [the term *paradigm*] I mean to suggest that some accepted examples of actual scientific practice—examples which include law, theory, application, and instrumentation together—provide models from which spring particular coherent traditions of scientific research. . . . The study of paradigms . . . is what mainly prepares the student for membership in the particular scientific community with which he will later practice. (10–11)

16. Black writes:

[T]here will be a correspondence among the intentions of a communication, the characteristics of his discourse, and the reactions of his auditors to that discourse. This postulate is justified by the fact that to deny it is to deny the possibility of language, as we normally understand that term. (16)

17. A good source on the theoretical compatibility of rhetoric with other critical theories of the late twentieth century is *The Rhetorical Tradition*; its editors, Patricia Bizzell and Bruce Herzberg, suggest that Michel Foucault, Jacques Derrida, and Julia Kristeva are themselves rhetorical theorists. Stanley Fish's essay "Rhetoric" is a good source on the theoretical fortunes of an encompassing theory of rhetoric.

18. Philip Wander is another rhetorical critic who believes that criticism is itself a kind of exhortation, a contribution to the public discourse that is its subject. Barbara Warnick writes about these "advocate critics" who enter texts polemically in order themselves "to persuade, to change readers' perspectives through the process of criticism" (233). Bernard L. Brock, Robert L. Scott, and James W. Chesebro write that "the critical impulse is directed towards some social objective or end. . . . [I]t seeks to change the human condition" (13).

19. The project, which ran from the 1930s into the 1970s, followed the progress of untreated syphilis in a test population of African American men. Antibiotic treatment for the disease was available during the time of the study.

1. A Kairology of Biomedicine

1. Joseph Dumit takes up questions of what it means to talk about the social element in certain illnesses, and he cautions against conservative uses of the social constructivist argument. To find a relation between social life and an illness, he says, is not to find that the illness is not *real*. On the social element in illness, see also Robert Aronowitz (*Making Sense*).

2. A chart in a recent issue of the *New York Times Magazine* exemplifies the narrative of progress. One of the charted "six illnesses stumbling toward a cure" is obsessive-compulsive disorder: "OCD was mistaken for demonic possession and treated with exorcism until the 19th century. . . . Genetic markers for OCD were discovered in lab animals in the early 1990's. Drugs like Prozac and Zoloft . . . became the cornerstone of treatment." From-ignorance-to-knowledge accounts are given also for pneumonia, irregular heart rhythms, preterm labor, ulcers, and melanoma (see Singer 30–31).

3. On rhetoric of science, see, for example, Charles Bazerman; Alan G. Gross; Randy Allen Harris; Greg Myers; and Lawrence J. Prelli. On rhetoric of medicine, see, for example, Celeste M. Condit; John Lyne; and Herbert W. Simons.

4. Rhetoricians are not the only ones to have challenged the notion that medicine exists outside of social life. Paul Starr explains that "our conceptions of disease and responses to it unquestionably show the imprint of our particular culture" (1). Howard F. Stein writes that biomedicine is not simply a part of culture, it is a culture itself, with roles, genres, rules, and values, all in the process of being created, negotiated, and revised (*American* 3). Barbara Duden says that "sociogenesis" includes the body itself: It is not just that biology is conditioned by social and cultural forces; rather, social, cultural, and biological constructs are "spun from the same historical material" (*Woman* 5). Thomas Laqueur writes:

> Visible flesh and blood cannot be regarded as the stable "real" foundation for cultural claims about it. Indeed, the interpretive problem is understanding the purchase of the "real" and the degree to which biology is only the expression of other and more pervasive truths. (43)

5. Allopathic medicine is a medicine of opposition in contrast to homeopathic medicine, a medicine of similarities: like curing like.

6. I am not attempting to provide an account of the rhetoric of the body—only to place the notion of a rhetoric of the body inside the notion of a rhetoric of health and medicine. There has been a great deal of interest recently in rhetorics of the body. See Katherine Galloway Young; Susan Bordo; Thomas Laqueur; and Jack Selzer and Sharon Crowley.

7. The rhetoric of the shift in medical attention from person to organ and disease is evident in the well-documented contemporary medical metonymy, "the liver in 409" or "the MI [myocardial infarction] that came in last night."

8. A comprehensive source on the "reign of technology" is Stanley J. Reiser. Dumit (*Picturing*) extends the discussion of technologies of visualization.

9. The prominent stethoscope reappeared in Canada in 2003 with the emergence of SARS (severe acute respiratory syndrome).

10. Duden is not sanguine about all public education on pregnancy and childbirth. In *Disembodying Women*, she records the history of what she calls the "invention" of the foetus as a "life."

11. As the chronology of access to the inside of the body is considered, it is interesting to note the persuasive strategies adopted by companies that sell access to internal-imaging technology. An advertisement for "Ultra-Fast CT scans now available without referral" invites its readers to "take charge" by *looking inside their own bodies* (see ScanQuest).

12. Life expectancy figures are often misleading, however, as gains are often calculated by averages and represent, above all, declines in infant mortality.

13. Bonaccorso and Sturchio are funded by Merck, whose motto "bringing out the best in medicine" brings to mind the figure of the helpful entrepreneur—like R. V. Pierce, whose "Favorite Prescription," "Golden Medical Discovery," and "Pleasant Pellets" were sold within the pages of his *People's Common Sense Medical Adviser*, first published in 1883.

14. The notion that the physician is more god than partner, though, is well established. The shelves of medical-school libraries still contain scores of volumes like Dr. George Surbled's *Medical Etiquette* of 1910, which describes each of the virtues of the physician—justice, charity, self-sacrifice, courage, patience, self-denial, discretion, dignity, honesty, and knowledge—in order to describe the physician to (in this case) himself, to idealize the physician *for* the physician. *Your Future as a Physician* (1962) tells the medical student that the "exaggerated idolatry surrounding some medical heroes of stage and screen is not too far from the truth" (Kalb 25).

15. See also Richard Gwyn and Glyn Elwyn on the question, "When is a shared decision not (quite) a shared decision?"

16. On sexual dysfunction and "manufacturing desire," see Jennifer R. Fishman. On disabling desire, see both Nikolas Rose and Mariana Valverde, who write about Naltrexone, an opiate-receptor antagonist, as a treatment for alcoholism.

2. Patient Audience: The Rhetorical Construction of the Migraineur

1. Recent studies of migraine (2004) note the prevalence of brain infarction (tissue death) and white-matter lesions in persons with migraine and suggest that migraine may be a chronic, progressive disease (see Mark Kruit et al.). Even more recently, migraine has been associated with risk of stroke (Picard, "Migraine"). So, there is no sense in which currently migraine itself is taken to be anything other than a serious medical condition.

2. Ian Hacking (*Social Construction of What?*) would distinguish between the social construction of migraine and the social construction of the idea of migraine and would find that migraine is an "interactive kind" (migraineurs interact with the idea of migraine). Following Hacking's discussion, no easy claim of the social construction of anything can be made—except, as Hacking says, of those things about which it is uninteresting to say that they are socially constructed, because they just are: for example, banking. For a review of literature on social construction in medicine, see Ludmilla Jordanova.

3. In 1921, before proposing his theory of dietary migraine (associated with "excessive intake of carbohydrates" or "intake of animal protein food"), Thomas R. Brown says the practitioner must first eliminate other possible etiological factors, including "intestinal toxemia or bacteremia," "gout," or "uncorrected eye strain, cerebral arteriosclerosis, disturbance of the nose and throat, various focal infections, nephritis, brain tumors, and pelvic disorders" (1396).

4. My research did not include collecting original transcripts of physician-patient interviews. I rely on accounts of physician-patient encounters published in books and in countless medical-journal articles on headache. These accounts are themselves contributions to the literature available to clinicians—and so the headache patient is continually reproduced. It stands to reason that a widely circulating description of "the headache patient" would have an effect on the physician's reception of a particular headache patient—and that, in turn, the

physician's reception would sponsor an interpellation, a calling forth, of the patient he or she addresses.

5. Liveing notes that female migraineurs "have rarely any one about them competent to divide the duties or share the responsibilities with them even where that is possible, or if they have, can be induced to make the trial" (434). A pathological reluctance to rely on domestic help is noted by other authors including Wolff, who offers this report from one of his female patients: "I had a maid once a week to clean house, but I couldn't let her wash the dishes. It irritated me too much to watch her" (323). Problems of the migraineur in relation to domestic help appear also in Walter Alvarez, who writes in the 1950s about the problematic home lives of women with migraine.

6. For the analogy with horoscopes, I am indebted to my colleague Siân Echard. The horoscope observation, in turn, brings to mind the (B. R.) Forer effect, also called the Barnum effect, in which vague and general personality descriptions come to seem pertinent to individual persons (see Dickson and Kelly).

7. The year 1913 saw the appearance of Ernest Playfair's translation into English of Siegmund Auerbach's original German.

8. Auerbach, incidentally, dismisses much of what had already become accepted migraine knowledge, thus demonstrating that knowledge about migraine is always knowledge-for-now:

> On the whole, more women than men are attacked by the complaint, but the difference is less than some authors have assumed. . . . Position and occupation probably exert little influence; it is certainly not true that the so-called upper classes are notably more affected by the disorder. (35)

9. Harold Maxwell, in 1966, finds that Wolff's "contributions to the understanding of all aspects of headache have been paramount and unsurpassed," and Wolff is cited as current in 1983 by Harold Geist (21). The American Headache Society (formerly the American Association for the Study of Headache) has been offering since 1966 the Harold G. Wolff Award for contributions to headache research.

10. See Robert Gatchel and James Weisberg; Ranjan Roy.

11. See Barbara Szekely et al. Menses-associated migraine continues to be of interest to researchers. See V. T. Martin et al.

12. The occurrence together of headache and depression in a significant number of people may suggest a common etiology, but it may also be the case that headache, especially chronic headache, is a cause of depression. For various reasons, depression may be the cause of headache.

13. One audience for Fabricant's book is headache patients themselves. Many publications over the period studied are directed at headache sufferers, and it is interesting to consider how people with headache are invited to imagine themselves. They are described in medical books, such as Fabricant's; in works of literature, such as *Les Misérables*; and they are described, for commercial purposes, by advertisements, such as this one for Hutchins's Headache Pills:

Nervous people are extremely liable to Headache, it also affects persons in whom the digestive organs are diseased, and who are troubled with dyspepsia, and a disease of the Nerves, and is sometimes brought on by hard study, anxiety, and perplexity in business. . . . Whatever distresses the nerves in general will bring on the Headache. (Hutchins 10)

People with headache do come to see themselves through the lens of available description; they, furthermore, self-describe in these terms to physicians. On diagnostic reflexivity in popular culture, see Elaine Showalter.

14. Nor is this view out of fashion (see Gabor Maté).

15. Specifically, Schmidt, Carney, and Fitzsimmons cite a meta-analysis identifying "five pitfalls" of interpretation of clinical findings:

(a) overinterpreting what is presented in a clinical session in order to derive expected or significant conclusions; (b) emphasizing certain patient weaknesses (overpathologizing) or characteristics (overpsychologizing) in line with the therapist's biases; (c) schematizing and/or simplifying material to fit the clinician's hypotheses; (d) drawing conclusions from insufficient data; (e) failure to externally verify conclusions. (Korchin qtd. in Schmidt, Carney, and Fitzsimmons 190)

16. A model "headache calendar" is supplied by the New England Center for Headache. An information brochure of the American Council for Headache Education recommends that people with headache make regular journal entries (15–16).

17. Migraine prophylaxis often includes along with beta-blockers and calcium-channel blockers low doses of antidepressants, particularly tricyclic ones.

18. Diamond and Dalessio do not mention that overprescription of headache medications is a frequent element in the overuse of them. That is, one might argue that "medication abuse" is, in part, an iatrogenic problem, a problem caused by medical treatment.

19. See Tepper. Reporting on a multi-site "landmark study" of clinical presentations of headache, Tepper says, "If a patient walks in complaining of headache, [there is a] 94% chance it's migraine-type. If a patient self-reports as having migraine, 99% of the time, they have migraine or migraine-type headache." Best practice for patients presenting with migraine is the earliest possible administration of a triptan medication (see Kaniecki).

20. I am not claiming that migraine is simply a disease that has passed from hysteria to biology or that the migraine patient is like the stomach-ulcer patient who was transformed from nervous wreck to person-with-*Helicobacter-pylori*-bacteria. That would be a reductive story (although, in 2002, medical news sources did raise the possibility that chronic headache might, like stomach ulcers, be a result of infection by *Helicobacter pylori*). But it is true that disorders for which there are chemical treatments are more respectable, generally, than those for which

there are only behavioral ones. See, for example, Peter Kramer's description of psychiatric disorders viewed through the lens of antidepressants (*Listening*).

21. Because of the association of nausea and vomiting with at least some migraine events, a delivery system that bypassed the stomach was desirable. Some newer triptans are available in other ingenious forms. Zomig (zolmitriptan) and Maxalt (rizatriptan), for example, come in tablets that disintegrate under the tongue.

22. See Lefevre on rhetorical elements in education about and advertisement of migraine pharmaceuticals.

23. According to Andrew Malleson, between one-half and three-quarters of North American and British children had tonsillectomies in the 1930s and early 1940s. Following World War II, Malleson reports, epidemiological studies demonstrated that these surgeries primarily had the effect of decreasing children's resistance to certain diseases (117).

3. The Epideictic Rhetoric of Pathography

1. One of the best-known scholars of "narrative medicine" is Rita Charon, professor of clinical medicine at Columbia University. Columbia's program in narrative medicine is a program of the College of Physicians and Surgeons.

2. The eleven-point scale has zero at the center (for "normal") and plus or minus five points in the direction of mania at the top and depression at the bottom. Martin is interested in, among other things, what zero as a line or a point on a chart suggests about the idea of normal.

3. A central problem for discussion of illness narrative is definition. Even commentators who describe the genre features of narrative may wind up counting as narratives first-person accounts, which do not, strictly speaking, qualify (see Greenhalgh and Hurwitz). In this chapter, I take a broad view of narrative. I am, for example, willing to see electronic journal entries as constituting narratives if they have threads of plot and character. There are, however, times in the chapter when the definition itself of narrative is what is at stake, as when I worry that the coherence requirement for narrative serves a coercive function.

4. Not only physicians, anthropologists, literary critics, and philosophers are interested in illness narratives; historians are interested, too. When Dorothy Porter and Roy Porter wrote their social history of doctors and patients in premodern medicine, they turned for source material primarily to the writings of patients, claiming that patients provide ampler and more abundant accounts than doctors do and not only of illnesses but also of medical encounters.

5. The 2003 Academy Awards were notable for their instances of genre violation. Indeed, a sense of anticipation among intending viewers was derived from their knowledge that, given divided feelings about the U.S. invasion of Iraq, genre violations could be expected.

6. From "Ana by Choice": "This is a site for those who ALREADY have an eating disorder and do not wish to go into recovery. Some material in here may be

triggering. If you do not already have an eating disorder, better it is that you do not develop one now. You may wish to leave."

7. This is the motto of Ana's Underground Grotto found at <http://plagueangel.com/grotto/>.

8. I first learned about pro-Ana web sites through the work of a then graduate student at my university—Karen Dias, working under the supervision of Isabel Dyck—who was interested in the Web postings of eating-disordered subjects for what the postings revealed about their motives and experience. Dias read the postings as a kind of narrative data.

9. Taking up the question of truth in narrative, Hawkins writes, "Pathographies may indeed be read as 'true stories,' but the emphasis must be as much on the word 'stories' as the word 'true'" (14). Pathographies "are of value to us not because they record 'what happened'—for they are not . . . factual accounts—but because they *are* interpretations of experience" (*Reconstructing* 25).

10. Carl Elliott credits Johns Hopkins psychologist John Money with the term *apotemnophilia*, literally, *love of amputation*. Money named the disorder in 1977. It has been renamed since, being called, in 1997, "factitious disability disorder"; in 2000, "amputee identity disorder"; and in 2004, "body integrity identity disorder."

11. This is Hawkins: "Over and over again, the same metaphorical paradigms are repeated in pathographies: the paradigm of regeneration, the idea of illness as battle, the athletic ideal, the journey into a distant country, and the mythos of healthy-mindedness" (*Reconstructing* 27).

12. Many pro-Ana sites are locations for diaries that read like Bridget Jones's diary, without the sense of humor. *Bridget Jones's Diary* begins, "*9st[one] 3 (but post-Christmas), alcohol units 14 (but effectively covers 2 days as 4 hours of party was on New Year's Day), cigarettes 22, calories 5424.*" Kate's "Anasway" entry for 10 January 2002:

> . . . Was 159 on Tuesday, now I am 155 again and am headed in the right direction.
>
> Had an unusually large breakfast today.
>
> 2 servings of plain oatmeal . . . 300 calories
>
> 1 whole cucumber . . . 40 calories

13. Hawkins (*Reconstructing*) also compares pathographies to conversion autobiographies of the seventeenth century.

14. Ehrenreich protests that the "mindless triumphalism" of survivorship "denigrates the dead and the dying. Did we who live 'fight' harder than those who've died?" ("Welcome" 53).

15. Hawkins notes that narratives "replace" memory: "The fragile terrain of memory is colonized by the written narrative" ("Writing"). A few years ago, following my mother's death, I wrote an account of her dying (see chapter 5). The

essay was not a pathography so much as a discourse study, but it is certainly true that my memory of events of the months leading up to my mother's death has been shaped by the story I came to tell about them. The story was accurate, but it was composed in the presence of the idea of readers of the *Journal of Medical Humanities*.

16. University of British Columbia graduate student Rachele Oriente suggested to me the idea of the infomercial as regards Cantor's narrative.

4. Hypochondria as a Rhetorical Disorder

1. According to a 2003 newspaper article, there is "buzz" that hypochondria is the next disease to be marketed to the public (McIlroy): Hypochondria is the new depression. Feature articles on hypochondria have appeared recently in the *New Yorker* (Groopman, "Sick"), *Time* (Lemonick), and the Canadian magazine *Walrus* (Gartner); these appearances testify to growing public interest in the disorder. Meanwhile, unprecedented attention is being paid to Munchausen's syndrome and Munchausen's syndrome by proxy, both, arguably, extreme hypochondrias (see McGill; Allison and Roberts; and Talbot).

2. These criteria vary in certain respects from those listed in the *ICD-10* (*International Classification of Diseases*, tenth edition). The latter include, most notably, a persistent belief in the presence of a specifically named serious physical disease.

3. Peggy J. Wagner and Julia E. Hendrich are among researchers who report that approximately 50 percent of physician visits each year are for complaints with no organic explanation. A. G. Barsky and G. L. Klerman say that no serious medical disease is found in 30 to 60 percent of all visits to primary-care physicians. Anecdotal reports from primary-care physicians can place numbers even higher. The "worried well" designation itself is, however, problematically post hoc. Physician Eric Cassell writes:

> Here are two people with persistent headache who come to a doctor; both are worried because they never had such a headache before. They see the doctor and one turns out to have a brain tumor. The other has "nothing."
> . . . Which one of those two, while they were in the waiting room with their new severe headaches, was the worried well? ("Worried")

4. George A. Ladee cites Forbes Winslow's 1863 edition of *Obscure Diseases of the Brain and Mind* for the first contemporary description of the condition— as a "morbid anxiety as to health," essentially, "a diseased concentration of physical sensibility, resulting from slight bodily ailments, which eventually assume to the distempered and deluded imagination a grave significant character" (qtd. in Ladee 13).

5. This is something like the way migraine has always been migraine although it has appeared under different names (bilious headache, sick headache, among others) and has been experienced differently by migraineurs. That is, Hildegard

of Bingen's migraine in the twelfth century was likely painful in the same sort of way that my neighbor's migraine was painful last week. But Hildegard experienced her auras as divine visions, whereas he just saw jagged lines of light and threw up. They had different migraine experiences in part because they inhabit different universes of discourse. Hypochondria is, in part, like migraine a set of complaints under a changing name (the hypochondria of the eighteenth century may be the neurosis of today, as Fischer-Homberger suggests), but hypochondria is also an enduring name for a set of associated and reinterpreted ills. A summary of the "history of the concept" of hypochondria is offered by German E. Berrios.

6. Brian Fallon, with others, is the author of a 1996 study of a placebo-controlled trial of antidepressant pharmacotherapy for hypochondria. Murray W. Enns, Kevin Kjernisted, and Mark Lander note in 2001 that this is the only such study (193). Also in 2001, Fallon reviews various related studies ("Pharmacologic Strategies").

7. A key idea of speech-act theory is that certain pronouncements have social force only when made by people licensed to make them and in places *where* they are licensed to make them. So, "The defendant is guilty as charged" has legal force when pronounced by a judge in a courtroom but not when pronounced by a cashier—or by a judge in a supermarket. Similarly, the force of "This person has diabetes" varies depending on who says it and where it is said. (On speech act theory, see Austin.)

8. It is no exaggeration to say that certain patients are reviled by their physicians. According to James Groves, for example, "hateful patients" are of four types: "dependent clingers, entitled demanders, manipulative help-rejecters and self-destructive deniers" (883). Not all hateful patients are hypochondriacs, and, no doubt, not all hypochondriacs are hateful patients. For a more recent discussion of hypochondriacal patients as "difficult" patients, see Lipsitt.

9. The self-diagnosing patient annoyed physicians even in the eighteenth century. Adair complained of patients who instead of offering "a detail of their symptoms, by which [the physician] might judge of the nature of the disease," rather said, "*Doctor, I am bilious*" and "had generally been in the habit of taking medicine to carry off the *supposed* offensive bile" (Adair 8).

10. The relation of patient complaints to established diagnoses is taken up by several authors who while they do not use the term *rhetoric* themselves nonetheless make rhetorically interesting points about that relation. Robert Aronowitz says, "[I]t should be of no surprise that the suffering of people can be only imperfectly mapped to a set of objective disease ideal-types" ("When" 808). Aronowitz raises the idea of idiosyncrasy and suggests a *script* (based on idiosyncrasy) to the physician to persuade the patient out of undue worry.

11. We may note an analogy here with a certain rhetoric of George W. Bush. Bush declared war on Iraq in March 2003 in the absence of evidence that Saddam Hussein had weapons of mass destruction; Bush argued that there was no evidence that Saddam Hussein did not have them. Part of the persuasive problem

for the Iraqis was meeting the demand for evidence of absence; the United Nations but not the United States was willing to be persuaded by absence of evidence.

12. Ironically, a checklist exists also for hypochondria—the Whitely Index, including questions like "Do you worry a lot about your health?" and "Is it hard for you to believe your doctor when he or she tells you there is nothing for you to worry about?" See Lemonick.

13. There is a growing literature on the relation between diagnoses (especially, but not only, psychiatric diagnoses) and pharmaceuticals. See Barbara Mintzes, who asks, "At what point does an understandable response to distressing life events become an indication for drug treatment—and a market opportunity?" ("For and Against" 908). David Healy ("Good Science"), Carl Elliott (*Better Than Well*), Peter Kramer (*Listening*), Joseph Dumit ("When Explanations"), Brendan I. Koerner, and Jennifer Fishman have all written about the reciprocity of diagnosis and treatment.

14. "The classification 'quark' is indifferent in the sense that calling a quark a quark makes no difference to the quark" (Hacking, *Social* 105). Depression is an interactive kind because depressed persons are changed in some way—not so much individually as collectively—by being classified as depressed. Hacking says, "By interaction I do not mean only the self-conscious reaction of a single individual to how she is classified. I mean the consequences of being so classified for the whole class of individuals and other people with whom they are intimately connected" (*Social* 115).

15. The following is noteworthy in respect to the diagnostic life of "social anxiety disorder." Physician Edward Foote writes, in 1902, that a person "suffering from hypochondria may dread to meet other persons, especially strangers, sometimes even friends, and for short we say he has anthrophobia" (674).

16. There is some widespread niggling suspicion that psychological states for which antidepressants are the treatment are at least in part if not socially constructed, then socially controlled. A character in *The Corrections* by Jonathan Franzen complains about the consumer economy driving the medication of his girlfriend:

> [A] lack of desire to spend money becomes a symptom of a disease that requires expensive medication. Which medication then destroys the libido, in other words destroys the appetite for the one pleasure in life that's free, which means the person has to spend even *more* money on compensatory pleasures. (31)

Depression—somewhat treatable, somewhat regulated, somewhat horrible, somewhat negotiable—has drawn public attention to the rhetorical element in diagnosis. However, recently, in response to various claims that depression is overdiagnosed and, in some cases, as Elliott has argued, more properly thought of as alienation or sadness, Kramer has written a book to make the case that depression is a grave illness, to be taken absolutely seriously (*Against Depression*).

17. Other excellent sources on drug advertising in the eighteenth and nineteenth centuries are Francis C. Doherty; Adelaide Hechtlinger; and A. Walker Bingham.

18. See also Sjaak Van der Geest and Susan R. Whyte: "[P]harmaceuticals predicate a graspable world of healing for the sufferer, giving the imagined 'itness' of the disease the countering 'itness' of the medicine and vice versa" (345).

19. Kramer (*Listening*) documents the idea that Prozac can leave its users feeling "better than well," but innumerable concoctions have been sold on the idea that everyone, really, suffers from some condition or other that a tonic with a wide enough reach can address. This nineteenth-century advertisement misses hardly anyone and suggests that even those who feel well can feel better:

> Do you have pains about the chest and sides, and sometimes in the back? Do you feel dull and sleepy? Does your mouth have a bad taste, especially in the morning? Is there a sort of sticky slime collects about the teeth? Is your appetite poor? Is there a feeling like a heavy load on the stomach, sometimes a faint, all-gone sensation at the pit of the stomach, which food does not satisfy? . . . Are your eyes sunken? . . . Do you feel tired all the while? Are you nervous, irritable and gloomy? Do you have evil forebodings? Is there a giddiness, a sort of whirling sensation in the head when rising up suddenly? . . . If you suffer from any of these symptoms, send me your name and I will send you, by mail, One Bottle of Medicine FREE. (reproduced in Hechtlinger 121)

20. Direct-to-consumer pharmaceutical advertising is legal in the United States and New Zealand and illegal in all other industrialized countries, including, at this moment, Canada (although existing restrictive legislation is under review). Canadians, however, are able to buy, on-line, drugs including human growth hormone, steroids, narcotic painkillers, sleeping pills, antidepressants, antibiotics, weight-loss pills, and cancer treatments. For a discussion of the pharmaceutical marketplace and the practices of consumers, see Barbara Mintzes et al. ("Influence") and André Picard ("Bypassing").

21. On consumerism itself as a disorder—and its relation to hypochondria, see Roy Porter:

> Frankenstein-like, the consumer society was giving birth to a new personality type: man the consumer, pained by deprivation and craving commodities. He thus grew addicted to "consumption"; it was his disease. Sickness, and the response to it through medicines in commodity form, was integral to this process. Quackery was the capitalist mode of production in its medical face. (*Health for Sale* 41)

22. Canada Diagnostic Centre's advertisement promises a full body scan that "is non-invasive, involves no intravenous injections and takes less than 20 minutes." The advertising of "a private imaging service provider" (as the centre describes itself on its Web site) is unusual in Canada, where health care is except by special provincial legislation publicly funded. ScanQuest advertises offices in

Washington state, offering special incentives to Canadians to compensate for travel expenses and unfavorable exchange rates. (Early in 2005, the *New York Times* reported that independent scanning operations were meeting with less commercial success than they had expected, and many were closing down. Apparently, fewer people than anticipated are enticed by the promise of test results outside the context of professional medical care; see Kolata, "Rapid.")

23. Haiken quotes psychologist Alfred Adler: "As we live in a group and are judged by the group, and as this group objects to any departure from normal appearance, . . . a facial deformity can have a very deleterious effect on behavior" (116).

24. In a letter to the editor of the *Globe and Mail*, G. Wilson writes that the "extreme makeover" of one contestant "took an interesting and attractive woman's face and turned it into the face of a wax-museum hooker." *Extreme Makeover* may be viewed as the twenty-first-century version of the 1924 *New York Daily Mirror* "Homely Girl Contest," in which, as Haiken reports, one young woman from New York won the opportunity to go under the knife of a "plastic surgeon [who] has offered to take the homeliest girl in the biggest city in the country and to make a beauty of her" (98).

25. This, from Darwin, appears in Ralph Colp Jr.: "I know well that my head would have failed years ago had not my stomach saved me from a minute's overwork" (70).

26. An account of the uses of Samuel Taylor Coleridge's hypochondria is in George Sebastian Rousseau and David Boyd Haycock.

27. Many of the worried well in Canada in 2003 feared they had SARS (severe acute respiratory syndrome). Here in evidence were fear of the marketplace and fear of contamination by public intercourse: anxieties of circulation. The surgical mask became a local icon—and because so many of the masks people wore during the SARS crisis were known to be ineffective against the virus in question, their status was *essentially* iconic.

28. In a dramatistic view, Burke says, we "consider the matter of motives in a perspective that, being developed from the analysis of drama, treats language and thought primarily as modes of action" (xxii). Burke's five questions for dramatistic analysis are these: "what was done (act), when or where it was done (scene), who did it (agent), how he did it (agency), and why (purpose)" (*Grammar* xv).

5. A Rhetoric of Death and Dying

1. Campbell's rhetorical theory is informed by faculty psychology, in which the mind has aspects differently acted upon by speakers. Campbell's idea, which assigns a procedure to the Ciceronian notion that the three aims of rhetoric are to delight, instruct, and move, has had a great deal of influence in rhetorical theory.

2. This chapter combines and revises two previously published essays: "Contesting Death, Speaking of Dying" and "What Is a Rhetoric of Death?: End-of-Life Decision-Making at a Psychiatric Hospital." The case study reported in

"Contesting Death" refers to events that took place in 1996. *Kairos* again is worth bearing in mind, for things change slowly in the medical establishment, but they do change. A hospice view of death—the preference for palliative care over life-sustaining care against all hope and comfort—has, in the meantime, become more widespread. The study described in "What Is a Rhetoric of Death?" is one sign of the willingness of some medical professionals to take the notions of advance directives and quality of death very seriously. Still, whenever I have given presentations on the topic of end-of-life decision making, and I have done so recently, audience members are forthcoming with personal stories that speak to the persistence of a biomedical rhetoric very much like the one described in my case-study report.

3. My claim about rhetorical disjunction is consistent with but not exactly same as the claims of Elliot Mishler and Robert L. Rubenstein. Mishler contrasts the "voice of biomedicine" and the "voice of the lifeworld": "[T]he physician's effort to impose a technocratic consciousness, to dominate the voice of the lifeworld by the voice of medicine, seriously impairs and distorts essential requirements for mutual dialogue and human interaction" (*Discourse* 126). Rubenstein is concerned specifically with discourses surrounding death, particularly with "the unmediated polarities of, on the one hand, life history, biography, or the person's interpretation of her own subjectivity . . . and, on the other, the 'external' realm of biomedicine" (262).

4. Schimmel's act is reviewed by Tod Hoffman.

5. This is a "Fisher" cartoon from 1997:

FIRST CHARACTER: What's that?
SECOND CHARACTER: It's a package from a funeral-planning company.
FIRST: No kidding!
SECOND: To encourage saving up for one's funeral they include a little piggy-bank.
FIRST: A piggy-bank?
SECOND: Well, not exactly.
FIRST: That's so cute.
SECOND: Want to start me off with a quarter? (*raising a small bank engraved* "RIP")

6. Gwyn and Elwyn's own case study is of a father of an ill child in conversation with a physician about the prescription of antibiotics for what the doctor believes actually to be a viral infection (antibiotics being useless in that case). Gwyn and Elwyn say that the decision about whether to administer antibiotics to this patient is not properly a shared one; rather, the physician solicits the preferences of the patient or family member but then engineers the making of the "right" decision. My chapter 7, on patient compliance, takes up questions of this type of decision making as well. A significant difference between the compliance problem and the end-of-life decision-making problem, however, is that medical

expertise may be the most important expertise for a decision on how to treat an infection but not the most important for a decision on how best to conduct an inevitable death.

7. I would not presume to call my method auto-ethnography; that would make it sound more social-scientific than it was. However, in the course of learning about auto-ethnography as a methodology, particularly from Susan Greenhalgh's work, I have come to understand in retrospect something about what I did when I paid attention to my own experience so carefully as a kind of participant-observer in the events of my own life. Greenhalgh says, helpfully, too, "Auto-ethnography differs from autobiography in that the focus is not on the writer, but on certain experiences in the writer's life that illuminate important or previously hidden aspects of the larger culture" (51).

8. Pain relief can be a euphemism for euthanasia. I understand now that I was wrong ever to ask my mother's caregivers questions that amounted to requests to kill her. Doctors, as I better understand now, remain bound by the received Hippocratic dictum "Do no harm" even if their resolve is anachronistic, coming, as it does, from a time when it simply was not possible to keep people alive artificially so that they might die naturally. (From the Oath: "I will use treatment to help the sick according to my ability and judgment, but never with a view to injury and wrong-doing. Neither will I administer a poison to anybody when asked to do so, nor will I suggest such a course" [14]). Doctors do not kill their patients, but they do relieve their patients' suffering. I might have asked my mother's doctors earlier to attend to her suffering and not have offended them by suggesting that they end her life. (For his comments on the humanity of physicians, I am indebted to Sholom Glouberman, who was at the time of our conversation director of the Health Network, Canadian Policy Research Networks.) The problem of the morphine treatment is also a concern of Michael J. Hyde in his essay on euthanasia.

9. The very idea of intervention encourages the illusion that by controlling the circumstances of death, one is somehow controlling death itself. It can be hard to remember that the question of *how* we will die is not a question of *if* we will— a difference that can be lost in comparisons of the death-control debate and the abortion-control debate (B. J. Logue, for example, compares them). In the latter, the issue actually is *whether* someone will be born.

10. Sociologist Sue Fisher reports on a similar ambivalence of experience when as a gynecology patient, she wants to insist on what she knows as a sociologist but can not quite be transformed from patienthood by that knowledge (see Fisher's introduction).

11. It is interesting to consider the effects on a contemporary death of its feminization—that, for example, the space of medicalized death is largely a feminine space. Women die older by about seven years than men. Their greater age means that women experience more illness, especially more chronic illness, than men. After age 65, women are three times more likely than men to reside in nursing

homes and to die there; one in four women, compared with one in seven men, ends life in such an institution (see Logue). It is partly because women are less likely to die swiftly and relatively young than slowly and relatively old that medical death is the death of women, and the politics of protracted, medicalized death is a feminine politics. Certainly, the nursing home, where, for the most part, women look after women—and most treatment decisions are made by men—is difficult to describe without some kind of recourse to a theory of gender. Still, the question is not how would my mother have died if she had been my father. If the new death is feminized, it is death for everyone in the grip of the metaphor *the patient is a woman.* So, for example, one feature of being a woman can be not to be taken seriously. That turns out also to be one feature of being old and sick.

12. The introduction to the SUPPORT study includes this description of typical care:

> Previous studies [on care of the seriously ill] indicate . . . that communication is often absent or occurs only during a crisis. Physicians today often perceive death as failure, they tend to be too pessimistic regarding prognoses, and they provide more extensive treatment to seriously ill patients than they would choose for themselves. (1592)

13. Notwithstanding the very human notion of advance directives elaborated later in this chapter, AD documents can also be treated just as more data. That is, advance directives are not in themselves the solution to rhetorical problems raised in this essay. Here, for example, is an illustration of the biomedical-institutional discourse in which the question of patient choice is often framed:

> The data suggest that nursing home patients are willing and eager to express advance directive preferences. Their capacity to render valid decisions was assessed by interview-based observer ratings and standardized measures with high intermethod agreement. The majority of patients prefer to forego life-sustaining measures, although patients with compromised decision making may be more likely to request aggressive therapeutic intervention. (E. Diamond et al. 625)

14. The problem of the patient not being taken seriously is part of a larger problem in the care of older adults. Patients are treated best when they surrender their autonomy without complaint and when they do not question judgments of their own incompetence to evaluate issues of their care. "Good" patients may be adopted by their caregivers, but when they are, they are adopted, often, not as adults but as children. This accounts, to some extent, for the phenomenon of institutional babytalk: "Are you going to be a good girl and take your medicine, Mrs. Smith?" (On the infantilization of older patients, especially women, see Patricia A. Sharpe.) In this context, it is not surprising that my mother's stated wish to die was taken, primarily, as something to get over.

15. The project's lead investigator was Maurice Bloch, then staff psychologist at Riverview Hospital.

16. The team as a whole was extremely conscientious about matters of clarity and, especially, clarity of terminology in the interviews. The social worker, for example, regularly made a point of welcoming questions of clarification. This is a sample quotation from the first transcript:

> So I want to make sure that you're always comfortable with the words that we're using, too. If any time you hear us say something that doesn't sound familiar, . . . please tell us. Because we tend to talk in hospital language, sometimes not in real world language. Common language. And please ask questions, anything you need to know. (3)

17. Transcriptions were done by my research assistant Nora Lusterio. The transcription method is based on that of G. H. Morris and Ronald Chenail, with minor modifications. There was no need, for example, for our purposes, to indicate length of pauses or other fine features of conversation, such as changes in intonation. Note also that in rendering transcriptions here, I have omitted habitual marks of hesitation (e.g., "um"), including only those hesitations or pauses that are needed for clarity because they signal a grammatical shift.

18. See Segal, Paré, Brent, and Vipond on the role of the outsider-researcher. It is especially important, for example, for a rhetorician not to be seen as (or, actually, to be) the annoying academic who presumes to be a critic of other people's professional practice.

19. Because the AD interview as videotaped comes after a meeting of family members with the team psychologist, medical information does not occupy the initial position in the process as a whole.

20. On the matter of using medical terms in physician-patient interviews, Gwyn and Elwyn say, "A paradox of using clinical terms with patients is that doctors are, on the one hand, including the patient within their professional discourse and, on the other, possibly excluding them" (445).

6. Values, Metaphors, and Health Policy

1. This chapter extends and elaborates an argument I made first in "Public Discourse and Public Policy: Some Ways that Metaphor Constrains Health (Care)."

2. Edward Shorter uses the phrase "longing for organicity" in the context of talking about the social stigma of psychiatric diagnoses, which may leave patients wishing for organic ones ("Borderland" 233). Of course, some psychiatric diagnoses are, at the same time, diagnoses of an organic disorder.

3. Writing about the overreliance of physicians on medical technology, Neil Postman blames patient demand for some overuse. He quotes a physician informant as saying, "Everyone who has a headache wants and expects a CAT scan" (101).

4. The specialists in question are Barron Lerner, Barry Kramer, and Don Berry, all of whom are featured in the documentary program "The Myth of Early Detection." Kramer, by the way, uses animal metaphors to describe the behaviors of different sorts of cancers. Fast-growing, metastasizing cancers, he says,

are birds; slow-growing, nonmetastasizing cancers are turtles; between birds and turtles are bears.

5. For example, Susan Sontag writes that metaphors of cancer overinvest the disease with meaning; Joan Boyle and James Morriss argue that the machine metaphor of the seventeenth century helped to produce a system of "disease cure" masquerading as "health care" (273); Emily Martin uses metaphor to anchor an anthropology of reproduction; Howard F. Stein writes about medical metaphors as metaphors of American culture, specifying metaphors of war, sports, and technology; Esther H. Condon writes about "caring" as a metaphor in nursing practice; Marlaine C. Smith rejects the "human being as machine" metaphor in favor of "the human being as organism" (48); Susan Bordo writes that the body is "mediated by language: by metaphors . . . and semantic grids" (288); Donna Haraway notes the "power of biomedical language . . . shaping the unequal experience of sickness and death for millions" (204).

6. See also Scott L. Montgomery, writing about metaphor and biomedical discourse:

> Over time, repetition and standardized usage gradually obscures the original figurative character of an image or term. By being endlessly repeated within a restricted context of meaning, such a term soon sinks into the institutional given of a particular discipline, becoming an element of its jargon. As such, it ceases to operate, and is no longer seen, as a figure of speech. (135)

7. Martin's "The Egg and the Sperm" makes succinctly an argument about metaphor that is elaborated in *The Woman in the Body*. See also *Flexible Bodies*. Barbara Tomlinson calls Martin's critical strategy "intensification:" "Strategies of intensification 'hijack' the language of texts under scrutiny in order to 'distil' or 'foreground' it, thereby demonstrating with vigor and emphasis the problems of underlying patterns of thinking" (9). Intensification is a strategy for exposing and dislodging discursive elements.

8. The project of waking up sleeping metaphors is paralleled for other structures of thought in Geoffrey C. Bowker and Susan Leigh Star's project of waking up sleeping classifications. Like metaphors do, standards and classifications organize our thinking in ways that are, in the usual course of events, invisible to us. "We have a moral and ethical agenda in our querying of these [classification] systems," Bowker and Star say. "Each standard and each category valorizes some point of view and silences another. This is not inherently a bad thing—indeed it is inescapable. But it *is* an ethical choice, and as such it is dangerous—not bad, but dangerous" (5).

Here is a conversation overheard taking place in the back seat of my car between Gabe (ten years old) and Raphael (eleven). The topic was the listing of kids for taking shots at hoops that day at basketball camp. Gabe says it isn't fair to use alphabetical order. But Raphael argues that it doesn't really matter; the names are going to be organized somehow. That is, some kid is going to be last—

and it doesn't matter if it's Daniel Zaitzow or not. This point is much like the one Bowker and Star make when they say classification is inescapable.

9. A discussion of health and metaphor would be incomplete without further acknowledgment of the contribution of Susan Sontag. With the publication of *Illness as Metaphor* and, later, AIDS *and Its Metaphors*, Sontag elaborates the relation of metaphor and illness. Making her case with reference to illness metaphors historically (citing, for example, tuberculosis and leprosy), she argues, "Nothing is more punitive than to give a disease a meaning—that meaning being invariably a moralistic one" (58). According to Sontag, the person with cancer, for example, is doubly afflicted—with the disease and with metaphors of the disease. Metaphorizations of cancer "manage to put the onus of the disease on the patient and not only weaken the patient's ability to understand the range of possible medical treatment but also, implicitly, direct the patient away from such treatment" (47).

Sontag is misread when she is taken simply to be "against metaphor." Her writing, as some of her critics have noted, is awash in metaphor itself; indeed, she begins *Illness as Metaphor* with "Illness is the night-side of life, a more onerous citizenship. Everyone who is born holds dual citizenship, in the kingdom of the well and in the kingdom of the sick" (3). Sontag is not urging us to abandon metaphor—how could we possibly?—but to pay attention to it and sometimes to reject it: to be able to "regard cancer as if it were just a disease—a very serious one, but just a disease. Not a curse, not a punishment, not an embarrassment. Without 'meaning'" (AIDS 102).

10. The biomedical model is perpetuated not by the action of independent biomedical metaphors but by a complex of forces—including a range of material ones, from the pharmaceutical lobby to conditions of practitioner licensing and the management of health maintenance organizations—in which certain metaphors operate. The relation of metaphor and model is complex and reciprocal. So, I dissociate my account from accounts such as this one from the Government of Canada's 1994 publication on the Status of Disabled Persons, which is too simple: "Attitudes and language reinforce each other. Negative attitudes toward disabled persons and patronizing terminology go hand-in-hand. Both must be changed, but the language must come first because words are easier to change than ideas" (204).

11. To compile this list, I relied on Arnold J. Heidenheimer, Hugh Heclo, and Carolyn Teich Adams and lurked for several months on the electronic discussion list HEALTHRE on health-care reform.

12. For further discussion of mechanical metaphors, see Scheper-Hughes and Lock.

13. One way of tracking the sway of body metaphors would be to examine diagrams of pathophysiological processes over time and note which diagrams betray a mechanistic imagination and which a cybernetic one.

14. On cyborgs, see Haraway. On prosthesis, see Wills.

15. On the war metaphor, see also Warren; Haraway; Montgomery; and Couser.

16. That medicine is a form of war is suggested also by procedures of medical training. Warren points out parallels between initiation into the medical profession and initiation into the military:

> The way of life of physicians-in-training prepares them for a life of fighting the enemy of disease, even as novice soldiers are prepared . . . for fighting a war. In both cases, status differentiation by rank is clearly maintained, and technical proficiency is stressed. There is little time for sleep, let alone time for reflection upon personal values and goals. (43)

17. The "market metaphor" for health care is also the topic of an essay by Ruth Malone, who writes that "the metaphor has been taken up readily, perhaps due to its compatibility with the economism of much health services research methodology, such as cost-benefit and cost-effectiveness studies" (18). Malone is interested in the moral element of the market metaphor and what it suggests for health policy.

18. See also Malone, who notes that a product-market conception of health policy and health care also

> helps to keep the experience of suffering safely at bay for us. . . . Health insurers speak of "adverse mortality rates" when too many of their patients die. People who are poor and sick . . . are called "medically indigent" or "the uninsured," terms that suggest deficiency in their capacity as consumers, rather than deficiencies in the system of health care. (19)

19. Genes are metaphors for persons; there are also *metametaphors* to consider: metaphors *of* the gene as metaphor, each with different implications when mobilized in public discourse. Celeste M. Condit and Deirdre M. Condit write about the difference in meaning of the blueprint metaphor (a variant of the coding metaphor) and the recipe metaphor for genes. See also Condit, *The Meanings of the Gene*.

20. One-gene, one-disease thinking has implications for individual decision making as well: If you know you lack the gene for lung cancer, you may be more inclined to smoke. If you know you carry the gene for depression, you may consider yourself a good candidate for antidepressants. See Peter Conrad ("Mirage") on OGOD (one-gene, one-disease) thinking and on the replication in gene theory of the germ-theory myth of specific etiology. See also Nelkin and Lindee.

21. Celeste Condit explains the rhetoric of the shift to a genetic world view:

> Each move a text makes establishes a position that disposes the audience toward the next move. Thus to understand the ways in which writers construct new models or worldviews, one must examine, in order, the progressive series of positions an author takes in a text that seeks to move an audience by stages from one ideological "place" to another. ("Women's" 126–27)

22. Conrad compares gene theory to germ theory as the latter was described by René Dubos in 1959. Dubos, writes Conrad, identified three interrelated assumptions underlying germ thinking: "the doctrine of specific aetiology; a focus on the internal rather than the external environment; and the metaphor of the body as a machine" (Conrad 230). The new genetics, Conrad says, has a parallel mythology.

23. For a discussion of caregiving and eldercare, see Dorazio-Migliore.

24. The Nexium advertisement appears in *Newsweek* magazine. In contrast, a Nexium advertisement directed at physicians and appearing in *Doctor's Review* does not mention "acid reflux disease" but talks about "heartburn" and "acid suppression."

25. I have searched popular magazines for similar messages not specifically aimed at product advertising. Examples are everywhere—perhaps most commonly these days in checklists for various disorders. A recent issue of *Cosmopolitan* contains an article called, "5 Aches You Should Never Ignore." Its sections begin as follows: "Your stomach has gone schizo. *You may have* Irritable Bowel Syndrome"; "You have very painful periods. *You may have* Endometriosis." "Your jaw gets achy for no apparent reason. *You may have* Temporomandibular Joint Disease" (Grumman, 194, 196; emphasis in original).

7. The Problem of Patient "Noncompliance":
Paternalism, Expertise, and the *Ethos* of the Physician

1. These numbers can be expected to be much higher now, especially as millions of prescriptions are written each year for new-generation antidepressants—selective serotonin reuptake inhibitors like Prozac, Paxil, and Zoloft. Depression itself is a risk factor for noncompliance in general, including noncompliance with treatment for depression (see DiMatteo, Lepper, and Croghan).

2. Haynes lists two hundred compliance variables in 1976. In 1987, Meichenbaum and Turk list fifty-two, including "relationship variables." In 2001, Vermeire et al. report, "More than 200 variables have been studied since 1975, but none of them can be considered as consistently predicting compliance" (332).

3. Augustine made the distinction between conviction and persuasion based on Cicero's three aims for rhetoric: to delight, to instruct, and to move. Conviction comes from instruction, but the audience is not persuaded until it is moved. George Campbell, in the eighteenth century, had recourse to faculty psychology to explain the difference. Conviction pertains to the understanding; persuasion pertains to the action of the understanding on the will. Chaim Perelman and Lucie Olbrechts-Tyteca take up the distinction in the twentieth century, also with the view that persuasion is an intensification of conviction leading to action.

4. At least two recent publications recognize the possibilities of identification as a strategy for improving compliance. The British Pharmaceutical Society authors of *From Compliance to Concordance* (Marinker) begin their report by citing their own experiences as noncomplying patients. Edward Morse, Patricia M.

Simon, and Paul M. Balson educate health-care practitioners about the difficulties of medication compliance in HIV-AIDS patients by having the practitioners follow their patients' pill-taking schedules, using placebos, for seven days.

5. Charles Anderson writes about vertical and horizontal relationships of physicians and patients.

6. Roberson refers here to a 1974 essay by G. V. Stimson, much cited in the critical literature on compliance.

7. Marinker's name comes up in an acknowledgment in an article by Silvia N. Bonaccorso and Jeffrey L. Sturchio on the virtues of direct-to-consumer advertising for prescription pharmaceuticals.

8. Fiona Stevenson et al. and other authors distinguish between intentional and unintentional nonadherence—and, in fact, it does not make sense to talk about a concordance model for unintentional nonadherence. Unintentional nonadherence is not, however, for that reason, outside the realm of interest for research on doctor-patient interviews: for example, patients may unintentionally not adhere because they have misunderstood physicians' or nurses' instructions. See also Fiona R. Ross on misplaced culpability for noncompliance.

9. The figure of the "careless consumptive" reappeared in the public imagination when, in Toronto in March and April 2003, surveillance and control efforts were stepped up to ensure that persons who had been exposed to SARS (severe acute respiratory syndrome) were conscientiously subjecting themselves to voluntary quarantine—the voluntariness of which was sometimes questionable. Meanwhile, the Canadian newspaper the *Globe and Mail* reported that in parts of China, the penalty for violating quarantine during the SARS crisis might be death (see York).

10. See Picard, who notes that in 2002, approximately 240,000 Canadians per month were buying prescription drugs online ("Bypassing").

11. The Marinker report actually violates its own main principle. The authors do hold that physicians have superior knowledge; "concordance" is best understood as a strategy for getting patients to take their advice. The document, in other words, betrays concordance as the new compliance. The authors explain, for example, that patients have various personal or cultural beliefs that cause them to resist the good evidence-based knowledge of their physicians, so physicians should not simply reassert their knowledge in the face of that resistance: "For the prescriber simply to reaffirm the views of medical science, and to dismiss or ignore these beliefs, is to fail to prescribe effectively" (7–8). Marinker and his colleagues do not, finally, so much suggest an ideologically new model for physician-patient interaction as they offer an overtly rhetorical plan for making the old model work. Their advice, they admit, is aimed at more effective patient *persuasion* (36–37). In a critique of concordance, Iona Heath argues that the model "clings to the conviction that there is, after all, a single objective account of reality and that this account is provided by medical science" (857).

12. See also Silverman who notes that the principle of disclosure is itself asymmetrical. With reference to their own case study, Richard Gwyn and Glyn Elwyn say that a physician could "by introducing new terminology, initiating the turn-taking sequences and controlling the topic choice, . . . effectively sabotag[e] the chances of a genuinely negotiated shared decision from the outset" (446).

13. On this "genrelizing" move, see also my "Problems of Generalization/Genrelization."

14. Parsons himself is associated by several commentators with a paternalist model of physician-patient relationship. See Charles, Gafni, and Whelan.

15. Inevitably, a concordance-equality-consumerist model of health care creates its own backlash. In a letter to the *British Medical Journal,* two physicians describe "at least three situations when treating the patient as a decision-maker . . . will fail." They ask, for example, "[I]n the case of an infectious and potentially lethal disease such as tuberculosis, can we as doctors ethically allow a patient the freedom of deciding which if any of the antibiotics he or she will take and how much?" (Milburn and Cochrane 1906).

16. E. P. Hamm and Alan W. Richardson note that measurement, "so frequently understood as the hallmark of disinterested knowledge," itself expresses human values and social choices (607). Measurement research in compliance takes for granted the quality of information being shared, the worth of medications being prescribed, and the advisability of following doctors' advice.

17. The question itself does not assume that all medical advice is, actually, good—and does not diminish the importance of what some patients know about their own illnesses. The problem of how to tell good advice from bad advice *in the particular case* is beyond the scope of this chapter.

18. J. Blake Scott contributes to this discussion of the rhetoric of HIV-AIDS. See also Richard M. Perloff on strategies for persuading people to have safer sex.

19. See Stevenson et al. on the role of experience, one's own and someone else's, in decision making.

20. Gwyn and Elwyn note that patients tend to reduce complex choices to dualistic ones.

21. On these topics, see Howard; Howe; and Mark; as well as "Was the Winnipeg Doctor Right" and "Wrong Smoke Signal."

22. The *Globe and Mail* noted that some women had managed to resist the idea that hormones were "a panacea against . . . the effects of declining estrogen levels of their heart, bones, memory, figure and sexual satisfaction" (K. Foss). The *New York Times* said the tide was turning from hormone replacement therapy as a "way for women to remain forever young" (Kolata, "Study").

Conclusion: The Usefulness of a Rhetoric of Medicine

1. For the idea of Club Dead, I am indebted to McGill University genre theorist Anthony Paré in conversation.

2. Rhetorical theory also suggests one answer to this question—on the idea of the presumption of a liaison between people and their actions (see Perelman and Olbrechts-Tyteca). If research is important, then the researcher is important, too.

3. When physician F. E. Kenyon suggested in 1976 that some hypochondriacs were only *ugly*, he was trying to make the case that body repairs can be made to faulty minds (X is hypochondriacal because she is miserable; she is miserable because she has an ugly nose). Does the argument hold for breast enhancement (Y is depressed because her breasts are small)?

4. While epidemiological studies make it clear that, in general, it is healthier not to be poor, it is also true that, out of many conditions, the wealthiest of us can not buy ourselves well.

5. In the discussion here and in other chapters about the commercial medicalization of moods, we might note the following from Arthur Kleinman on the biomedical transformation of them: "[A]n aspect of the ideological influence [of biomedicine] is the euphemization of suffering, which becomes medicalized as a psychiatric condition, thereby transforming an inherently moral category into a technical one" (36).

6. Moreover, many health researchers, including many excellent and irreproachable ones, are funded in their research by pharmaceutical companies.

7. Public reporting around the Toronto SARS outbreaks is suggestive for problems of trust and expertise more generally. For example, while some experts were announcing to the public that the coronavirus had been isolated as the cause of SARS, others were saying that evidence of the coronavirus was only to be found in 40 percent of positive cases. While some experts were saying drastic measures were needed to contain the spread of the disease, others had pronounced the outbreak over. The problem was not that experts disagreed, but that, sometimes, experts seemed not to be expert at all. Could people in the know agree on the diagnostic criteria for SARS? Did it make sense to count "suspect" cases along with "probable" ones in public reporting? Was the cumulative count of cases a more accurate reflection of spread than a comparative count of new cases? Risk management is one thing; uncertainty management, another.

8. I said in chapter 6 that we should not confuse the question of how we die with the question of if we die (mentioning the analogy of the right-to-die question and the right-to-abortion question, only the latter being a question of *if* life). The distinction of *how* and *if* is important also in decision making for treatments such as HRT. Given that we are all going to die, any one of us might think that dying quickly of a heart attack at sixty-eight is preferable to dying slowly of cancer at seventy, the risk of heart attack then being something to weigh.

9. As I have mentioned, Gwyn and Elwyn analyze the transcripts of an interview between a physician and the father of a child-patient, where the physician, having diagnosed a viral infection, does not wish to prescribe antibiotics, and the father, relying on previous experience with a sick child, wants antibiotics

prescribed. Gwyn and Elwyn are interested in the extent to which the "shared decision [is] not (quite) a shared decision." But I am interested in the difference between the patient/family "decision maker" as *informed* and the patient/family "decision maker" as *knowledgeable*. The father in Gwyn and Elwyn's case can be given a great deal of information, but he can not be made to think with knowledge of medicine like a physician.

Works Cited

Abrams, M. H. *The Mirror and the Lamp*. London: Oxford UP, 1953.

Adair, James M. *Essays on Fashionable Diseases. The Dangerous Effects of Hot and Crouded Rooms. The Clothing of Invalids. Lady and Gentlemen Doctors. And on Quacks and Quackery . . . With a Dedication to Philip Thicknesse . . . to Which Is Added, a Dramatic Dialogue*. London: Bateman, 1790.

Allemang, John, Miro Certenig, and Shawna Richer. "Club Medical." *Globe and Mail* 3 Aug. 2002: F1+.

Allison, David B., and Mark S. Roberts. *Disordered Mother or Disordered Diagnosis: Munchausen by Proxy Syndrome*. Hillsdale, NJ: Analytic, 1998.

Althusser, Louis. *Lenin and Philosophy and Other Essays*. Trans. Ben Brewster. New York: Monthly, 1971.

Alvarez, Walter. *How to Live with Your Migraine (Sick) Headaches*. Chicago: Wilcox, 1952.

———. *The Neuroses: Diagnosis and Management of Functional Disorders and Minor Psychoses*. Philadelphia: Saunders, 1951.

Amanda. *Amanda Smith!* 5 June 2002 <http://www.appstate.edu/~as42281/>.

American Council for Headache Education. "Headache Prevention: Finding What Works for You." Pamphlet. Mount Royal, NJ. 1999.

American Psychiatric Association. *Diagnostic and Statistical Manual of Mental Disorders*. 4th ed. Washington, DC: Amer. Psychiatric Assoc., 1994.

Ana by Choice. 5 June 2002 <http://www.ana-by-choice.com>.

Ana's Underground Grotto. 5 June 2002 <http://plagueangel.com/grotto/>.

Anasway. "Diary. January 2002." Online posting. 5 July 2002 <http://www.ana-by-choice.com/January%202002.htm>.

Anderson, Charles M. *Richard Selzer and the Rhetoric of Surgery*. Carbondale: Southern Illinois UP, 1989.

Anderssen, Erin. "Graveside Manners." *Globe and Mail* 30 Nov. 2002: F3.

Andrews, James R. *The Practice of Rhetorical Criticism*. 2nd ed. White Plains, NY: Longman, 1990.

Annas, George J. "Reframing the Debate on Health Care Reform by Replacing Our Metaphors." *New England Journal of Medicine* 333 (1995): 744–47.

Aristotle. *The Rhetoric of Aristotle*. Trans. Lane Cooper. Englewood Cliffs, NJ: Prentice, 1960.

Aronowitz, Robert A. *Making Sense of Illness: Science, Society, and Disease*. Cambridge: Cambridge UP, 1998.

———. "When Do Symptoms Become a Disease?" *Annals of Internal Medicine* 134 (2001): 803–8.

Asmundson, Gordon J. G., Steven Taylor, and Brian J. Cox. *Health Anxiety: Clinical and Research Perspectives on Hypochondriasis and Related Conditions*. Chichester, Eng.: Wiley, 2001.

Atkinson, Paul. "Discourse, Descriptions, and Diagnosis: Reproducing Normal Medicine." *Biomedicine Examined.* Ed. Margaret Lock and Deborah R. Gordon. Dordrecht: Kluwer, 1988. 57–93.

Auerbach, Siegmund. *Headache, Its Varieties, Their Nature, Recognition and Treatment. A Theoretical and Practical Treatise for Students and Practitioners.* Trans. Ernest Playfair. London: Hodder, 1913.

Austen, Jane. *Emma.* London: Oxford UP, 1971.

Austin, J. L. *How to Do Things with Words.* Cambridge: Harvard UP, 1962.

Bacon, Francis. *The Advancement of Learning.* Series ed. Stephen Jay Gould. New York: Modern Lib., 2001.

Barofsky, I. "Compliance, Adherence, and the Therapeutic Alliance: Steps in the Development of Self-Care." *Social Science and Medicine* 12 (1978): 369–76.

Barsky, A. G., and G. L. Klerman. "Hypochondriasis." *Harvard Medical School Mental Health Letter* 2 (1985): 4.

Bauby, Jean-Dominique. *The Diving Bell and the Butterfly.* Trans. Jeremy Leggatt. New York: Knopf, 1997.

Baur, Susan. *Hypochondria: Woeful Imaginings.* Berkeley: U of California P, 1988.

Bayley, John. *Iris: A Memoir of Iris Murdoch.* London: Duckworth, 1998.

Bazerman, Charles. *Shaping Written Knowledge: The Genre and Activity of the Experimental Article in Science.* Madison: U of Wisconsin P, 1988.

Benson, Herbert. Foreword. *Encounters with Qi: Exploring Chinese Medicine.* Ed. David Eisenberg and Thomas Lee Wright. New York: Norton, 1985.

Benson, Thomas W. Introduction. T. Benson xi–xxii.

———, ed. *Landmark Essays on Rhetorical Criticism.* Davis, CA: Hermagoras, 1993.

Berrios, German E. "Hypochondriasis: History of the Concept." *Hypochondriasis: Modern Perspectives on an Ancient Malady.* Ed. Vladan Starvevic and Don R. Lipsitt. Oxford: Oxford UP, 2001. 3–20.

Binder, S. "Tobacco Report Offensive, Lobbyist Says." *Vancouver Sun* 5 Sep. 1994: A5.

Bingham, A. Walker. *The Snake-Oil Syndrome: Patent Medicine Advertising.* Hanover, MA: Christopher, 1994.

Bitzer, Lloyd, and Edwin Black, eds. *The Prospect of Rhetoric: Report of the National Development Project.* Englewood Cliffs, NJ: Prentice-Hall, 1971.

Bizzell, Patricia, and Bruce Herzberg. *The Rhetorical Tradition.* Boston: Bedford, 1990.

Black, Edwin. *Rhetorical Questions: Studies of Public Discourse.* Chicago: U of Chicago P, 1992.

Bonaccorso, Silvia N., and Jeffrey L. Sturchio. "For and Against: Direct to Consumer Advertising Is Medicalising Normal Human Experience: Against." *British Medical Journal* 324 (13 Apr. 2002): 910–11.

Booth, Wayne C. *Modern Dogma and the Rhetoric of Assent*. Notre Dame, IN: Notre Dame UP, 1974.

Bordo, Susan. *Unbearable Weight: Feminism, Western Culture, and the Body*. Berkeley: U of California P, 1993.

Boswell, James. *The Hypochondriack. Being the Seventy Essays by the Celebrated Biographer, Appearing in the London Magazine, from November, 1777, to August, 1783, and Here First Reprinted*. Ed. Margaret Bailey. Stanford: Stanford UP, 1928.

Bowen, Deborah J., Almut Helmes, and Erika Lease. "Predicting Compliance." *Compliance in Healthcare and Research*. Ed. Lora E. Burke and Ira S. Ockene. Armonk, NY: Futura, 2001. 25–41.

Bowker, Geoffrey C., and Susan Leigh Star. *Sorting Things Out: Classification and Its Consequences*. Cambridge, MA: MIT, 1999.

Boyle, Joan, and James Morriss. "The Crisis in Medicine: Models, Myths, and Metaphors." *ETC: A Review of General Semantics* 36 (1979): 261–74.

Bratman, Steven. *Health Food Junkies: Overcoming the Obsession with Healthful Eating*. New York: Broadway, 2000.

Brock, Bernard L., Robert L. Scott, and James W. Chesebro. *Methods of Rhetorical Criticism*. Detroit: Wayne State UP, 1989.

Brook, M. G., et al. "Adherence to Highly Active Antiretroviral Therapy in the Real World: Experience of Twelve English HIV Units." *AIDS Patient Care and STDS* 15.9 (2001): 491–94.

Brown, Barry. "Doctor's Ultimatum Forces Smokers to Quit or Leave." *Buffalo News* 3 Mar. 2002: A8. Lexis-Nexis Academic Universe, Canada. 15 July 2002 <http://web.lexis-nexis.com/universe>.

Brown, Thomas R. "Role of Diet in Etiology and Treatment of Migraine and Other Types of Headache." *Journal of the AMA* 77 (1921): 1396–1400.

Browne, Janet. "I Could Have Retched All Night: Charles Darwin and His Body." *Science Incarnate: Historical Embodiments of Natural Knowledge*. Ed. Christopher Lawrence and Steven Shapin. Chicago: U of Chicago P, 1998. 240–87.

Broyard, Anatole. *Intoxicated by My Illness: And Other Writings on Life and Death*. New York: Ballantine, 1992.

Bryant, Donald Cross. *Rhetorical Dimensions in Criticism*. Baton Rouge: Louisiana State UP, 1973.

———. *The Rhetorical Idiom: Essays in Rhetoric, Oratory, Language, and Drama Presented to Herbert August Wichelns with a Reprint of His Literary Criticism of Oratory (1925)*. Ithaca, NY: Cornell UP, 1958.

Buchan, William. *Domestic Medicine: Or, a Treatise on the Prevention and Cure of Diseases by Regimen and Simple Medicines*. Edinburgh: Balfour, 1769.

Burke, Kenneth. *A Grammar of Motives*. Berkeley: U of California P, 1969.

———. *Language as Symbolic Action*. Berkeley: U of California P, 1966.

————. *Philosophy of Literary Form: Studies in Symbolic Action.* 3rd ed. Berkeley: U of California P, 1973.

————. *A Rhetoric of Motives.* Berkeley: U of California P, 1969.

————. "Rhetoric—Old and New." *Journal of General Education* 5 (1951): 202–9.

Burke, Lora E., and Ira S. Ockene. *Compliance in Healthcare and Research.* Amer. Heart Assoc. Monograph Series. Armonk, NY: Futura, 2001.

Burton, Russell P. D., and Teresa Hudson. "Achieving Individually Sustained Commitment to Treatment Through Self-Constructed Models of Medical Adherence." *Sociological Spectrum* 21 (2001): 393–422.

Campbell, Harry. *Headache and Other Morbid Cephalic Sensations.* London: Lewis, 1894.

Campbell, John Angus. "Charles Darwin: Rhetorician of Science." *The Rhetoric of the Human Sciences: Language and Argument in Scholarship and Public Affairs.* Ed. John S. Nelson, Allan Megill, and Donald N. McCloskey. Madison: U of Madison P, 1987. 69–86.

Canada. Parliament. House of Commons. Standing Committee on Human Rights and the Status of Disabled Persons. *Report of the Standing Committee on Human Rights and the Status of Disabled Persons.* Ottawa: House of Commons, 1994.

Canada. Royal Commission on New Reproductive Technologies. *Proceed with Care: Final Report of the Royal Commission on New Reproductive Technologies.* Submitted by Patricia Baird et al. Ottawa: Minister of Govt. Services Canada, 1993.

Canada Diagnostic Centres. Advertisement. *Vancouver Magazine* June 2002: 39.

Canadian Institute for Health Information. "Quick Stats by Topic: Macro Spending." 16 June 2005 <http://secure.cihi.ca/cihiweb/dispPage.jsp?cw_page=statistics_topic_e#healthspending>.

Cantor, Carla, with Brian Fallon. *Phantom Illness: Shattering the Myth of Hypochondria.* Boston: Houghton, 1996.

Carmichael, Mary. "Medical Testing at Home." *Newsweek* 19 May 2003: 67–68.

Cassell, Eric J. *The Nature of Suffering: And the Goals of Medicine.* 2nd ed. New York: Oxford UP, 2004.

————. E-mail to the author. 3 Feb. 2001.

————. "What Is Pain? When Is Suffering?" Keynote address. CIHR Networking Workshop on Pain and Suffering. University of British Columbia, Vancouver. 25 Jan. 2001. "The Relationship Between Pain and Suffering—Summary." *Pain and Suffering Interdisciplinary Research Network.* 10 Jan. 2001 <http://www.english.ubc.ca/projects/PAIN/windex.htm>.

————. "Worried Well." E-mail to the author. 19 Dec. 2001.

Cathell, D. W. *Book on the Physician Himself: And Things That Concern His Reputation and Success.* 9th rev. and enl. ed. Philadelphia: Davis, 1889.

Charland, Maurice. "Constitutive Rhetoric: The Case of the *Peuple Québécois*." T. Benson, *Landmark* 213–34.

Charles, Cathy, Amiram Gafni, and Tim Whelan. "Shared Decision-Making in the Medical Encounter: What Does It Mean? (or It Takes at Least Two to Tango)." *Social Science and Medicine* 44 (1997): 681–92.

Cialdini, Robert B. *Influence: How and Why People Agree to Things*. New York: Quill, 1984.

Cicourel, Aaron V. "The Reproduction of Objective Knowledge: Common Sense Reasoning in Medical Decision Making." *The Knowledge Society: The Growing Impact of Scientific Knowledge on Social Relations*. Ed. G. Bohme and N. Stehr. Dordrecht: Reidel, 1986. 87–122.

Civil Action, A. Book by Jonathan Harr. Screenplay and dir. by Steven Zaillian. Buena, 1998.

Collins, Harry M., and Trevor J. Pinch. *The Golem: What You Should Know about Science*. 2nd ed. Cambridge: Cambridge UP, 1998.

Colp, Ralph, Jr. *To Be an Invalid: The Illness of Charles Darwin*. Chicago: U of Chicago P, 1977.

Condit, Celeste M. *The Meanings of the Gene: Public Debates about Human Heredity*. Madison: U of Wisconsin P, 1999.

———. "Women's Reproductive Choices and the Genetic Model of Medicine." *Body Talk: Rhetoric, Technology, Reproduction*. Ed. Mary M. Lay. Madison: U of Wisconsin P, 2000. 125–41.

Condit, Celeste M., and Deirdre M. Condit. "Blueprints and Recipes: Gendered Metaphors for Genetic Medicine." *Journal of Medical Humanities* 22.1 (2001): 29–40.

Condon, Esther H. "Nursing and the Caring Metaphor: Gender and Political Influences on an Ethics of Care." *Nursing Outlook* 40.1 (1992): 14–19.

Conrad, Peter. "Medicalization and Social Control." *Annual Review of Sociology* 18 (1992): 209–32.

———. "A Mirage of Genes." *Sociology of Health & Illness* 21.2 (1999): 228–41.

Corbett, Edward P. J. *Classical Rhetoric for the Modern Student*. 3rd ed. New York: Oxford UP, 1990.

———, ed. *Rhetorical Analyses of Literary Works*. New York: Oxford UP, 1969.

Couser, G. Thomas. *Recovering Bodies: Illness, Disability, and Life-Writing*. Madison: U of Wisconsin P, 1997.

Cox, Barbara G., and Charles G. Roland. "How Rhetoric Confuses Scientific Issues." *IEEE Transactions on Professional Communication* 16.3 (1973): 140–42.

Crowther, Prudence. Letter. *Harper's Magazine* 304 (Feb. 2002): 4.

Culler, Jonathan. *Structuralist Poetics*. London: Routledge, 1975.

Cuthbertson, Brian H., and David W. Noble. "Compliance: A Broken Concept." *British Medical Journal* 314 (8 Mar. 1997): 690–91.

Darwin, Charles. *On the Origin of Species*. Cambridge, MA: Harvard UP, 1964.

Davis, M. S., and R. L. Eichhorn. "Compliance with Medical Regimens: A Panel Study." *Journal of Health and Human Behavior* 4 (1963): 240–49.

Day, William Henry, ed. *Headaches: Their Nature, Causes, and Treatment*. 2nd ed. London: Churchill, 1878.

Derrida, Jacques. "The Rhetoric of Drugs. An Interview." *differences* 5.1 (1993): 1–25.

Diamond, Eric L., et al. "Decision-Making Ability and Advance Directive Preferences in Nursing Home Patients and Proxies." *Gerontologist* 29 (1989): 622–26.

Diamond, Seymour, and Donald J. Dalessio. *The Practicing Physician's Approach to Headache*. New York: Medcom, 1973.

Dickson, D. H., and I. W. Kelly. "'The Barnum Effect' in Personality Assessment: A Review of the Literature." *Psychological Reports* 57 (1985): 367–82.

DiMatteo, M. Robin, and D. Dante DiNicola. *Achieving Patient Compliance*. New York: Pergamon, 1982.

DiMatteo, M. Robin, and Heidi S. Lepper. "Promoting Adherence to Courses of Treatment: Mutual Collaboration in the Physician-Patient Relationship." *Health Communication Research: A Guide to Developments and Directions*. Ed. Bernard K. Duffy and Lorraine D. Jackson. Westport, CT: Greenwood, 1998. 75–86.

DiMatteo, M. Robin, Heidi S. Lepper, and Thomas W. Croghan. "Depression Is a Risk Factor for Noncompliance with Medical Treatment." *Archives of Internal Medicine* 160 (24 July 2000): 2101–7.

DiNicola, D. Dante, and M. Robin DiMatteo. "Practitioners, Patients, and Compliance with Medical Regimens: A Social Psychological Perspective." *Handbook of Psychology and Health*. Ed. Andrew Baum, Shelley E. Taylor, and Jerome E. Singer. Vol. 4. Hillsdale, NJ: Erlbaum, 1984. 55–84.

Doherty, Francis C. *A Study in Eighteenth-Century Advertising Methods: The Anodyne Necklace*. Lewiston, NY: Mellen, 1992.

Donnelly, William. "The Language of Medical Case Histories." *Annals of Internal Medicine* 127.11 (1997): 1045–48.

Donovan, Jenny L. "Patient Decision Making: The Missing Ingredient in Compliance Research." *Intl. Journal of Technology Assessment in Health Care* 11.3 (1995): 443–55.

Dorazio-Migliore, Margaret Louise. "Eldercare in Context: Narrative, Gender, and Ethnicity." Diss. University of British Columbia, Vancouver, 1999.

Duden, Barbara. *Disembodying Women: Perspectives on Pregnancy and the Unborn*. Trans. Lee Hoinacki. Cambridge: Harvard UP, 1993.

———. *The Woman Beneath the Skin: A Doctor's Patients in Eighteenth-Century Germany*. Trans. Thomas Dunlap. Cambridge, MA: Harvard UP, 1991.

Dumit, Joseph. *Picturing Personhood: Brain Scans and Medical Identity*. Princeton: Princeton UP, 2004.

———. "When Explanations Rest: 'Good-Enough' Brain Science and the New Socio-Medical Disorders." *Living and Working with the New Medical Technologies: Intersections of Inquiry*. Ed. Margaret Lock, Alan Young, and Alberto Cambrosio. Cambridge: Cambridge UP, 2000. 209–32.

Eagleton, Terry. *Literary Theory: An Introduction*. Oxford: Blackwell, 1983.

Edmeads, John. "The Dark Side of Medication Abuse." Editorial. *Headache* 29 (1989): 190–91.

———. "Narcotic Alternatives in Acute Migraine." Editorial. *Headache* 25 (1985): 343.

———. "Placebos and the Power of Negative Thinking." Editorial. *Headache* 24 (1984): 342–43.

Edson, Margaret. *Wit: A Play*. New York: Faber, 1999.

Ehrenreich, Barbara. Response to letter. *Harper's Magazine* 304 (Feb. 2002): 5+.

———. "Welcome to Cancerland: A Mammogram Leads to a Cult of Pink Kitsch." *Harper's Magazine* 302 (Nov. 2001): 43–53.

Ehrenreich, Barbara, and Deirdre English. *For Her Own Good: 150 Years of the Experts' Advice to Women*. New York: Doubleday, 1978.

Ehrlich, Richard. *The Healthy Hypochondriac: Recognizing, Understanding, and Living with Anxieties about Our Health*. Philadelphia: Saunders, 1980.

Elliott, Carl. *Better Than Well: American Medicine Meets the American Dream*. New York: Norton, 2003.

———. "A New Way to Be Mad." *Atlantic Monthly* 286.6 (Dec. 2000): 72–84.

———. "Pursued by Happiness and Beaten Senseless: Prozac and the American Dream." *Hastings Center Report* 30.2 (2000): 7–12.

Engel, George L. "The Need for a New Medical Model: A Challenge for Biomedicine." *Science* 196 (1977): 129–36.

Engelhardt, H. Tristram. "The Concepts of Health and Disease." *Evaluation and Explanation in the Biomedical Sciences: Proceedings of the First Trans-Disciplinary Symposium on Philosophy and Medicine, Held at Galveston, May 9–11, 1974*. Ed. Engelhardt and Stuart F. Spicker. Dordrecht: Reidel, 1975. 125–41.

Enns, Murray W., Kevin Kjernisted, and Mark Lander. "Pharmacological Management of Hypochondriasis and Related Disorders." *Health Anxiety: Clinical and Research Perspectives on Hypochondriasis and Related Conditions*. Ed. Gordon J. G. Asmundson, Steven Taylor, and Brian J. Cox. Chichester, Eng.: Wiley, 2001. 193–219.

Erin Brockovich. Screenplay by Susannah Grant. Dir. Steven Soderbergh. Universal, 2000.

Eugenides, Jeffrey. *Middlesex*. Toronto: Vintage Canada, 2003.

Evans, Robert G., and Gregory L. Stoddart. "Producing Health, Consuming Health Care." *Social Science and Medicine* 31 (1990): 1347–63.

Evans, Robert G., Morris Lionel Barer, and Theodore R. Marmor, eds. *Why Are Some People Healthy and Others Not?: The Determinants of Health of Populations.* New York: Gruyter, 1994.

Fabricant, Noah D. *Headaches, What Causes Them, How to Get Relief.* New York: Staples, 1949.

Fallon, Brian. Foreword. Cantor i–xiii.

———. "Pharmacologic Strategies for Hypochondriasis." *Hypochondriasis: Modern Perspectives on an Ancient Malady.* Ed. Vladan Starvevic and Don R. Lipsitt. Oxford: Oxford UP, 2001. 329–54.

Fallon, Brian A., et al. "The Pharmacotherapy of Hypochondriasis." *Psychopharmacology Bull.* 32 (1996): 607–11.

Farrell, Thomas B. *Norms of Rhetorical Culture.* New Haven: Yale UP, 1993.

Fayerman, Pamela. "Elective Surgery Benefits Most Patients: Study." *Vancouver Sun* 29 May 2001: B1+.

———. "Two City Hospitals Discharged Heart Patients Too Quickly." *Vancouver Sun* (6 July 2004): A1+.

Fein, Esther B. "Failing to Discuss Dying Adds to Pain of Patient and Family." *New York Times* 5 Mar. 1997: A1+.

Fielding, Helen. *Bridget Jones's Diary.* London: Picador, 1996.

Fischer-Homberger, Esther. "Hypochondriasis of the Eighteenth Century— Neurosis of the Present Century." *Bull. of the Hist. of Medicine* 46 (1972): 391–401.

Fish, Stanley. "Rhetoric." *Critical Terms for Literary Study.* Ed. Frank Lentricchia and Thomas McLaughlin. Chicago: U of Chicago P, 1990. 203–22.

Fisher, Sue. *In the Patient's Best Interest: Women and the Politics of Medical Decisions.* New Brunswick, NJ: Rutgers UP, 1988.

Fishman, Jennifer R. "Manufacturing Desire: The Commodification of Female Sexual Dysfunction." *Social Studies of Science* 34 (2004): 187–218.

Fissell, Mary E. "The Disappearance of the Patient's Narrative and the Invention of Hospital Medicine." *British Medicine in an Age of Reform.* Ed. Roger K. French and Andrew Wear. London: Routledge, 1991. 92–109.

Fletcher, Suzanne W., and Graham A. Colditz. "Failure of Estrogen Plus Progestin Therapy for Prevention." Editorial. *Journal of the AMA* 288.3 (2002): 366–68.

Foote, Edward B. *Dr. Foote's Home Cyclopedia of Popular Medical, Social and Sexual Science.* New York: Murray, 1902.

———. *Plain Home Talk about the Human System—the Habits of Men and Women—. . . Embracing Medical Common Sense Applied to Causes, Prevention, and Cure of Chronic Diseases.* New York: Bancroft, 1871.

Foss, Krista. "Hormone Study Sparks Debate." *Globe and Mail* 11 July 2002: A6.

Foss, Sonja K. *Rhetorical Criticism: Exploration and Practice.* Prospect Heights, IL: Waveland, 1989.

Foucault, Michel. *The Birth of the Clinic: An Archaeology of Medical Perception.* Trans. A. M. Sheridan Smith. New York: Pantheon, 1973.

France, Karen Russo, and Rejiv Grover. "What Is the Health Care Product?" *Journal of Health Care Marketing* 12.2 (1992): 31–38.

Frank, Arthur. *The Wounded Storyteller: Body, Illness, and Ethics.* Chicago: U of Chicago P, 1995.

Frankford, David M. "Scientism and Economism in the Regulation of Health Care." *Journal of Health Politics, Policy, and the Law* 19 (winter 1994): 774–807.

Franzen, Jonathan. *The Corrections.* Toronto: HarperFlamingo, 2001.

Freeman, Michael A. "Perspectives on the Future of Network-Based Managed Behavioral Health Care Systems." *Assoc. of Preferred Provider Organizations Journal* (Apr./May 1992): 17–22.

Fuller, Steve. *Philosophy, Rhetoric, and the End of Knowledge: The Coming of Science and Technology Studies.* Madison: U of Wisconsin P, 1993.

———. "'Rhetoric of Science': Double the Trouble?" *Rhetorical Hermeneutics: Invention and Interpretation in the Age of Science.* Ed. Alan G. Gross and William M. Keith. Albany: State U of New York P, 1997. 279–98.

Future Perfect. 12 July 2002 <http://www.hiddenmia.diaryland.com>.

Gartner, Zsuzsi. "You Are Here: An Anatomy of Hypochondria." *Walrus* (Oct. 2004): 24–27.

Gatchel, Robert, and James Weisberg, eds. *Personality Characteristics of Patients with Pain.* Washington, DC: Amer. Psychological Assoc., 2000.

Gaylin, Willard. "Faulty Diagnosis: Why Clinton's Health-Care Plan Won't Cure What Ails Us." *Harper's Magazine* 207 (Oct. 1993): 57–64.

Geist, Harold. *Migraine: Psychological, Psychiatric, and Physiological Aspects.* Malabar, FL: Krieger, 1983.

Gerbino, P. P. Foreword. *Annals of Pharmacotherapy* 27 (1993).

Gergen, Kenneth J., with Mary Gergen. "Life Narrative: A Fractured Restorying." Speaker series. *Interdisciplinary Inquiry into Narratives of Disease, Disability, and Trauma.* University of British Columbia, Vancouver. 3 July 2001.

Gieryn, Thomas F. "Boundary-Work and the Demarcation of Science from Nonscience: Strains and Interests in Professional Ideologies of Scientists." *Amer. Sociological Rev.* 48 (1983): 781–95.

Gilbert, G. Nigel, and Michael J. Mulkay. *Opening Pandora's Box: A Sociological Analysis of Scientists' Discourse.* Cambridge: Cambridge UP, 1984.

———. "The Transformation of Research Findings into Scientific Knowledge." *Social Studies of Science* 6 (1976): 281–306.

Gilman, Charlotte Perkins. "The Yellow Wallpaper." *"The Yellow Wallpaper" and Other Stories.* Mineola, NY: Dover, 1997. 1–15.

Goldsmith, Jeff C. "Technology and the End to Entitlement." *Healthcare Forum Journal* (Sep./Oct. 1993): 16–23.

Golub, Edward S. *The Limits of Medicine: How Science Shapes Our Hope for the Future*. New York: Random, 1994.

Gorman, Christine. "The Science of Anxiety." *Time* 10 June (2002): 34–42.

Grady, Denise. "The Hard Facts Behind a Heartbreaking Case." *New York Times* 19 June 2005, week in review: 5.

Graham, John R. *Treatment of Migraine*. Boston: Little, 1956.

Grandin, Temple. *Thinking in Pictures: And Other Reports from My Life with Autism*. New York: Vintage, 1996.

Grashof, John F. "Abstract of 'In Pursuit of Pregnancy' by Paula Mergenbagen Dewitt." *Journal of Health Care Marketing* 13.3 (1993): 68.

Greene, Jeremy A. "Therapeutic Infidelities: 'Noncompliance' Enters the Medical Literature, 1955–1975." *Social History of Medicine* 17 (2004): 327–43.

Greenhalgh, Susan. *Under the Medical Gaze: Facts and Fictions of Chronic Pain*. Berkeley: U of California P, 2001.

Greenhalgh, Trisha, and Brian Hurwitz. "Why Study Narrative?" *British Medical Journal* 318 (2 Jan. 1999): 48–50.

Groopman, Jerome. "Sick with Worry." *New Yorker* (11 Aug. 2003): 28–34.

Gross, Alan G. *The Rhetoric of Science*. Cambridge, MA: Harvard UP, 1990.

Gross, Alan G., and William M. Keith. Introduction, Gross and Keith 1–22.

———, eds. *Rhetorical Hermeneutics: Invention and Interpretation in the Age of Science*. Albany: State U of New York P, 1997.

Grove, Stephen J., and Gregory M. Pickett. "Root Canals and Retailing." *Journal of Health Care Marketing* 14.4 (1994): 36–40.

Groves, James. "Taking Care of the Hateful Patient." *New England Journal of Medicine* 298.16 (1978): 883–87.

Grumman, Rachel. "Five Aches You Should Never Ignore." *Cosmopolitan* (May 2003): 194, 196.

Gunn, John C. *Gunn's Domestic Medicine, or, a Poor Man's Friend, in the Hours of Affliction, Pain and Sickness*. Knoxville, TN: Gunn, 1830.

Gwyn, Richard, and Glyn Elwyn. "When Is a Shared Decision Not (Quite) a Shared Decision? Negotiating Preferences in a General Practice Encounter." *Social Science and Medicine* 49 (1999): 437–47.

Hacking, Ian. *Mad Travelers: Reflections on the Reality of Transient Mental Illness*. Charlottesville: UP of Virginia, 1998.

———. "Risk and Dirt." *Risk and Morality*. Ed. Richard V. Ericson and Aaron Doyle. Toronto: U of Toronto P, 2003. 22–47.

———. *The Social Construction of What?* Cambridge, MA: Harvard UP, 1999.

Haiken, Elizabeth. *Venus Envy: A History of Cosmetic Surgery*. Baltimore: Johns Hopkins UP, 1997.

Halloran, S. Michael. "The Birth of Molecular Biology: An Essay in the Rhetorical Criticism of Scientific Discourse." *Rhetoric Rev.* 3 (1984): 70–83.

Hamm, E. P., and Alan W. Richardson. "Measurement of the People, by the

People, and for the People." *Studies in Hist. and Philosophy of Science* 32.4 (2001): 607–12.

Haraway, Donna. *Simians, Cyborgs, and Women: The Reinvention of Nature.* New York: Routledge, 1991.

Harris, Randy Allen. Introduction. *Landmark Essays on Rhetoric of Science: Case Studies.* Mahwah, NJ: Hermagoras, 1997. xi–xlv.

Harrison, Barbara. "Profound Hypochondria." *Ms.* 5 (1977): 71+.

Hart, Roderick. "Wandering with Rhetorical Criticism." Nothstine, Blair, and Copeland 71–81.

Hawkins, Anne Hunsaker. *Reconstructing Illness: Studies in Pathography.* 2nd ed. West Lafayette, IN: Purdue UP, 1999.

———. "Writing about Illness and Disability: Treatment or Testimony." Keynote address. *Narratives of Disease, Disability, and Trauma: An Interdisciplinary Conference.* University of British Columbia, Vancouver. 9 May 2002.

Haynes, R. Brian. "Improving Patient Adherence: State of the Art, with a Special Focus on Medication Taking for Cardiovascular Disorders." *Compliance in Healthcare and Research.* Ed. Lora E. Burke and Ira S. Ockene. Armonk, NY: Futura, 2001. 3–21.

Haynes, R. Brian, D. Wayne Taylor, and David L. Sackett. *Compliance in Health Care.* Baltimore: Johns Hopkins UP, 1979.

Healy, David. *The Antidepressant Era.* Cambridge, MA: Harvard UP, 1997.

———. "Good Science or Good Business?" *Hastings Center Report* 30.2 (2000): 19–22.

Heath, Iona. "A Wolf in Sheep's Clothing: A Critical Look at the Ethics of Drug Taking." *British Medical Journal* 327 (2003): 856–58.

Hechtlinger, Adelaide. *The Great Patent Medicine Era: Or, Without Benefit of Doctor.* New York: Grosset, 1970.

Heidenheimer, Arnold J., Hugh Heclo, and Carolyn Teich Adams, eds. *Comparative Public Policy: The Politics of Social Choice in America, Europe, and Japan.* New York: St. Martin's, 1990.

Hering, R., and T. J. Steiner. "Abrupt Outpatient Withdrawal of Medication in Analgesic-Abusing Migraineurs." *Lancet* 337 (15 June 1991): 1442–43.

Hippocrates. "The Oath." *Source Book of Medical History.* Comp. Logan Clendening. New York: Dover, 1942. 14–15.

Hoffman, Geoffrey. Interview with Mark Forsythe. CBC Radio, Vancouver. 5 May 1995.

Hoffman, Tod. "Completely Incorrect." *Globe and Mail* 12 July 2002: R5.

Holm, Søren. "What Is Wrong with Compliance?" *Journal of Medical Ethics* 19 (1993): 108–10.

Howard, Robert. "Doctor's Aren't Free to Pick Their Patients." *Hamilton Spectator* 2 Mar. 2002: D4.

Howe, Brian. "Legalities Versus Ethics in Doctor Response on Tobacco: Doctor's Response on Tobacco While Legally Correct Is Not Ethical." *Cape Breton Post* 13 Mar. 2002: B6. Lexis-Nexis Academic Universe, Canada. 15 July 2005 <http://web.lexis-nexis.com/universe>.

Hunter, Kathryn Montgomery. *Doctors' Stories: The Narrative Structure of Medical Knowledge.* Princeton, NJ: Princeton UP, 1991.

Hutchins, H. *Hutchins' Receipt Book Containing Valuable and Choice Receipts . . . to Which Is Added Important Information Concerning Cephalalgia or Headache.* Springfield, MA: Hutchins, 1862.

Hyde, Michael. "Medicine, Rhetoric, and Euthanasia: A Case Study in the Workings of a Postmodern Discourse." *QJS* 79 (1993): 201–24.

Illich, Ivan. *Medical Nemesis: The Expropriation of Health Limits to Medicine.* London: Boyars, 1976.

Isler, Hansruedi. "The Galenic Tradition and Migraine." *Journal of the History of the Neurosciences* 1 (1992): 227–33.

Jarratt, Susan C. *Rereading the Sophists: Classical Rhetoric Refigured.* Carbondale: Southern Illinois UP, 1991.

Jordanova, Ludmilla. "The Social Construction of Medical Knowledge." *Social History of Medicine* 7 (1995): 361–81.

Kalb, S. William. *Your Future as a Physician.* New York: Rosen, 1963.

Kaniecki, Robert. "Putting It Together for Clinical Practice." Symposium. "New Advances and Understandings in the Diagnosis and Care of Migraine Patients." *Forty-fourth Annual Scientific Meeting of the American Headache Society.* Sheraton Seattle Hotel and Towers, Seattle. 21 June 2002.

Kant, Immanuel. *Anthropology from a Pragmatic Point of View.* Trans. Mary J. Gregor. The Hague: Nijhoff, 1974.

Kate. "Hi, I'm New." Online posting. 2 June 2002. Discussion forum *Anasway/ Ana by Choice.* 6 June 2002 <http://www.ana-by-choice.com/> <http://www.angelsforum.org/>.

Keller, Evelyn Fox. *Refiguring Life: Metaphors of Twentieth-Century Biology.* New York: Columbia UP, 1995.

Kelner, Merrijoy J., and Ivy L. Bourgeault. "Patient Control over Dying: Responses of Health Care Professionals." *Social Science and Medicine* 36 (1993): 757–65.

Kennedy, Robert F., Jr. "Deadly Immunity." *Salon.com.* 16 June 2005 <http://www.salon.com/src/pass/gateway/demo2.html?> <http://www.salon.com/news/feature/2005/06/16/thimerosal/index_np.html>.

Kenyon, F. E. "Hypochondriacal States." *British Journal of Psychiatry* 129 (1976): 1–14.

Kirmayer, Laurence J. "Mind and Body as Metaphors: Hidden Values in Biomedicine." *Biomedicine Examined.* Ed. Margaret Lock and Deborah R. Gordon. Dordrecht: Kluwer, 1988. 57–93.

Klein, Bonnie Sherr, with Persimmon Blackbridge. *Slow Dance: A Story of Stroke, Love, and Disability*. Toronto: Knopf, 1997.

Kleinman, Arthur. *The Illness Narratives: Suffering, Healing, and the Human Condition*. New York: Basic, 1988.

Klyn, Mark. "Toward a Pluralistic Rhetorical Criticism." Nilsen 146–57.

Knorr-Cetina, Karin D. *The Manufacture of Knowledge: An Essay on the Constructivist and Contextual Nature of Science*. Oxford: Pergamon, 1981.

Koerner, Brendan I. "Disorders Made to Order." *Mother Jones* (July/Aug. 2002): 58–63+.

Kolata, Gina. "Rapid Rise and Fall for Clinics That Market Scans to Patients." *New York Times* 23 Jan. 2005: A1, A17.

———. "Study Is Halted over Rise Seen in Cancer Risk." *New York Times* 9 July 2002: A1.

Kolata, Gina, and Melody Petersen. "Hormone Replacement Study a Shock to the Medical System." *New York Times* 10 July 2002: A1+.

Kramer, Peter. *Against Depression*. New York: Viking, 2005.

———. "The Anatomy of Melancholy." *New York Times Book Review* 7 Apr. 1996: 27.

———. *Listening to Prozac*. New York: Viking, 1993.

Kruit, Mark C., et al. "Migraine as a Risk Factor for Subclinical Brain Lesions." *Journal of the AMA* 291 (2004): 427–34.

Kuhn, Thomas S. *The Structure of Scientific Revolutions*. 3rd ed. Chicago: U of Chicago P, 1996.

Kushner, Howard. "The Biological Revolution in Psychiatry and the Deauthorization of Pain and Suffering." Discussion paper. *CIHR Networking Work-shop on Pain and Suffering*. University of British Columbia, Vancouver. Jan. 2001. *Pain and Suffering Interdisciplinary Research Network*. 15 Jan. 2001 <http://www.english.ubc.ca/projects/PAIN/windex.htm>.

Ladee, George A. *Hypochondriacal Syndromes*. Amsterdam: Elsevier, 1966.

Lakoff, George, and Mark Johnson. *Metaphors We Live By*. Chicago: U of Chicago P, 1980.

Laqueur, Thomas. *Making Sex: Body and Gender from the Greeks to Freud*. Cambridge, MA: Harvard UP, 1990.

Latour, Bruno, and Steve Woolgar. *Laboratory Life: The Social Construction of Scientific Facts*. Beverly Hills: Sage, 1979.

Lear, Martha Weinman. *Heartsounds*. New York: Simon, 1980.

Lefevre, Karen Burke. "Introducing Imitrex to Migraine Patients: The Rhetoric of Pharmaceutical Innovation." Conf. on Coll. Composition and Communication. Palmer House Hilton Hotel, Chicago. 2 Apr. 1998.

Leff, Michael. "Things Made by Words: Reflections on Textual Criticism." *QJS* 78 (1992): 223–31.

Lemonick, Michael D. "How to Heal a Hypochondriac." *Time* (6 Oct. 2003): 38–39.

Lerner, Barron H. "From Careless Consumptive to Recalcitrant Patients: The Historical Construction of Noncompliance." *Social Science and Medicine* 45.9 (1997): 1423–31.

———. Letter. *Harper's Magazine* 304 (Feb. 2002): 4.

Lingard, Lorelei, and Richard Haber. "Learning Medical Talk: How the Apprenticeship Complicates Current Explicit/Tacit Debates in Genre Instruction." *The Rhetoric and Ideology of Genre: Strategies for Stability and Change.* Ed. Richard M. Coe, Lingard, and Tatiana Teslenko. Cresskill, NJ: Hampton, 2002. 155–70.

Lipsitt, Don R. "The Patient-Physician Relationship in the Treatment of Hypochondriasis." *Hypochondriasis: Modern Perspectives on an Ancient Malady.* Ed. Vladan Starvevic and Lipsitt. Oxford: Oxford UP, 2001. 265–90.

Liveing, Edward. *On Megrim, Sick-Headache, and Some Allied Disorders.* London: Churchill, 1873.

Lo, Bernard. "Improving Care near the End of Life: Why Is It So Hard?" *Journal of the AMA* 274 (1995): 1634–36.

Lobel, H. O., et al. "Use of Malaria Prevention Measures by North American and European Travelers to East Africa." *Journal of Travel Medicine* 8.4 (2001): 167–72.

Lock, Margaret. "Breast Cancer: Reading the Omens." *Anthropology Today* 14 (1998): 7–16.

Logue, B. J. "Taking Charge: Death Control as an Emergent Women's Issue." *Women and Health* 17.4 (1991): 97–121.

Lorde, Audre. *The Cancer Journals.* San Francisco: Spinster, 1980.

Love, Myron. "Manitoba FP Wields 'Stick' Against Smokers." *Medical Post* 38.3 (22 Jan. 2002): 6.

Mairs, Nancy. *Waist-High in the World: A Life among the Nondisabled.* Boston: Beacon, 1996.

Malleson, Andrew. *Whiplash and Other Useful Illnesses.* Montreal: McGill-Queen's UP, 2002.

Malone, Ruth E. "Policy as Product: Morality and Metaphor in Health Policy Discourse." *Hastings Center Report* 29.3 (1999): 16–22.

Marinker, Marshall. *From Compliance to Concordance: Achieving Shared Goals in Medicine Taking.* London: Royal Pharmaceutical Soc., 1997.

———. "Personal Paper: Writing Prescriptions Is Easy." *British Medical Journal* 314 (8 Mar. 1997): 747–48.

Mark, Patricia. "The Downside of Dropping Patients with Bad Habits." *Medical Post* 38.16 (23 Apr. 2002): 15.

Marsten, Wendy. *The Hypochondriac's Handbook.* San Francisco: Chronicle, 1998.

Martin, Emily. "The Egg and the Sperm: How Science Has Constructed a

Romance Based on Stereotypical Male-Female Roles." *Signs: Journal of Women in Culture and Society* 16 (1991): 485–501.

———. *Flexible Bodies: Tracking Immunity in American Culture from the Days of Polio to the Age of AIDS.* Boston: Beacon, 1994.

———. "Monitoring the Mind." The New Politics of Surveillance and Visibility: A Green College Conference. University of British Columbia, Vancouver. 25 May 2003.

———. *The Woman in the Body: A Cultural Analysis of Reproduction.* Boston: Beacon, 1987.

Martin, V. T., et al. "Does the Phase of the Menstrual Cycle Have an Effect on Headache?" *Forty-fourth Annual Scientific Meeting of the American Headache Society.* Sheraton Seattle Hotel and Towers, Seattle. 22 June 2002.

Maté, Gabor. *When the Body Says No: The Cost of Hidden Stress.* Toronto: Knopf. 2003.

Maxwell, Harold. *Migraine: Background and Treatment.* Bristol: Wright, 1966.

McCarthy, Mary. *The Group.* 1954. New York: Avon, 1980.

McGill, Craig. *Do No Harm? Munchausen Syndrome by Proxy.* London: Vision, 2002.

McIlroy, Anne. "High Anxiety." *Globe and Mail* (20 Sept. 2003): F1+.

Mead, Beverly T. "Management of Hypochondriacal Patients" *Journal of the AMA* 192 (5 Apr. 1965): 33–35.

Meichenbaum, Donald, and Dennis C. Turk. *Facilitating Treatment Adherence: A Practitioner's Guidebook.* New York: Plenum, 1987.

Melito, Richard. "The 'Business' Metaphor in the Delivery of Human Services." *Psychiatric Quarterly* 54.1 (1982): 43–55.

Merton, Robert King. *Sociological Ambivalence and Other Essays.* New York: Free, 1976.

Mickleburgh, Rod. "Hospitals Call for Market-Style Competition." *Globe and Mail* 10 June 1993: A6.

Milburn, H. J., and G. M. Cochrane. Letter. "Treating the Patient as a Decision Maker Is Not Always Appropriate." *British Medical Journal* 314 (28 June 1997): 1906.

Miller, Carolyn. "The Presumptions of Expertise: The Role of *Ethos* in Risk Analysis." *Configurations* 11 (2003): 163–202.

Mintzes, Barbara. "Doctor, about That Medicine I Saw Advertised . . . " 2001. *In Motion Magazine.* 28 June 2002 <http://www.inmotionmagazine.com/hcare/mintzes.html>.

———. "For and Against: Direct to Consumer Advertising Is Medicalising Normal Human Experience: For." *British Medical Journal* 324 (13 Apr. 2002): 908–9.

Mintzes, Barbara, et al. "Influence of Direct to Consumer Pharmaceutical Advertising and Patients' Requests on Prescribing Decisions: Two Site Cross Sectional Survey." *British Medical Journal* 324 (2 Feb. 2002): 278–79.

Mishler, Elliot. *The Discourse of Medicine: Dialectics of Medical Interviews.* Norwood, NJ: Ablex, 1984.

———. "Viewpoint: Critical Perspectives on the Biomedical Model." *Social Contexts of Health, Illness, and Patient Care.* Ed. Mishler. Cambridge, MA: Cambridge UP, 1981. 1–23.

Mitchell, S. Weir. *Doctor and Patient.* Philadelphia: Lippincott, 1904.

Molière, Jean-Baptiste. "The Hypochondriac." Trans. John Wood and David Coward. *The Miser and Other Plays.* London: Penguin, 2000.

Montgomery, Scott L. *The Scientific Voice.* New York: Guilford, 1996.

Moore, Marjorie A. "Nursing: A Scientific Discipline?" *Nursing Forum* 7.4 (1968): 340–48. *Nursing Forum* 28.1 (1993): 28–33.

Morris, G. H., and Ronald J. Chenail. *The Talk of the Clinic: Explorations in the Analysis of Medical and Therapeutic Discourse.* Hillsdale, NJ: Erlbaum, 1995.

Morse, Edward V., Patricia M. Simon, and Paul M. Balson. "Using Experiential Training to Enhance Health Professionals' Awareness of Patient Compliance Issues." *Academic Medicine* 68.9 (1993): 693–97.

Myers, Greg. *Writing Biology: Texts on the Social Construction of Scientific Knowledge.* Madison: U of Wisconsin P, 1990.

"Myth of Early Detection." *Health Matters.* CBC. Newsworld Network. 30 May 2003.

Nelkin, Dorothy, and M. Susan Lindee. *The DNA Mystique: The Gene as a Cultural Icon.* New York: Freeman, 1995.

Nelson, Hilde Lindemann. "Seven Things to Do with Stories." *Narratives of Disease, Disability, and Trauma: An Interdisciplinary Conference.* University of British Columbia, Vancouver. 11 May 2002.

———. *Stories and Their Limits: Narrative Approaches to Biomedicine.* New York: Routledge, 1997.

"Nexium." Advertisement. *Doctor's Review* Feb. 2003.

"Nexium." Advertisement. *Newsweek* 19 May 2003.

Nichols, Marie Hochmuth. "Burkeian Criticism." Nilsen 75–85.

———. "Kenneth Burke and the 'New Rhetoric.'" *QJS* 38 (1952): 133–44.

Nilsen, Thomas R., ed. *Essays in Rhetorical Criticism.* New York: Random, 1968.

Nothstine, William L., Carole Blair, and Gary A. Copeland, eds. *Critical Questions: Invention, Creativity, and the Criticism of Discourse and Media.* New York: St. Martin's, 1994.

Nuland, Sherwin B. *How We Die: Reflections on Life's Final Chapter.* New York: Knopf, 1994.

O'Keefe, Daniel J. *Persuasion: Theory and Research.* Newbury Park, CA: Sage, 1990.

Ong, Walter J. "The Writer's Audience Is Always a Fiction." *PMLA* 90.1 (1975): 9–21.

Organization for Economic Cooperation and Development. United States. 16
June 2005 <http://www.oecd.org/country 0,3021,en_33873108_33873886_
1_1_1_1,00.html>.

Osheron, Samuel, and Lorna AmaraSingham. "The Machine Metaphor in
Medicine." *Social Contexts of Health, Illness, and Patient Care.* Ed. Elliot
Mishler. Cambridge: Cambridge UP, 1981. 219–49.

Parsons, Talcott. "Illness and the Role of the Physician: A Sociological
Perspective." *Amer. Journal of Orthopsychiatry* 21 (1956): 452–60.

———. *The Social System.* Glencoe, IL: Free, 1951.

Pascalev, Assya. "Images of Death and Dying in the Intensive Care Unit."
Journal of Medical Humanities 17 (1996): 219–36.

Pennebaker, James W. *Opening Up: The Healing Power of Expressing
Emotions.* New York: Guilford, 1997.

Perelman, Chaim, and Lucie Olbrechts-Tyteca. *The New Rhetoric: A Treatise
on Argumentation.* Trans. John Wilkinson and Purcell Weaver. Notre
Dame, IN: Notre Dame UP, 1969.

Perloff, Richard M. *Persuading People to Have Safer Sex: Applications of
Social Science to the AIDS Crisis.* Mahwah, NJ: Erlbaum, 2001.

Pesman, Curtis. "Looking for Trouble." *Esquire* (Aug. 2002): 60–64.

Petty, Richard E., Thomas M. Ostrom, and Timothy C. Brock. *Cognitive
Responses in Persuasion.* Hillsdale, NJ: Erlbaum, 1981.

Picard, André. "Bypassing Their MD's, Canadians Go On-line for Drugs."
Globe and Mail 2 Mar. 2002: A1.

———. "Migraine Doubles Risk of Stroke, Research Finds." *Globe and Mail*
13 Dec. 2004: A6.

———. "Unnecessary Operations May Be Rife, Study Finds." *Globe and Mail*
29 May 2001: A1+.

Pierce, R. V. *The People's Common Sense Medical Adviser in Plain English, or,
Medicine Simplified.* 57th ed. Buffalo, NY: World's Dispensary, 1895.

Polanyi, Michael. *Personal Knowledge: Toward a Post-Critical Philosophy.*
Chicago: U of Chicago P, 1958.

Porter, Dorothy, and Roy Porter. *Patient's Progress: Doctors and Doctoring in
Eighteenth-Century England.* Oxford: Polity, 1989.

Porter, Roy. *The Greatest Benefit to Mankind: A Medical History of Humanity
from Antiquity to the Present.* London: HarperCollins, 1997.

———. *Health for Sale: Quackery in England 1660–1850.* Manchester:
Manchester UP, 1989.

Postman, Neil. *Technopology: The Surrender of Culture to Technology.* New
York: Vintage, 1993.

Prelli, Lawrence J. *A Rhetoric of Science: Inventing Scientific Discourse.*
Columbia: U of South Carolina P, 1989.

Rachman, Stanley. Foreword. *Health Anxiety: Clinical and Research Perspectives on Hypochondriasis and Related Conditions.* Ed. Gordon J. G.

Asmundson, Steven Taylor, and Brian J. Cox. Chichester, Eng.: Wiley, 2001. xvii–xviii.

Radner, Gilda. *It's Always Something*. New York: Simon, 1989.

Reiser, Stanley J. *Medicine and the Reign of Technology*. Cambridge, MA: Cambridge UP, 1978.

Richards, Sarah. "Death Becomes You." *Globe and Mail* 26 Oct. 2002: L1.

Richer, Shawna. "The New Millennium's Malady." *Globe and Mail* 15 June 2002: F7.

Roberson, Mildred H. B. "The Meaning of Compliance: Patient Perspectives." *Qualitative Health Research* 2.1 (1992): 7–26.

Robey, William H. *Headache*. Philadelphia: Lippincott, 1931.

Rodin, Judith, and Irving L. Janis. "The Social Influence of Physicians and Other Health Care Practitioners as Agents of Change." *Interpersonal Issues in Health Care*. Ed. Howard S. Friedman and M. Robin DiMatteo. New York: Academic, 1982. 33–50.

Rose, Nikolas. "The Neurochemical Self and Its Anomalies." *Risk and Morality*. Ed. Richard V. Ericson and Aaron Doyle. Toronto: U of Toronto P, 2003. 407–37.

Rosenau, Pauline Vaillancourt. "Post-Modernity: Its Meaning and Implications for Community Health Organizing." *Journal of Health Politics, Policy, and Law* 19 (1994): 303–33.

Rosenberg, Charles. *Explaining Epidemics and Other Studies in the History of Medicine*. Cambridge: Cambridge UP, 1992.

Ross, Fiona R. "Patient Compliance—Whose Responsibility?" *Social Science and Medicine* 32.1 (1991): 89–94.

Ross, Frederick. "A Physician Who Refuses to Treat Patients Who Smoke." Interview with Jeff Hutcheson. *Canada AM*. CTV Television. 1 Mar. 2002. Lexis-Nexis Academic Universe, Canada. 15 July 2002 <http://web.lexis-nexis.com/universe>.

Roter, Debra L., et al. "Effectiveness of Interventions to Improve Patient Compliance. A Meta-Analysis." *Medical Care* 36.8 (1998): 1138–61.

Roth, Philip. *Portnoy's Complaint*. New York: Vintage, 1994.

Rousseau, George Sebastian, and David Boyd Haycock. "Framing Samuel Taylor Coleridge's Gut: Genius, Digestion, Hypochondria." *Framing and Imagining Disease in Cultural History*. Ed. Miranda Gill, David Haycock, and Malte Herwig. New York: Palgrave, 2003. 231–66.

Roy, Ranjan. *Child Abuse and Chronic Pain: A Curious Relationship?* Toronto: U of Toronto P, 1998.

Rubenstein, Robert L. "Narratives of Elder Parental Death: A Structural and Cultural Analysis." *Medical Anthropology Quarterly* 9.3 (1995): 257–76.

Sackett, David L., and R. Brian Haynes, eds. *Compliance with Therapeutic Regimens*. Baltimore: Johns Hopkins UP, 1976.

ScanQuest. Advertisement. *Vancouver Magazine* Summer 2002.

Scheper-Hughes, Nancy, and Margaret M. Lock. "The Mindful Body: A Prolegomenon to Future Work in Medical Anthropology." *Medical Anthropology Quarterly* 1.1 (1987): 6–41.

Scheurich, Neil. "Hysteria and the Medical Narrative." *Perspectives in Biology and Medicine* 43.4 (2000): 461–76.

Schmidt, F. N., P. Carney, and G. Fitzsimmons. "An Empirical Assessment of the Migraine Personality Type." *Journal of Psychosomatic Research* 30 (1986): 189–97.

Scott, J. Blake. *Risky Rhetoric: AIDS and the Cultural Practices of HIV Testing.* Carbondale: Southern Illinois UP, 2003.

Segal, Judith Zelda. "Contesting Death, Speaking of Dying." *Journal of Medical Humanities* 21 (winter 2000): 29–44.

———. "Patient Compliance, the Rhetoric of Rhetoric, and the Rhetoric of Persuasion." *RSQ* 23.3/4 (1994): 90–102.

———. "Problems of Generalization/Genrelization: The Case of the Doctor-Patient Interview." *The Rhetoric and Ideology of Genre: Strategies for Stability and Change.* Ed. Richard M. Coe, Lorelei Lingard, and Tatiana Teslenko. Cresskill, NJ: Hampton, 2002. 171–84.

———. "Public Discourse and Public Policy: Some Ways That Metaphor Constrains Health (Care)." *Journal of Medical Humanities* 18 (1997): 217–31.

———. "Reading Medical Prose as Rhetoric: A Study in the Rhetoric of Science." Diss. University of British Columbia, Vancouver, 1988.

———. "What Is a Rhetoric of Death?: End-of-Life Decision-Making at a Psychiatric Hospital." *Technostyle* 16 (winter 2000): 67–86.

Segal, Judy, Anthony Paré, Doug Brent, and Douglas Vipond. "The Researcher as Missionary: Problems with Rhetoric and Reform in the Disciplines." *CCC* 50 (1998): 71–90.

Selzer, Jack, and Sharon Crowley, eds. *Rhetorical Bodies.* Madison: U of Wisconsin P, 1999.

Shapin, Steven. *A Social History of Truth: Civility and Science in Seventeenth-Century England.* Chicago: U of Chicago P, 1994.

Sharf, Barbara F. "Poster Art as Women's Rhetoric: Raising Awareness about Breast Cancer." *Literature and Medicine* 14 (1995): 72–86.

Sharpe, Patricia A. "Older Women and Health Services: Moving from Ageism Toward Empowerment." *Women and Health* 22 (1995): 9–23.

Shorter, Edward. "The Borderland Between Neurology and History: Conversion Reactions." *Neurologic Clinics* 13.2 (1995): 229–39.

———. *From Paralysis to Fatigue: A History of Psychosomatic Illness in the Modern Era.* Toronto: Maxwell, 1992.

Showalter, Elaine. *Hystories: Hysterical Epidemics and Modern Media.* New York: Columbia UP, 1997.

Shryock, Richard H. *The History of Nursing: An Interpretation of the Social and Medical Factors Involved.* Philadelphia: Saunders, 1959.

Silberstein, Stephen D. "Evaluation and Emergency Treatment of Headache." *Headache* 32 (1992): 396–407.

Silverman, D. R. "Narrowing the Gap Between the Rhetoric and the Reality of Medical Ethics." *Academic Medicine* 71.3 (1996): 227–37.

Silverman, David. *Communication and Medical Practice: Social Relations and the Clinic.* London: Sage, 1987.

Simons, Herbert W. "Are Scientists Rhetors in Disguise?: An Analysis of Discursive Processes Within Scientific Communities." *Rhetoric in Transition: Studies in the Nature and Use of Rhetoric.* Ed. Eugene E. White. University Park: Pennsylvania State UP, 1980. 115–30.

———. "The Rhetoric of the Scientific Research Report: 'Drug-Pushing' in a Medical Journal Article." *Recovery of Rhetoric: Persuasive Discourse and Disciplinarity in the Human Sciences.* Ed. R. H. Roberts and J. M. M. Good. Charlottesville: UP of Virginia, 1993. 148–63.

Singer, Michael. "Six Illnesses Stumbling Toward a Cure." *New York Times Magazine* 16 Mar. 2003: 30–31.

Smith, Marlaine C. "Metaphor in Nursing Theory." *Nursing Quarterly* 5.2 (1992): 48–49.

Solomon, Martha. "Commentary." Nothstine, Blair, and Copeland 301–6.

———. "The Rhetoric of Dehumanization: An Analysis of Medical Reports of the Tuskegee Syphilis Project." Nothstine, Blair, and Copeland 307–22.

Sontag, Susan. *Illness as Metaphor* and AIDS *and Its Metaphors.* 1978 and 1989. New York: Anchor, 1990.

Sprat, Thomas. *The History of the Royal-Society of London, for the Improving of Natural Knowledge.* London: Martyn, 1667. *History of the Royal Society.* Ed. Jackson I. Cope and Harold Whitmore Jones. St. Louis: Washington UP, 1958.

Stang, David J., and Lawrence S. Wrightsman. *Dictionary of Social Behavior and Social Research Methods.* Monterey, CA: Brooks, 1981.

Starr, Paul. *The Social Transformation of American Medicine.* New York: Basic, 1982.

Stein, Howard F. *American Medicine as Culture.* Boulder, CO: Westview, 1990.

———. "Domestic Wars and the Militarization of American Biomedicine." *Journal of Psychiatry* 22 (1995): 406–16.

Stevenson, Fiona A., et al. "Perceptions of Legitimacy: The Influence on Medicine Taking and Prescribing." *Health: An Interdisciplinary Journal for the Social Study of Health, Illness and Medicine* 6.1 (2002): 85–104.

Stewart, Charles J. "Historical Survey: Rhetorical Criticism in Twentieth Century America." *Explorations in Rhetorical Criticism.* Ed. G. P. Mohrmann, Charles J. Stewart, and Donovan J. Ochs. University Park: Pennsylvania State UP, 1973. 1–31.

Stewart, Moira, and Debra Roter. *Communicating with Medical Patients.* London: Sage, 1989.

Stimson, G. V. "Obeying Doctor's Orders: A View from the Other Side." *Social Science and Medicine* 8 (1974): 97–104.

SUPPORT (The Study to Understand Prognoses and Preferences for Outcomes and Risks of Treatment). "A Controlled Trial to Improve Care for Seriously Ill Hospitalized Patients." *Journal of the AMA* 274 (1995): 1591–98.

Surbled, George. *Medical Etiquette: Handbook of Elementary Deontology.* Trans. W. P. Grant. London: Sherrat, 1910.

Szekely, Barbara. "Nonpharmacological Treatment of Menstrual Headache: Relaxation-Biofeedback Behavior Therapy, and Person-Centered Insight Therapy." *Headache* 26 (1986): 86–92.

Talbot, Margaret. "Diagnosis: Bad Mother." *New Yorker* (9, 16 Aug. 2004): 62–75.

Tepper, Stewart. "Co-Prescription of Triptans with Other Medications: A Cohort Study Involving 240,268 Patients." *Forty-fourth Annual Scientific Meeting of the American Headache Society.* Sheraton Seattle Hotel and Towers, Seattle. 21 June 2002.

———. "Presentations of Headache." Symposium. "New Advances and Understandings in the Diagnosis and Care of Migraine Patients." *Forty-fourth Annual Scientific Meeting of the American Headache Society.* Sheraton Seattle Hotel and Towers, Seattle. 21 June 2002.

Theobald, John. *Every Man His Own Physician. Being a Complete Collection of Efficacious and Approved Remedies. For Every Disease Incident to the Human Body: With Plain Instructions for Their Common Use. Necessary to Be Had in All Families, Particular Those Residing in the Country.* London: Griffin, 1764.

Thomas, Lewis. *The Youngest Science: Notes of a Medicine-Watcher.* New York: Viking, 1983.

Tomlinson, Barbara. "Intensification and the Discourse of Decline: A Rhetoric of Medical Anthropology." *Medical Anthropology Quarterly* 13.1 (1999): 7–31.

Trostle, James A. "Medical Compliance as an Ideology." *Social Science and Medicine* 27.12 (1988): 1299–309.

"Trouble with What the Doctor Ordered." Editorial. *Globe and Mail* 11 July 2002: A12.

Valverde, Mariana. "Targeted Governance and the Problem of Desire." *Risk and Morality.* Ed. Richard V. Ericson and Aaron Doyle. Toronto: U of Toronto P, 2003. 438–58.

Van der Geest, Sjaak, and Susan R. Whyte. "The Charm of Medicines: Metaphors and Metonyms." *Medical Anthropology Quarterly* 3.4 (1989): 345–67.

Vermeire, E., et al. "Patient Adherence to Treatment: Three Decades of Research. A Comprehensive Review." *Journal of Clinical Pharmacy and Therapeutics* 26 (2001): 331–42.

Wagner, Peggy J., and Julia E. Hendrich. "Physician Views on Frequent Medical Use: Patient Beliefs and Demographic and Diagnostic Correlates." *Journal of Family Practice* 36.4 (1993): 417–22.

Walter, Otis. "On the Varieties of Rhetorical Criticism." Nilsen 158–72.

Wander, Philip. "The Rhetoric of American Foreign Policy." Nothstine, Blair, and Copeland 389–416.

Warnick, Barbara. "Life in Context: What Is the Critic's Role?" *QJS* 78 (1992): 232–37.

Warren, Virginia. "The 'Medicine Is War' Metaphor." *HEC Forum* 3.1 (1991): 39–50.

"Was the Winnipeg Doctor Right to Refuse Smokers as Patients?" *Winnipeg Sun* 10 Mar. 2002: M14. Lexis-Nexis Academic Universe, Canada. 15 July 2002 <http://web.lexis-nexis.com/universe>.

Weaver, Richard M. "Concealed Rhetoric in Scientistic Sociology." *Language Is Sermonic: Richard M. Weaver on the Nature of Rhetoric*. Ed. Richard L. Johannesen, Rennard Strickland, and Ralph T. Eubanks. Baton Rouge: Louisiana State UP, 1970. 139–58.

———. "Language Is Sermonic." Johannesen, Strickland, and Eubanks 201–25.

Weber, Frederick Parkes. "Two Strange Cases of Functional Disorder with Remarks on the Association of Hysteria and Malingering." *Intl. Clinics* 1 (1912): 125–38.

Weigert, Andrew J. "The Immoral Rhetoric of Scientific Sociology." *American Sociologist* 5 (1970): 111–19.

Weingarten, Gene. *The Hypochondriac's Guide to Life. And Death*. New York: Simon, 1998.

Wenegrat, Brant. *Theater of Disorder: Patients, Doctors, and the Construction of Illness*. Oxford: Oxford UP, 2001.

Wente, Margaret. "Who's a Woman to Trust?" *Globe and Mail* 11 July 2002: A13.

West, Candace. *Routine Complications: Troubles with Talk Between Doctors and Patients*. Bloomington: Indiana UP, 1984.

Wichelns, Herbert A. "The Literary Criticism of Oratory (1925)." T. Benson, *Landmark* 1–32.

Wills, David. *Prosthesis*. Stanford: Stanford UP, 1995.

Wilson, G. Letter. *Globe and Mail* 3 Aug. 2002: A12.

Wilson, Robert A. *Feminine Forever*. New York: Evans, 1966.

Wolff, Harold G. *Headache and Other Head Pain*. Ed. Donald J. Dalessio and Stephen D. Silberstein. 6th ed. New York: Oxford UP, 1993.

Wong, Carol A. "Commentary." *Nursing Forum* 28.1 (1993): 32–33.

"Wrong Smoke Signal." *Record* (Kitchener-Waterloo) 2 Mar. 2002: A16. Lexis-Nexis Academic Universe, Canada. 15 July 2002 <http://web.lexis-nexis.ccom/universe>.

Yandle, Sharon. Letter. *Harper's Magazine* 304 (Feb. 2002): 4–5.

York, Geoffrey. "China's War Against SARS Now Includes Death Penalty." *Globe and Mail* 16 May 2003: A9.

Young, Katherine. "Narrative Embodiments: Enclaves of the Self in the Realm of Medicine." *Texts of Identity*. Ed. John Shotter and Kenneth J. Gergen. London: Sage, 1989. 152–65.

Young, Katherine Galloway, ed. *Bodylore*. Knoxville: U of Tennessee P, 1993.

Index

Judy Z. Segal is an associate professor of English at the University of British Columbia, where she teaches the history and theory of rhetoric, as well as the rhetoric of science and medicine. Her essays have appeared in such journals as *Rhetoric Review, Rhetoric Society Quarterly, Social Science and Medicine,* and *Journal of Medical Humanities.* She is a member of the President's International Advisory Committee of the Canadian Institutes of Health Research.